POST-CARTESIAN MEDITATIONS

An Essay in
Dialectical Phenomenology

by

JAMES L. MARSH

Fordham University Press
New York
1988

Printed in the United States of America

TO

VINCE, LARRY, BUFORD, AND JOHN

COMPANIONS IN THE STRUGGLE

CONTENTS

PREFACE

This is an essay in dialectical phenomenology in the tradition of such thinkers as Hegel and Marx, Husserl and Heidegger, Merleau-Ponty and Sartre, Ricoeur and Gadamer, Paci and Kosík. The essay consciously situates itself in relation to Descartes' *Meditations* and Husserl's *Cartesian Meditations* in taking up developments that have since occurred in phenomenology and philosophy generally. What would Descartes and Husserl write now if they were alive?

This essay began as a straightforward exercise in eidetic, descriptive phenomenology. However, because I found that I could not ignore the extent to which such phenomenology depends on and emerges from history, I had to affirm a backward-looking, hermeneutical moment of retrieval that complements the eidetic and descriptive. Moreover, I found not only that phenomenology and history stretch backward but that they stretch forward into the future. I found it necessary, therefore, to affirm a moment of suspicion or critique on a psychological and social level. Retrieval, description, and suspicion corresponding to the three temporal modalities of past, present, and future are essential to a fully adequate phenomenological method.

Such a conclusion seemed less outrageous when I reflected on the history of twentieth-century phenomenology, which has moved from the transcendental eidetics of Husserl through the existential phenomenology of Sartre, Heidegger, Merleau-Ponty, and Ricoeur to the hermeneutical phenomenology of Gadamer and the later Ricoeur. One could legitimately say that the history of phenomenology traces a path from suspension, present in Husserl's "bracketing" of all common-sense and scientific claims, to suspicion, present in Freudian, Nietzschean, and Marxian critiques of experience and incorporated by Ricoeur into his conception of phenomenology. This path from suspension to suspicion is the logical, phenomenological path of this book. In tracing such a path phenomenology logically and historically moves away from the abstract, Cartesian subject toward the concrete, historical subject. Phenomenology, though historically indebted to Cartesianism, is essentially oriented to overcoming it.

Such overcoming has several dimensions or aspects. The first is the "triumph of ambiguity," a move away from meaning conceived as abstract, universal, clear, exact, and apodictic to meaning conceived as concrete, pluralistic, contextualistic, implicit, and tentative. Both Merleau-Ponty and the later Wittgenstein make such moves, and it is from reflection on their agreement and disagreement that my own method in phenomenology emerges.

Second, there is a hermeneutical, historical turn that Husserl begins to make at the end of his life in *The Crisis of European Sciences and Transcendental Phenomenology*, where phenomenology in its own internal becoming is essentially related to the history of philosophy. Husserl sees this historical turn as necessary, but does not execute it fully; nor does he see its implication for such issues as certainty in phenomenology, the possibility of thinking without presuppositions, and the relation of idea to fact.

Third, there is the phenomenon of embodiment, again hinted at and partially developed but not fully worked out by Husserl. Because of embodiment human beings are in the world, and any distinction between the transcendental and embodied ego has to be given up.

Fourth, there is the linguistic turn that has occurred in both phenomenology and analytic philosophy. Consequently, consciousness as rooted in the life-world is necessarily expressive and linguistic. The phenomenon of language is then further evidence against the notion of an isolated *cogito* shut up inside itself and in full possession of itself.

Fifth, there is the discovery of the free, existential subject. Human persons are free; they not only know but create a world through forceful intervention in that world. Consequently, a phenomenology intending to do full justice to experience must incorporate this experience of freedom into its account and try to understand it.

Sixth, there is the question of intersubjectivity: How do I come to know and choose the other person as distinct from me in the life-world? This is an issue raised by Husserl but not adequately treated because of the affirmation of the transcendental ego. As I argue in the book, the rejection of the transcendental ego and the affirmation of the person in the world are necessary in order to resolve this problem.

Seventh, there are the various anti-philosophies arising on the ruins of exaggerated claims for transcendental philosophy. One can answer Rorty's problems with representation, however, or Derrida's problems with presence without rejecting philosophy itself. Philosophy as rigorous science finally realizes that there is such a thing as too much rigor and too much exactness.

Eighth, there is a critical turn insofar as history reveals itself as contradictory, at odds with the incarnate, intelligent, free social subject. If phenomenology is to be fully descriptive, then it has to describe the particular historical experiences of alienation rooted in such structures as capitalism. If phenomenology is to be fully critical, it must reflect on the contradiction between its own affirmation of the incarnate, free subject and

the practical negation of that subjectivity in industrial society. If phenomenology is to fulfill its own ambition of achieving full lucidity and clarity,
then it must reflect upon itself as a product of the form of life that is
capitalism. Suspicion culminating in ideology critique, then, has to be a
part of phenomenology itself.

Ninth, there are the questions we must confront that are raised by the
post-modern critique of modernist, evidential rationality. Is such rationality simply to be jettisoned, as late Heidegger, Derrida, Foucault, Caputo, and others claim, or can it be critically redeemed? My option is
that of critical redemption, in which I steer a middle course between
the extremes of a narrow, foundationalist, Cartesian rationality and a
post-modernist rejection and transcendence of Western, modern rationality. This middle course might be described as a "critical modernism," taking its bearings from such thinkers as Hegel and Marx, Husserl
and Merleau-Ponty, Ricoeur and Habermas.

Phenomenology as it operates in this book, then, is involved in a
triple reduction, hermeneutical, phenomenological, and critical, each
grounded in a specific modality of time consciousness. The hermeneutical inquiry into tradition and history is rooted in the past; the phenomenological, in the present; and the critical, in the future. Past, present, and
future are present in all three modes of inquiry, of course, but only one
temporal aspect is explicit and thematic in each reduction.

Reflection on the present encompasses what Husserl and others have
described as the phenomenological reduction, which has three aspects:
description of lived experience with as few presuppositions as possible,
eidetic analysis uncovering certain, invariant structures of experience, and
affirmation of self and life-world as ultimate, correlative, ontological
grounds for experience.

Phenomenology as I conceive it, therefore, is not only descriptive but
dialectical in several different senses. (*a*) Experience reveals itself as a
unity of opposites, subject and object, determination and indetermination, self and other, conscious and unconscious, universal and particular.
(*b*) Dialectic is present insofar as this book is written from a moving
standpoint, with a movement from less to more complex wholes—for example, from perception to language to the relationship between perception and reflection to objectivity to freedom. At the beginning of each new
chapter and section, the previous synthesis is revealed as inadequate and
incomplete in various ways, and contradictions uncovered in various attempts at new syntheses. The organization of the argument in the book
and in each chapter is, therefore, similar to that in Hegel's *Phenomenology
of Spirit*.

(*c*) The method is dialectical insofar as critique and suspicion become a crucial part of phenomenology itself. Only with suspicion directed toward alienating psychological and social structures that inhibit self-conscious living does phenomenology become fully complete as phenomenology. Only with explicit reflection on the relationship of phenomenology to alienating social structures such as capitalism does phenomenology become fully self-reflective. This book, then, consciously relates to and continues the phenomenological Marxist tradition of such thinkers as Sartre and Merleau-Ponty, Kosík and Paci.

(d) Phenomenology is dialectical insofar as it emerges from history as a result of a dialectic between objectivism and subjectivism. Insofar as Cartesianism defines modern philosophy in the narrow sense of a critical, transcendental turn into the knowing subject and in a broader sense of giving rise to two different, opposed philosophies of subjectivism and objectivism, a division corresponding to the Cartesian separation of thinking and extended substances and the reduction of the objective world to a set of primary qualities known scientifically, this book is a reflection on the entire tradition of modern philosophy.

These Meditations, then, are post-Cartesian insofar as they both retain Descartes' valid insights into subjectivity, critical radicality, and the values of full, self-conscious, autonomous living and knowing, and integrate these insights with new insights into the lived body, the life-world, the limits of science, language, intersubjectivity, freedom, and the personal and social unconscious. Descartes has to be both preserved and overcome insofar as he is the philosopher of bourgeois modernity *par excellence.* The dualism that emerges in his philosophy between objectivity and subjectivity, mind and body, science and common sense corresponds with and legitimizes the same dualism as that emerges within capitalism itself. Descartes' valid insights pointing toward a different, non-bourgeois form of existence are in tension with the bourgeois aspects of his philosophy, and it is this tension that this book claims to overcome. Full recovery of the world, of the subject–object relationship in all its integrity, demands the theoretical and practical overcoming of alienation in that world, an alienation that Cartesianism both reflects and attempts to transcend.

In another way, as the title indicates, this book is a synthesis of Cartesian and dialectical traditions in phenomenology. The former with its emphasis on subjectivity, consciousness, and the abstract universal common to all epochs, and the latter with its emphasis on history, critique, and the historically specific particular, must be brought together in a phenomenology that is both descriptive and dialectical, ontological and critical, aware of its universal foundations and yet able to interpret and criticize particular social systems. Only in such a theory do we avoid the relativism of a phenomenology unsure of its foundations and the naïveté of ascribing to human nature what is really a particular, historical result of particular social relations.

Because one of the themes of my book is the overcoming of alienation, it would be supremely un–self-conscious of me to use sexist language. At the same time I have not wished to deny myself altogether the use of the personal pronoun, "he" or "she," "him" or "her"; or to overuse the awkward "her or she." Following the advice of the Guidelines for *Nonsexist Use of Language in NCTE Publications* published by the National Council for Teachers of English, I have, therefore, in each chapter begun with the feminine and alternated in the use of feminine and masculine within paragraphs and between paragraphs.

If one of the central theses of this book is correct, no book is a product simply of the author. Many have collaborated and contributed to the final result. I owe a special debt to the members of the local Saint Louis area phenomenological group, Herbert Spiegelberg, Bill Hamrick, Bob Wolfe, and Frank Flinn, who have listened and responded sympathetically—critically—to many parts of this work over the years. I am grateful to Martin Denys, Jack Caputo, Roslyn Bologh, and Bernie Dauenhauer for reading and criticizing earlier drafts, and to Buford Farris for reading and criticizing Chapters 8 and 9. Over the years I have tried out early versions of many chapters on graduate seminars. Student-colleagues deserving special mention are Russell Hittinger and Gary Percesepe, whose enlightened, critical response has been very helpful; Tom Jeannot, whose enlightenment, criticism, encouragement, proofreading of the whole manuscript, and very generous typing of two long chapters meant a great deal; and Mike Mahon, who subjected several chapters to a very rigorous proofreading. Linda Lashley has been a typist of extraordinary patience and competence, and a summer grant from the Saint Louis University Beaumont Fund made a final typing possible. Mary Beatrice Schulte proved to be an excellent editor, who has contributed immeasurably to whatever literary artistry this book possesses.

I also wish to acknowledge the following journals and publishers for permission to use material initially appearing under their auspices: *Philosophy Today*, for parts of Chapters 1 and 8; *Man and World*, for part of Chapter 1; *The Modern Schoolman* and *Southwestern Journal of Philosophy*, for parts of Chapter 2; *International Philosophical Quarterly* and the State University of New York Press, for parts of Chapter 3; Martinus Nijhoff and *Poetics Today*, for parts of Chapter 4; and *The British Journal of the Society of Phenomenology*, for part of Chapter 8.

Fordham University

POST-CARTESIAN
MEDITATIONS

1

The Historical Reduction

IF WE ARE to avoid doing philosophy from on high, muttering empty nothings that do not relate to real people and real situations, we must reflect on our real practical and theoretical situation. But to begin with our real situation is to be plunged into history. We must begin with practical and theoretical reflection on our contemporary historical situation, an historical reduction. The first part of this chapter, therefore, is the practical reduction; the second part, the theoretical historical.[1]

A PRACTICAL HISTORICAL REDUCTION

If philosophy begins in wonder before the mystery of being, it is appropriate that I begin by reflecting on human beings and nature within a total context. In scrutinizing and reflecting on the paradox of the human person in relation to the world, both in the world and yet transcending it with questions, both determined and free, both perceiving and reflecting, I begin to wonder and, therefore, to think philosophically.

Yet equally noteworthy and constituting another possible beginning for philosophy is the experience of alienation, estrangement of human beings from the world and from themselves. Rather than mystery, the awareness of ourselves in a context that thought can never exhaust, we have the obviousness of scientific problems. Rather than stressing the free, open person, we stress the producing and consuming of commodities. Rather than being, there is having, or, more precisely, we reduce being to having, possessing, controlling.[2]

Such alienation or covering over never totally succeeds; for the thoughtful, the mystery of nature, human persons, and being keeps breaking through the reified appearance. Nonetheless, the most thought-provoking experience seems to be this passage back and forth between mystery and problem, quality and quantity, respectful openness toward reality and domination. This experience motivates the practical question "What shall I do with my life?" or "What kind of person will I be?" Yet we cannot answer the practical question without answering the theoretical question "What does it mean to be a person?" or "What is a person in his or her own deepest reality?" The practical question gives rise to the theoretical, and the theoretical in turn makes it possible to answer the practical question.

To live in Western industrial society, however, is already to be confronted with lived answers to both these questions. The dominant practical answer is that one should possess, consume, produce, and control; the dominant theoretical answer is that human beings are individuals or things manipulable and knowable by empirical science alone. Day in and day out this lived ontology of human existence confronts us, constantly inviting us to live a thing-like existence as members of a crowd. Such alienation has at least three aspects: reification, individualism, and scientism.[3]

Reification has four manifestations: idle talk, curiosity, ambiguity, and fallenness.[4] Idle talk occurs when I understand and say something without previously making it my own. I simply repeat what the crowd is saying and follow what the crowd is doing. I pick up my opinions from *The New York Times*, my tastes from Madison Avenue, and my morality from convention—everyone else does it. Curiosity is a questing after novelty for its own sake, not to understand it but simply to pass from it to another novelty. "Distracted from distraction by distraction,"[5] I flee from myself into ever newer and more extreme forms of sensation and consumption—I substitute sensation for deep experience.

Ambiguity, understood here in a negative sense different from its meaning in the last part of this chapter, occurs because of the confusion and inability to distinguish between genuine understanding and its opposite. In my refusal to slow down to think about what I am doing in trying to be up to date, I am continually going wrong in my idle talk. I understand the other in terms of what "they" have said and what "they" think. I am constantly, competitively listening in and observing others in order to get the jump on them; my hostility and aggressiveness masquerade as courtesy and friendliness.

Human beings, because they are reified through idle talk, curiosity, and ambiguity, are fallen. Fallenness has several characteristics as well: temptation, tranquillity, estrangement, self-entanglement. To live in Western industrial society is continually to be tempted to do things the way "they" do them and to think the way "they" think, conforming like a thing. In so doing I have reassurance and security that I am like everyone else and so have tranquillity. The risks of being an independent, autonomous thinker and chooser are risks I do not care to run. Living life according to Gallup Polls, the Top Ten, and the Nielsen Ratings is easier and causes less anxiety.

But giving up the project of autonomous living means that I have lost myself, have become estranged from myself. Because such estrangement still leaves me with myself, I become entangled with myself. I plunge from genuine, autonomous living into the inauthentic life of the "they" who assure me that I am doing the right thing. Loss of self presents itself as gaining the self, and real individuality is rejected as eccentricity and pride—"Who does she think she is?"

Most work, for example, is geared toward efficiency and is unenjoyable and uncreative. Work in the office as well as in the factory is increasingly subject to the division of labor as the mind and skill of the work passes to the capitalist manager or machine. Even work organized around a computer, work that could be fulfilling and challenging, is for the most part reduced to keypunch operators filing cards, hour after hour, day after day.[6]

When workers leave the job to go home, they find that they have been preceded by advertisers, managers, and experts telling them to define their leisure in terms of consumption. Neither at work nor at home are workers really at home in the sense of being one with themselves. Rather, they are under constant pressure to buy the latest television set, suit of clothes, set of golf clubs, or automobile in order to exist more fully. Human beings are what they make, and the more they have, the more they are. Through such pressure a conformism develops in which everyone becomes like everyone else, with no room for individuality or dissent. Idle talk, curiosity, and ambiguity prevail as individuals become members of a mass only numerically distinct from one another, with no qualitative distinction or inner life.[7]

Not only is there social alienation; there is political alienation, manifested in growing disenchantment with the political process, lower percentages of eligible voters turning out to vote every year, and increasing cynicism about the possibility of social change. Rather than being political subjects actively and critically participating in the electoral process, human beings have become political objects, observed by Gallup Polls, manipulated by the latest version of selling the president, and controlled by experts like Kissinger, Brezinski, and Weinberger.[8] More and more the methods of the White House tend to imitate those of Madison Avenue, and serious discussion of issues is minimized or ignored. To watch a television debate between two presidential candidates, for example, is often to witness a substitution of rhetoric for argument, manipulation for dialogue, and triviality for profundity—idle talk and ambiguity reign supreme.

Such reification is accompanied by individualism, a pursuing of my own self-interest with little recognition of social ties beyond my immediate self or family. In line at a supermarket, for example, or waiting for a subway, or driving in traffic, I am aware of myself as an individual externally related to others in a series. I am pursuing my own goals, thinking my own thoughts, looking out for my own interests. Others in the series arc present to me as obstacles, means, or objects merely indifferent to my achieving my own ends. Others become an issue explicitly when there is a breakdown: the cash register goes on the blink, the train is late, or the traffic is jammed. I do not value the society of others as an end in itself. I use others as means to my ends, and they use me. I use sales clerks to buy groceries, and they use me to take my money and make a living.

When the series is generalized beyond my individual experience, it becomes impersonal and objectivized. Watching a television show in the privacy of my own home, for example, I can almost completely forget that other people in other homes are watching the same show. This fact becomes explicit later when the Nielsen Ratings tell me that ten million people watched the program that night and that I was one of them. But at the same time I was at best only marginally aware that others were watching the program. Here again, constructed into a social fact by the Nielson Ratings, are the same externality, indifference, and individualism as in the more local examples.[9]

The underlying notion of reason behind these phenomena of reification and individualism is positivistic and scientistic. I understand positivism, here and in the rest of the book, in Ayer's sense of confining knowledge to actual or possible knowledge of an empirical state of affairs. I understand scientism in Comte's sense of equating genuine knowledge with science. Positivism and scientism, therefore, overlap at least in theory and often are identical in practice.[10] As I shall argue in the rest of this book, one theoretical and practical implication of a fully consistent scientism is the rejection of prescientific, common-sense knowledge as legitimate. The rational is that which I can quantify, predict, and control. All else is irrelevant and unreal.

When I am interviewing for a position and I fill out a form on myself, I list the facts about myself that can easily be verified. I leave out all the intangible, emotional, intellectual, and spiritual dimensions of my experience that are more fundamental and that define my identity as a person. These inner dimensions, not accessible to a scientific approach conducted after the model of positive science, are irrational according to this model of reason.

The dominance of technology as a form of control manifests this dominance by science. More and more, science is a method for getting results in the economic, social, and political arenas. The economic sphere requires such technical control if it is not to fall into recession or depression; the social, if people are to buy the goods produced by the system; and the political, if society is to keep a lid on social unrest and exclude unacceptable alternatives. Technique, the use of science and technology for commodious living, is part of the taken-for-granted context of life, in which we assume that all problems are technical problems and that only the useful is the real. Technique is the common sense of the contemporary era.[11]

Alienation manifesting itself in reification, individualism, and scientism is very prevalent. Nonetheless someone such as Skinner asks whether or not this alienation stems from an outmoded belief in an inner self.[12] If there is no inner self to exclude, repress, or exploit, then the feeling of alienation is inappropriate, and I shall have to see through it. I should simply accept my status as an object and not worry about human dignity, freedom, or consciousness.

A theoretical inquiry, therefore, into what a human person is, what reason is, what human knowing, doing, and community are in their full range and variety is necessary. I must move from practical, lived alienation to theoretical reflection on that alienation, from the practical question "What should I do?" to the theoretical question "What and who am I?"

A Theoretical Historical Reduction

Descartes and Husserl

Doing theory requires one to begin somewhere, and beginning involves the question of a starting point. After some reflection, I can see that there is no fully immediate beginning, no obvious starting point, without unexamined presuppositions. Searching for such a beginning, Husserl in his *Cartesian Meditations* begins with the Enlightenment "prejudice against prejudice." The attempt to be free from history reveals itself to be historically influenced. Also assumed by Husserl are the legitimacy and desirability of philosophy as rigorous science.[13]

What Husserl saw, therefore, in the *Crisis*, is that an historical reduction was necessary, an inquiry into history itself as forming his own philosophy. Rather than attempting to leave history behind, the philosopher should inquire into it if he would fully understand himself as philosopher. Husserl thus conducted an inquiry into the history of modern philosophy in order to understand it as leading up to his own philosophy.[14]

Descartes · Like Husserl, I begin with Descartes because he decisively and clearly takes the turn into the subject that is decisive for modern philosophy and the modern era. With him, philosophy becomes *methodical, critical, reflexive,* and *comprehensive* in a way that it was not before. With him also a one-sidedness emerges that is the obverse side of his achievement and that will be one of the main concerns of this book. Without him, as Husserl saw so clearly, phenomenology in a contemporary vein would be impossible.[15]

With Descartes, the methodical effort to ground philosophy in the human subject begins. We should not leave philosophical conclusions to chance or to an intuition reserved for the metaphysical elect, but work them out from the ground up in such a way that we can justify each step evidentially. Descartes no longer naïvely accepts previous presuppositions in philosophy such as the knowability of the external world or of God, but, rather, critically questions these presuppositions. Such grounding occurs through a radical reflection on the self's experience of the world that leaves no question unanswered, no claim unexamined, no hypothesis untested. Whereas philosophers previously had discussed the human subject in metaphysical terms such as potency and act initially derived from the natural world, now for the first time the possibility emerges of doing justice to human experience on its own terms and comprehensively relating this new self-knowledge to the world.

I begin in my own historical reduction, therefore, with Descartes' move in the seventeenth century from naïveté to criticism, metaphysics to epistemology, object to subject. Confronted with a welter of conflicting philosophies uncertain about their foundations, the growth of new science, and an emerging skepticism about religious claims, he resolves to find an absolutely certain, secure foundation for philosophy. Because nothing is certain, he finds it necessary to set aside all presuppositions about truth, reality, and value.

Descartes, then, begins his inquiry by applying himself earnestly and freely to the general overthrow of all his previous opinions. To achieve this end he suggests that what is necessary is, not showing the whole as false, but rejecting the whole of his previous knowledge if each part leaves grounds for doubt; what is necessary is, not considering individual beliefs, but rather criticizing the principles on which the beliefs rest.

One of these principles is the senses. Although all that he has accepted as true up to this point he has received through the senses, these nonetheless sometimes mislead us. Prudence dictates that we not place full trust in that which can mislead us. Someone may object that even though the senses may occasionally mislead us, they nonetheless present much other information impossible to doubt—that I am in this place, for example, and seated by this fire. Descartes answers this objection by stating that many times he has dreamed of himself in just such a situation. Consequently, such information cannot be fully trusted.

Someone could also object, however, that certain representations could not originate except through the commerce of the senses with real objects. Even if this representation of a chair is imaginary, it had to arise through interaction with a real chair. On the same principle, although certain general objects such as eyes, body, and head might be imaginary, we are obliged to admit the reality of other objects simpler than these, from which they are formed. Even if physics and astronomy are doubtful because their objects are composite, arithmetic and geometry, which regard simple objects, are indubitable.

Whether I am awake or dreaming, it remains true that two and three make five.

At this point in his argument Descartes introduces the notion of an evil demon who may have arranged things such that I am systematically deceived even about mathematical propositions. People certainly do sometimes think they have certain knowledge even when they really do not. In the assumption that all things that I think are false, what is it that I can know for sure? In the assumption also that there is an evil demon who is a deceiver, I can nonetheless say that it is truly I myself who am deceived in thinking those false thoughts. If deception implies a deceiver, deception also implies someone who thinks mistakenly and, therefore, who exists in such aberrant intellectual activity.

If I know that I am, however, it is not clear yet what I am. Descartes pursues this question by first considering what he previously thought himself to be, a rational animal. That answer no longer is adequate, for inquiry into the meanings of "animal" and "rational" would be necessary, and such inquiry would take us into even more difficult questions. Attending, on the contrary, to thoughts that emerge of their own accord in my mind, it seems clear that I do have a body, understood here as that which can terminate in a certain figure, occupy space, and be sensibly perceived and moved. Self-motion, as well as perceiving and thinking, do not necessarily pertain to the nature of body as such.

What am I then? Do I have any of the attributes essentially pertaining to body? Descartes answers that none of them can be said to belong to me essentially. Am I then capable of nutrition or walking or perceiving? Since these activities are impossible without the body, Descartes denies that they are essential to my identity as a thinking self. Since we can admit only what is necessarily true, only one candidate is left: thinking itself. This alone is what necessarily pertains to me as a thing. I can imagine or doubt coherently that I have a body, but not that I am thinking, since that very activity of doubt itself is an activity of thinking.

What is a thinking thing? "It is a thing that doubts, understands, [conceives], affirms, denies, wills, refuses, that imagines, also, and perceives. . . ." Even if what I perceive or imagine is false, nonetheless the activities themselves of imagining and perceiving are present. Perceiving and imagining are identical with thinking, then, and I begin to know what I am with a bit more distinctness and clarity than before.

Nonetheless it does seem true that sensible things are known with greater clarity and distinctness than my intangible thinking self. Descartes ascribes this semblance to the weakness of the mind, its tendency to disorder, and, therefore, he more attentively considers what bodies are. Is the true body, the genuine piece of wax, that which I can touch, taste, see, smell, and hear? Clearly not, since when I place the wax near the fire, all that I perceived through the senses changes. Nonetheless the same piece of wax remained after the change, something extended, flexible, and movable. What is meant by "flexible" and "movable" is not that I imagine that the wax as round can become square or as square can become triangular, because an infinity of such changes is thinkable. The real piece of wax I think thematically as an object of mental inspection.[16]

Emerging from such self-affirmation is that the criteria of truth are clarity and distinctness. "Clear" is that which is present to an attentive mind; "distinct" is that which is so precise and different from all other objects as to comprehend in itself only what is clear. With these criteria in mind, Descartes next moves to consider the question of God. Can God be known clearly and distinctly? On this issue Descartes constructs three different proofs. The first moves from the idea of God to God as the cause of that idea. If the objective reality of one of my ideas cannot exist in me formally or eminently and if, as follows from this, I cannot be the cause of this idea, it follows necessarily that He exists. By God is understood an infinite, independent, all-knowing, all-powerful substance who has created all things. The idea of God is not present in me formally as a property of my being; nor is it present eminently, as something I could have caused, because the less perfect cannot give rise to the more perfect. There can be in the effect only as much as there is in the cause. But if I am imperfect, changeable, finite, prone to error, how should I be able to give rise to the idea of a perfect, unchangeable, infinite, infallible being?

Descartes' second proof moves from the existence of himself to the existence of God. From whom can I derive my existence? Perhaps from myself, my parents, or other causes less perfect than God. If I were the cause of my existence, I should doubt nothing, desire nothing, lack nothing. Since I manifestly really doubt, desire, and lack, I cannot be the author of my being. Nor can the cause be my parents or some being less than God, for the cause would have to explain my origin as a thinking thing who possesses the idea of God in myself, and the cause cannot possess less reality or content than the effect.[17]

Descartes' third proof is the ontological proof. Since I conceive God as all-perfect and existence is a perfection, it necessarily follows that God exists. It is no valid objection to such a proof that mountains do not exist simply because we conceive them; mountains in this respect are not analogous to God. God is *sui generis* in that His essence necessarily implies His existence. Similarly it is no adequate objection to this thesis that the original supposition of the proof, that God has all perfections, is not necessary. Descartes admits that it is not necessary to conceive the idea of deity at any time or all the time, but once I do, I necessarily think deity as perfect and, therefore, existent.[18]

It necessarily follows, then, from the notion of God's perfection that He cannot be a deceiver, since all fraud and deception spring from some deficit. Errors arise in me because my will sometimes extends farther than the understanding will allow. Properly restrain the will, Descartes argues, and you will live in the truth.

At this point in the argument, Descartes returns to considering our knowledge of the external world. Armed with the knowledge that God is not a deceiver, I am equipped to restore in chastened, qualified form my belief in the reality of the external world. First, I know that I exist and that as a thinking thing I am distinct from my body, since what is clearly and distinctly conceived as existing separately must exist separately.

Second, because there is in me a passive faculty of perception that is aware of being affected by corporeal things, these things must exist outside of me, at least insofar as they can be known through the clear and distinct ideas of speculative geometry. If there were no such things, then God would be a deceiver since He has given a strong inclination to believe in such things and no way of discovering that they do not exist.

Third, even with regard to other things that are only particular—for example, that the sun is of such a size and figure, or impressions of light, sound, pain, and so on—I can see in each of these dictates of nature some truth. By "nature" here I should understand God Himself or the order and disposition placed by God in particular things. By my own particular nature, I understand the assemble of all that God has given to me. Nature, however, teaches me nothing more expressly than that I have a body that feels hunger, pleasure, and pain. Also, it is a body in which I am not lodged merely as a pilot in a ship, but to which I am intimately conjoined. Mind and body in this conjunction are experienced as a unity. For were that not so, I should not feel pain when my body is hurt, seeing that I am merely a thinking being, but should perceive the wound by the understanding alone, just as a pilot perceives by sight when any part of his vessel is damaged.[19]

Descartes, here, has moved in his *Meditations* from doubt about the external world through self-affirmation and affirmation of God to a reinstating of the external world. Although the argument is brilliant and ingenious and represents a new point of departure for philosophy, there are difficulties that seem apparent. First, there is the question about the possibility, necessity, and desirability of a presuppositionless approach to philosophy. Is not Descartes in his approach actually employing all kinds of presuppositions, such as the clarity and distinctness of mathematical science, the Galilean distinction between primary and secondary qualities, the medieval notion of substance in discussing thinking things and extended things? Is he not, as Gadamer suggests, subject to an uncritical "prejudice against prejudice" that overlooks the possibly legitimate, illumining role of prejudice?

Second, we can ask about the legitimacy of indubitability as a criterion of truth in philosophy. What seems to be missing here is a prior descriptive inquiry into the kinds of evidence appropriate to different levels and kinds of conscious experience, perception, reflection, common sense, science, and metaphysics. If indubitability is perhaps a legitimate criterion for mathematical truth, is it equally so for perception? Does perception not have a corrigible, probable quality about it that would make indubitability an inappropriate criterion for perceptual truth? If so, then is the movement from error or the possibility of error in the perceptual world to total doubt about that world in the first meditation legitimate? Is not the enterprise self-contradictory to the extent that Descartes knows that he has erred only through subsequent true perceptions that overturn the erroneous one? I discover that the bent stick in the water is really straight and so on.

Third, terms that have meaning in one context, where they are related to others by contrast, lose their meaning when taken out of that context and absolutized. Talking about a dream makes sense in a contrast to veridical perception in the full public world of other persons. "Dream" here would have its meaning in contrast to "perception" and "perceived reality." But when "dreaming" or "imagining" is absolutized, such that the whole world is a fantasy caused by an evil demon, then these meaningful contrasts are lost. "Dreaming" and "imagining," because they include everything, mean nothing. Descartes, indeed, in the sixth meditation recognizes such a contrast when he discusses the difference between being awake and being asleep: "for I now find a very marked difference between the two states, in that our memory can never connect our dreams with each other and with the course of life, as it is in the habit of doing with events that occur when we are awake."[20]

Fourth, the criterion of clarity and distinctness is suspect. (a) It tilts the balance in favor of some kinds of evidence that approach a mathematical paradigm of exactness over other kinds. The undesirable consequences of such a move emerge when we see Descartes, for example, preferring a definitional separation of mind and body over a more vague, imprecise experience of their togetherness and intermingling: "I am not only lodged in my body as a pilot in a vessel, but . . . so intimately conjoined, and as it were intermixed with it, that my mind and body compose a certain unity."[21] Without such an initial bias toward evidence that is clear and distinct, Descartes might have been able to take more advantage of the evidence for unity that he himself noticed, and, therefore, have avoided some of the virulent dualism that plagued his own thought.

(b) The preference for the clear and distinct also ignores the necessary interrelation of contraries in experience, such as mind with body, dreaming with perception, and so on. If certain concepts and realities have their meaning only in relation to other concepts and realities, then trying to isolate a distinct meaning only obscures matters. Many, if not all, such concepts and realities seem to have their meaning in relationship to what is other. "Red" is a color that has its meaning only in relation to "black," "blue," "white," and so on; the tone of C, only in relation to other tones on the scale. Difference is essential to meaning. Something means only by meaning something else. Something is identical only in a context of difference.

(c) The focus on clarity and distinctness ignores the role of context in determining meaning. If the red table that I am looking at has meaning only in contrast to the background from which it emerges, the "red" has meaning only in relation to an implicitly understood language of color words.

Fifth, as the discussion of Husserl later in this chapter will show more fully, the seeds of a later scientism and positivism are present in Descartes' taking over of the distinction between primary and secondary qualities. Because of the above-mentioned difficulties, mind–body dualism and subject–object dualism emerge as problems that Descartes bequeaths to later modern philosophy. If all I know for certain are my own ideas, I remain locked up inside my *cogito*, problematically related to the external world. Because I am incapable of any direct commerce with the world, I have the difficulty of knowing whether my ideas correspond with it. Since I cannot leap outside my skin to compare my ideas with reality, it becomes necessary to seek a divine guarantor of the truth of such ideas.

Mind–body dualism is a problem because Descartes uncritically uses criteria of clarity and distinctness and overlooks or minimizes other more vague, less distinct, less clear evidence of a primordial unity. A contradiction emerges between a felt, experienced unity and conceptual, reflective dualism that will haunt philosophy well into the twentieth century.

Finally, there is the problem of circularity in the proofs for the existence of God. If clarity and distinctness are the criteria of truth, then we have ideas from physics that seem clear in themselves, apart from any recourse to God. If, on the other hand, God is necessary to guarantee the truth of clear and distinct ideas, then the question arises about how we can use clear and distinct ideas to infer a divine guarantor of the truth of those clear and distinct ideas. In Descartes' proofs, not only the idea of God but other ideas, such as the principle of causality, are such clear and distinct ideas.

Husserl · In the Introduction to *Cartesian Meditations*, Husserl begins his reflection by arguing in the spirit of Descartes that philosophy must begin with the withdrawal of the philosopher into himself: "Philosophy—wisdom (*sagesse*)—is the philosophizer's quite personal affair. It must arise as *his* wisdom, as his self-acquired knowledge tending toward universality, a knowledge for which he can answer from the beginning, and at each step, by virtue of his own absolute insights."[22] Added to the urgency of such philosophical reflection are the fragmented situation of philosophy today and the uncertainty of the sciences about their own foundations.[23]

In the first meditation, Husserl undertakes an inquiry into the beginning of his own project. Throwing out of play all the convictions we have accepted up to now, we are invited to reflect, not upon the results of any science or fully worked-out logic of any science, but upon the idea of science itself as embodied in scientific striving. We prescind from the *de facto* validity of the sciences in order to reflect on the intentionality of scientific striving itself.[24]

What we discover, first of all, is that science is oriented toward judgments, and a distinction emerges between immediate and mediate judgments. Mediate judgments are those grounded in the sense and truth of other judgments. Immediate judgments are grounded beliefs that can be reactivated at will in reflection, either to recapture the ground of the immediate judgments or to ground mediate judgments further.[25]

Because true judgments are grounded judgments, mediately or immediately, they are based upon evidence. Judgments can be formulated in propositions as meant, but they are known as true or false when they are related to appropriate states of affairs. For example, my anticipations about a person I am about to meet are fulfilled or not fulfilled when she steps off the train; a scientific hypothesis is confirmed or disconfirmed when the appropriate experiments are made; and my judgment that a department store dummy is a beautiful woman is put to the test when I try to touch her or ask her out.[26]

Evidence in a broad sense is "an '*experiencing*' of something that is, and is thus; it is precisely a mental seeing of something itself."[27] Perfect evidence and its correlate, pure and genuine truth, are given as ideas lodged in the striving for knowledge, for fulfillment of one's meaning intention. A first methodological principle emerges from reflection on the idea of evidence: that I as a beginning philosopher must not accept any judgment not grounded on evidence.[28]

As we reflect further, the idea of evidence becomes differentiated. In our striving for perfect evidence, the idea of "perfect" becomes that of either inadequacy or apodicticity. Adequate evidence is evidence that is complete. A perfect induction in science or exhaustive examination of all the sides of a thing would be examples of such completeness. I am not sure myself that one can give an example of perfect evidence in this sense that actually occurs. Most of the time, perhaps all the time, we experience the idea of adequacy negatively through experienced inadequacy or incompleteness of evidence. There are always unconsidered examples, unseen sides, and vague obscurities.[29]

A different sense of evidence, apodicticity, has a higher dignity and can occur even in evidence that is inadequate. This apodicticity has the property of being absolutely indubitable, and its superiority is evinced in the scientist's endeavor to ground further already adequate claims in principles that are apodictic. Apodicticity has the "signal peculiarity of being *at the same time the absolute unimaginableness* (inconceivability) of their [states of affairs] *non-being*, and thus excluding in advance every doubt as 'objectless', empty."[30]

Husserl's reflection then turns to inquiring into what starting point is apodictic. Is the existence of the world apodictic? Though its existence is obvious and its evidence is prior to all other evidence, nonetheless we become doubtful that the world is apodictic. Not only can the perception of an individual thing prove to be an illusion, but the world itself as a whole could be but a coherent dream. Not only all the sciences based upon the evidence of the world, but the world itself, therefore, must be put in brackets and treated only as an acceptance phenomenon.[31]

What, then, is an absolutely impregnable starting point? If we must bracket the thesis of the world, that move affects the intramundane existence of all other egos as well, since I know them only through their bodily behavior in the world. If other men must be bracketed, then so also must all the cultural and political formations that presuppose other human beings.[32]

Whether the phenomena of the world are illusory or true, however, still these phenomena as mine are not nothing. And even if I abstain from all belief in the world, still this abstaining is mine and cannot be doubted. When I abstain from belief in the world or particular things or persons within it, what is still present are these phenomena as phenomena. The universal depriving of acceptance, therefore, allows me to gain not only the world as phenomenon, as meant, but also the pure life of the ego, aware of itself as intending the world through perceiving, remembering, imagining, thinking, and choosing. Thus the being of the ego, because it is more certain, is prior to the being of the world. The method whereby we recover the ego in its pure intending life is the transcendental, phenomenological *epoche* or reduction.[33]

Because the ego is absolutely, apodictically certain of itself, it is distinct from the psychophysical, embodied ego, which is part of the bracketed world. By phenomenological *epoche*, I reduce my psychological self-experience to transcendental, phenomenological self-experience. The world that exists for me, including my own embodied, psychophysical self, derives its sense and existential status from me as transcendental ego. But just as the ego is not a piece of the world, so the world is not an inherent part of the ego. Even in the presence of the reduced world to the conscious self there is a minimal "transcendence" as part of the essence of anything worldly. Because this transcendence is constituted as part of the sense of the world, the ego is legitimately called "transcendental" in the phenomenological sense.[34]

Husserl in this extremely Cartesian moment of his thought is, therefore, oriented to a presuppositionless approach, not accepting any judgment that has not been grounded in evidence, wiping the slate clean of any judgments not so grounded. However, in so striving to be free from prejudice, Husserl seems to give into a prejudice against prejudice. Although as beginning philosophers we do not accept any normative idea of science, "this does not imply that we renounce the general aim of grounding science absolutely."[35] An absolute grounding of science, however, implies no ungrounded presuppositions if such a science is to avoid judgments that are not grounded or are only partially grounded. Husserl, therefore, seems to be implicitly indebted to the tradition of modern philosophy, especially to Descartes, in a way that is at odds with his attempt to be presuppositionless. Even at this stage Husserlian immanence tends to explode itself from within.

It is because of such problems that Husserl explicitly takes up historical reflection in the *Crisis*. History is not just an example of truth or of falling away from the truth that we know outside of history. Rather, historical reflection by the philosopher is essential for the philosopher himself because he is essentially temporal and social. As Husserl himself puts it, "Only an understanding from within of the movement of modern philosophy from Descartes to the present, which is coherent despite all its contradictions, makes possible an understanding of the present itself. . . . Philosophy and science would accordingly be the historical movement through which universal reason, 'inborn' in humanity as such, is revealed."[36]

Motivating Husserl's inquiry here is the crisis of the sciences expressing itself in a positivistic misunderstanding of their own method and truth. Present especially in human sciences such as psychology, this crisis also becomes a practical lived crisis of humanity as such. Subjectivity is ignored in the worship of fact. "Merely fact-minded sciences make merely fact-minded people."[37] As a result, there is a scientific and practical turning away from questions essential for the meaning of human existence. To understand how such a crisis originated we must inquire back into history.

It is the very orientation to exposing and bringing to light all presuppositions, therefore, that motivates Husserl's turn toward history. If there are historically acquired prejudices as well as natural prejudices, full, lucid grounding in evidence demands that I unpack those prejudices. If certain historically acquired prejudices are internal to the philosophical, phenomenological enterprise itself—for example, the history of modern philosophy giving me a language and set of questions out of which and about which I think—then phenomenology itself has to reflect historically on its own genesis. Let me quote Husserl again.

> What is clearly necessary (what else could be of help here?) is that we *reflect back*, in a thorough *historical* and *critical* fashion, in order to provide, *before all decisions*, for a radical self-understanding: we must inquire back into what was originally and always sought in philosophy, what was continually sought by all the philosophers and philosophies that have communicated with one another historically; but this must include a *critical* consideration of what, in respect to the goals and methods [of philosophy], is ultimate, original, and genuine and which, once seen, apodictically conquers the will.[38]

There is, then, an historical reduction that complements the phenomenological reduction. The philosopher as the historical functionary of mankind should inquire back into the fundamental reshaping of the task of philosophy that took place at the beginning of the modern era. What is new and unprecedented is the ideal of a rational mastery of the totality of being. The ideal of a total systematic rational comprehension of the universe receives its first scientific expression in Galileo and its first philosophical expression in Descartes.[39]

In Galileo, the project takes the form of the mathematization of nature. Prescientifically the world is given in a subjectively relative manner. To each of us the world appears somewhat different, and for each of us these appearances count as valid. Even though we believe in one world, we all are aware of discrepancies among individual perceptions. My "green" is not necessarily identical to yours; nor is your "cold" identical to mind.[40]

When we render the shapes of our world more abstract by imagining them or drawing figures for the sake of practical projects such as surveying, we do not initially reach ideal geometrical shapes, but only shapes more or less straight, flat, circular, and so on. When we go further and act as geometers to construct not just images of triangles and circles but definitions and proofs, then we reach an exactness not attainable in prescientific, pre-mathematical knowing.[41] Geometry-idealized shapes and objectivities initially developed in the prescientific art of measuring. The geometry and astronomy that Galileo took over as worked out by Euclid and others was already pregiven to Galileo, as was the art of measurement, with its increasing exactness. Because the art of measurement and sciences of geometry and astronomy were so given, Galileo felt no need for a "passionate *praxis of inquiry*" into their genesis from prescientific modes of encounter with the world.[42]

But in taking over these achievements, Galileo gives them a new twist by attempting to universalize them. He attempts a totally systematic, scientific comprehension of the material world, even the qualities not directly quantifiable, such as color. As a result, there is a move to make quantification an index of what is real. Primary qualities that can be described, thought, and measured quantitatively are real; secondary qualities are merely subjective.[43]

As modern science develops within this perspective, there is movement toward greater and greater abstractness, from measuring to Euclidean geometry to concentration on formulas to arithmetization of geometry to formalization of meaning in formal logic to technization, which uses the formulas in science and technology but has forgotten the original thinking that gave rise to them. As a result, in a "fallacy of misplaced concreteness,"[44] the formulas themselves are taken for the total truth. "Mathematics and mathematical science, as a garb of ideas, or the garb of symbols of the symbolic mathematical theories, encompasses everything which, for scientists and the educated generally, *represents* the life-world, *dresses it up* as 'objectively actual and true' nature. It is through the garb of ideas that we take for *true being* what is actually a *method....*"[45]

What is forgotten in such misplaced concreteness is the life-world as the prescientific context from which and out of which all scientific theorizing goes on. "For the human being in his surrounding world there are many types of praxis, and among them is this peculiar and historically late one, theoretical praxis." Forgotten also is the genesis of scientific truth from its original beginnings in prescientific perceiving and measuring of bodies. This forgetfulness has portentous consequences for the history of modern philosophy and modern life.[46]

Descartes takes over from Galileo the idea of philosophy as universal mathematics. He takes over the Galilean notion of a world-in-itself, and he reifies the ego into soul only problematically, contingently related to what is not itself. But ideas that upset this rationalism are also present in the *Meditations*. Descartes discovers intentionality, the self's presence in its own conscious activity to what is not itself—and discovers an entirely new beginning for philosophy by grounding it in subjectivity. But if intentionality is real, the notion of an "outside" to the ego makes no sense.[47]

The result of accepting Galileo's notion that all bodies are real only as knowable scientifically leads to dualism, between primary qualities and secondary qualities and between mind and body. This confidence in a physicalistic, rationalistic model takes two forms, the all-encompassing, rationalistic systems of Leibniz and Spinoza and the naturalizing empiricism that moves from Locke through Hume. In such empiricism there are two basic assumptions: that the soul is a psychic thing similar to physical things and that the method of knowing the soul, moving from description to explanation, is similar to biophysics.[48]

Empiricism works out the implications of Descartes' psychologically adulterated transcendentalism. In Locke there is a complete overlooking of the intentionality discovered by Descartes and a curious mixture of skepticism and dogmatism. He takes over the idea of ego as soul. Problems present in Descartes, such as the question about how the self-enclosed subject is able to transcend his own subjectivity to reach objective being, turn into questions of psychological genesis. That sense data are affections from the outside is not a problem for him but something taken for granted. The soul is taken as something passive and thing-like, which receives representations from without but has no *a priori* structure or content of its own. At the same time Locke develops a skepticism about the ability of science to know things in themselves. "We have adequate representations and knowledge only of what is in our own soul." [49]

Locke's inconsistent mixture of dogmatism and skepticism becomes more strictly, purely skeptical in Berkeley and Hume. Berkeley draws the proper skeptical conclusion about external space from Locke's premises that we know only our own ideas and representations and that we do not know the essences of external things. External space itself is a fiction and construction. Hume takes such skepticism to its logical conclusion. All categories of objectivity—mathematics, space, external things—are simply fictional constructions out of given sense data. Even the "I" is a psychological fiction. "To be consistent, we must say: reason, knowledge, including that of true values, of pure ideals of every sort, including the ethical—all this is fiction." [50]

From a starting point in objectivism, modern philosophy comes in Hume to subjectivistic solipsism, for how could inferences from data to other data ever reach objective being? Hume did not ask the question about the status of the reason that established his theory as truth. Would not that reasoning itself be just another datum, another association, another fiction? Like all skepticism or irrationalism, therefore, Hume's cancels itself out. But his comfortable academic skepticism, which tries to disguise as harmless or absurd his absurd results, fathers an effective, unhealthy positivism that stays on the surface of the philosophical abyss and contents itself with the successes of the positive sciences and their psychologistic elucidation. [51]

Nonetheless, there is in Hume a shaping of a naïve, dogmatic objectivism, an awareness that all objectivities are "accomplishments" of consciousness itself. What Hume did, from Husserl's perspective, was to misinterpret the results of such discovery skeptically because of his own naïve notions of experience and reason. But Hume's skeptical results lay the groundwork for a new kind of objectivity grounded in conscious, intentional experience. [52]

With Kant, a new kind of transcendental subjectivism emerges, one that has learned from Hume but one that more properly is the successor to the rationalist tradition as that has developed up through Christian Wolff. Kant's is the first fully worked-out transcendental philosophy attempting to exhibit the *a priori* structure of human knowing, moral activity, and aesthetic perception. To that extent he takes a step forward. He does, however, accept the world as described by science and does not inquire into the life-world as the ground of science. There is the lack of an intuitive exhibiting method in Kant's approach, which leads him to attempt to deduce concepts *a priori* rather than to disclose them reflectively through eidetic description. Because he is too much influenced by the naturalism and objectivism of modern philosophy, his concept of experience is too narrow, confined to either external or internal sensations. For these reasons he falls into paradoxes and contradictions, such as claiming that things-in-themselves exist but claiming at the same time that we cannot know them; or using categories such as cause or substance or existence, initially restricted to phenomena, to talk about things-in-themselves.[53]

The history of modern philosophy as that culminates in Kant, therefore, is a dialectic between transcendentalism and objectivism.[54] Transcendental phenomenology emerges as the truth of such a dialectic. In contrast to Descartes', Husserl's ego is intentionally present to the world. In contrast to Kant's, Husserl's mode of theorizing is an eidetic description that intuitively reveals and understands all human experience. In contrast to Kant's world, the life-world comes into explicit, thematic focus as the ground of science. In contrast to Kant's and the empiricists' experience, human experience is not simply experience of sensuous objects, but experience of myself as a conscious self perceiving, imagining, remembering, understanding, judging, and choosing. As Husserl says in the *Ideas*, "If by '*Positivism*' we are to mean the absolute unbiased grounding of all science on what is 'positive', i.e., on what can be primordially apprehended, then it is *we* [phenomenologists] who are the genuine positivists."[55]

When we theorize phenomenologically, the life-world initially appears as the subjective–relative in contrast to the objective revealed by science. The life-world appears simply as a partial problem appended to thinking the objectivity of the sciences. However, as we reflect, this contrast between subjective and objective begins to turn on its head. For we discover that perceptions in the life-world, which in their own way are objective, are necessary to ground science. The falling bodies I think about are initially perceived by me, and experiments verifying the law of falling bodies terminate in life-world perceptions. If these are merely subjective and not objective, therefore, the hypotheses of science itself would be merely subjective. Moreover, certain presuppositions, such as the intersubjective nature of truth, are themselves derived from the life-world. Einstein uses the Michelson experiments and the corroboration of them by other researchers.

> But Einstein could make no use whatever of a theoretical psychological-psychophysical construction of the objective being of Mr. Michelson; rather, he made use of the human being who was accessible to him, as to everyone else in the prescientific world, as an object of straightforward experience, the human being whose existence, with this vitality, in these activities and creations within the common life-world, is always the presupposition for all of Einstein's objective-scientific lines of inquiry, projects, and accomplishments pertaining to Michelson's experiments.[56]

Not only does the life-world ground science, but the life-world in another sense includes science. When we see that science is just one project among many that human beings undertake in the life-world and that the results of science are themselves products of an activity that is chosen and that operates according to certain criteria and values, then we see scientific theorizing as part of the life-world conceived as the totality of projects. In two senses, therefore, Husserl relativizes claims of science to be absolutely the only form of knowing: science is founded on life-world perceptions and science is part of the life-world.[57] Still another overcoming of scientism and positivism occurs when we reflect on phenomenological theorizing itself. For what we have been doing is reflectively trying to ground science in the life-world. An ungrounded science, one that leaves its presuppositions unexamined, is not fully scientific. But the only way to ground science fully is to transcend it as positive science and recover it phenomenologically as grounded in the life-world. Not only does phenomenology emerge as a crucial counter-instance to scientism, but the life-world, rather than being a part, a mere subjective appendage to the objective sciences, has become the whole. Science has been seen to be not only objective but subjective, not whole but part. The life-world has been seen to be not only subjective but objective, not part but whole.

In *Crisis*, therefore, Husserl makes a breakthrough to history and the life-world. On the other hand, these very breakthroughs tend to explode even more the Cartesian immanence with which he began in *Cartesian Meditations*. If history is essential for philosophical self-understanding, and historical judgments about history and history of philosophy are contingent and not apodictic, how can apodicticity be possible in phenomenology? Moreover, if the very turn to history uncovers some presuppositions, does not this same turn make it seem unlikely that a total account of all presuppositions is possible? Recovery of the life-world as the ground of all thought gives us another inexhaustible fount that can never be exhaustively thematized. We are tempted to say, with Merleau-Ponty, that "The most important lesson which the reduction teaches us is the impossibility of a complete reduction."[58]

Finally, if perception founds all thought and if perception is essentially embodied, can the distinction between transcendental and embodied ago, established in *Cartesian Meditations* and reiterated in *Crisis*, be maintained? Is not such a distinction a Cartesian remnant in Husserl that his discovery of the life-world should force him to expunge? Husserl's very attempt to expand his project of presuppositionless phenomenology leads him to discoveries that undermine that project.[59]

The Triumph of Ambiguity

This section has a twofold purpose. The first is to show that within their respective traditions of analytic philosophy and phenomenology Wittgenstein and Merleau-Ponty make equivalent moves away from meaning conceived as concrete, pluralistic, contextualistic, implicit, and tentative. In a word, meaning is ambiguous. Whereas earlier thinkers, Descartes and Husserl, tried to overcome ambiguity and leave it behind, the later Wittgenstein and Merleau-Ponty accept ambiguity and make it the basis of their philosophies. The first part of this section establishes the fact and meaning of this triumph of ambiguity.

The second part assesses the limits of the triumph. Although there are deep affinities between Wittgenstein and Merleau-Ponty on the issue of meaning, there are also significant differences. One of these is the issue of family resemblances *vs.* universal eidetic patterns as the foundation of meaning in the common-sense world. Has ambiguity triumphed to the extent that no essences remain, only a rough, overlapping family of similarities? The second part of this section explores this question.

One might ask what the point is in comparing thinkers so dissimilar in orientation, products of the very different traditions of analytic philosophy and phenomenology. The answer is that philosophical isolation is not good. If I can show that common ground is present, then fruitful philosophical dialogue can take place.[60] Also, in any discussion of analytic philosophy and phenomenology, two errors have to be avoided. The first is perceiving nothing but disagreement; the second, stressing excessively the common ground and thus risking a too facile synthesis or harmony. My treatment, arguing for both deep affinities and at least one important difference, avoids both these errors.

The Fact and Meaning of the Triumph · Meaning for both Wittgenstein and Merleau-Ponty is essentially descriptive, not explanatory. Meaning is not hidden in some entity behind or above the phenomena of experience, but present in these phenomena. Philosophy, Wittgenstein says, simply puts everything before us. It does not interfere with the actual use of language, but can only describe it. Philosophy leaves everything as it is because every sentence in our language is in order as it is. "[D]on't think, but look!"[61]

Merleau-Ponty's phenomenology also describes rather than explaining or analyzing. If one takes seriously Husserl's advice to return to the things themselves as they are immediately experienced, one must reject scientific explanation as an adequate account of oneself. One cannot rightly conceive of oneself simply as a part of the world, as the outcome of certain objective causal processes. Nor is one a pure Cartesian subject divorced from the world. The phenomenological reduction, the attempt to describe human experience without common-sense, scientific, or idealistic prejudices, reveals an embodied subject in the world who initially experiences the world from a point of view.

I experience such a world, not as the outcome of a series of syntheses, but as the pre-reflective setting or context in which such syntheses take place. To be in a room reading a book is to be explicitly aware of the book and its meaning and implicitly, vaguely aware of the room, noises outdoors, the city, nature, and so on. This setting or field is the ultimate horizon within which human subjects perceive, reflect, and interact with one another. This horizon is "world" in a phenomenological sense.[62]

Consequently, both the later Wittgenstein and Merleau-Ponty react against excessively logicist, abstract, ideal notions of meaning because such notions are not descriptive. Both thinkers bring philosophy down to earth. Wittgenstein, rejecting his own earlier idea of a philosophy modeled on an ideal calculus, affirms the priority and importance of ordinary language. Merleau-Ponty, rejecting the Husserlian ideal of a complete reduction wherein the human subject knows himself with total clarity, asserts that the life-world is the ground of meaning. Ordinary language, the total family of common-sense uses of language, and the life-world, the total, pretheoretical lived context within which all human projects take place, are not to be transcended and left behind for some ideal, metaphysical realm of meaning, but to be explored for the meanings they already contain.[63] "What *we* do is to bring words back from their metaphysical to their everyday use," says Wittgenstein.[64] "The perceived world is the always presupposed foundation of all rationality, all value and all existence," says Merleau-Ponty.[65]

A consequence of such a philosophical move is that both affirm the priority of concrete speech over abstract systems of language. Meaning is not some ideal, mathematical system, says Wittgenstein, but the way we use the word or sentence in concrete situations—the meaning is the use. Meaning is found primarily not in some Husserlian phenomenology of all possible languages, suggests Merleau-Ponty, but in the specific situation in which speaking subjects interact with one another in a particular language.[66]

For both thinkers this return to the rough ground of the common-sense world means a rejection of Cartesianism. Meaning is public and expressive, not private and internal. For Wittgenstein meaning is not a second, independent process running alongside the external language games we play, but is rather inextricably linked to these very language games. Most of the time an accompanying feeling or thought is as inessential to the meaning of the language game as the addition of a paper crown, which leaves the use of the piece unaltered, to a white king in a chess game. "I have been trying in all this to remove the temptation to think that there '*must* be' what is called a mental process of thinking, hoping, wishing, believing, etc., independent of the process of expressing a thought, a hope, a wish, etc."[67]

Expressions such as "having an idea before one's mind" can be quite misleading. They suggest that there is already a complete, fully articulated idea that has only to be translated into external words. Most of the time something very different happens. The "idea" before the mind becomes complete only in the process of expressing it. This process is what happens when a person gropes for a word, several words are proposed and rejected, finally the right one is proposed, and he says "That is what I meant." The proof for the impossibility of trisecting the angle with ruler and compasses does not just analyze our idea of the trisection of an angle; rather it gives us a new idea of trisection, one which we did not have prior to the proof.[68]

Merleau-Ponty's rejection of Cartesianism is grounded in his affirmation of the lived body. The Cartesian dilemma of how to bridge the gap between a pure intellectual subject and a world of objective bodies is solved by such a move. "The experience of our own body, on the other hand, reveals to us an ambiguous mode of existing."[69] The lived body is not an object like other things in the world, but is that whereby a person is able to know things at all. To perceive a table in a room is to be aware implicitly of oneself as the embodied, incarnate perceiver—the body is subject, not object. It is that whereby a person is able to be present to the world. A person observes external objects with her body; but she does not observe her body. To do so she would need a second body, which itself would be unobservable, and would thus be involved in an infinite regress. A person's body is a permanent presence, an absolute "here" that cannot be distinguished from herself.[70]

Because of the primacy of the lived body, there is no thought that is complete in itself apart from external expression. "The orator does not think before speaking, nor even while speaking; his speech is his thought." When a person reads a text, there is no thought marginal to the text itself, for the words fully occupy the mind. A person speaks not just to communicate but also to know, herself, what she intends. Speech enables a person to take possession of meanings otherwise present only in a muffled way. The relation between speech and thought is internal, not external.[71]

For both thinkers the meaning of an expression is essentially related to the context in which it is uttered. Meaning is holistic. Language for Wittgenstein is a family of language games. Just as the move of a pawn in a game of chess cannot be understood apart from the other possible moves and rules of the game, so also the meaning of a word, phrase, or sentence cannot be understood apart from the language game in which it is played. The meaning of a sentence such as "I would like the bed made" will vary, depending on whether the language game is one of describing, exhorting, commanding, or prescribing.

Meaning is not simply explicit, but implicit, part of the context of the language game. If someone had said "Napoleon was crowned in 1804," and we asked him "Did you mean the man who won the battle of Austerlitz?" he might say "Yes, I meant him." But this does not imply that the idea of Napoleon, the victor in the battle of Austerlitz, was present when the speaker said that Napoleon was crowned in 1804. The sentence "Bring me a brick" has its meaning in contrast with other sentences in the language—for instance, "Take these two bricks away." But a person need not have the latter sentence in mind when he speaks the former. All that is important is "that these contrasts should exist in the system of language which he is using, and that they need not in any sense be present in his mind when he utters his sentence."[72]

For Merleau-Ponty as well, meaning is a function of context, a context that is always partially latent and implicit, a "cohesive whole of convergent linguistic gestures, each of which will be defined less by a signification than by a use value." The elements of a language form a synchrony in the sense that each of them signifies only in relation to the others. Each sign used singly alludes to the meaning of the whole, even though this whole is never an explicit object. Two people talking about the latest symphony orchestra concert use words like "movement," "scherzo," and "sonata form" that presume a systematic whole of shared, implicit musical understanding. Such speaking subjects, always projecting a future, make use of this habitual or sedimented system of language to say what has never been said before.[73]

Such contextualism leads both thinkers to a rejection of atomism. Wittgenstein, renouncing his own earlier notion that language can be broken down into clear, definite atomic statements referring to ultimately simple atomic facts, asks "What are the simple parts of a chair? Are they the pieces of wood, the molecules, or the atoms?"

His answer is that it makes no sense to speak absolutely of the simple parts of the chair. If the language game is common-sense description, simples in that language game could be the bits of wood. If the language game is chemistry, the simples could be molecules. Simples are defined in the context of the language game being played.[74]

Is not a chessboard composed of ultimate simples, the thirty-two white and thirty-two black squares? Wittgenstein answers that we could also say that it was composed of the colors black and white and the schema of squares. Considering a complex of red, green, white, and black monochrome squares, he says that under certain circumstances it makes sense to call a monochrome square composite, consisting perhaps of two rectangles or of the elements of color and shape. It makes no sense to talk about simples outside a particular language game.[75]

Wittgenstein's rejection of atomism is also present in his account of perception, where he denies any hard and fast distinction between atomic, sensible givens and interpretation, between "seeing" and "seeing as." Seeing a drawing as a cube, he says, is not two experiences: seeing it as a plane figure, plus seeing it in depth. "Seeing something as a swastika" does not mean seeing something as something else. "Seeing dashes as a face" does not involve a comparison between a group of dashes and a real human face. There is one visual object, not two, and the dashes have their meaning as parts of the real human face. When I see a picture of a rabbit, I do not necessarily say that I am seeing it now as a rabbit, any more than I would say that I am seeing these utensils now as a knife and a fork. If I begin to see a picture of a rabbit as a duck, then my visual experience itself changes. The so-called sensible givens are related to the interpretation and vice versa.[76]

For Merleau-Ponty, perception is essentially of a gestalt, a figure-on-ground in which all the elements are essentially related to a whole. A white patch on a homogeneous background can be perceived only against that background. Each point in the patch has meaning as part of a shape, and even a mere point can be perceived only as a figure on a background. That which is perceived is always in the middle of something else, is always part of a field. Sensation as pure atomistic impression is a myth. "[E]xistence is not a set of facts (like 'psychic facts') capable of being reduced to others or to which they can reduce themselves, but the ambiguous setting of their inter-communication. . . ."[77] The red patch seen on the carpet is red only in virtue of a shadow that lies across it, and its quality is apparent only in relation to the play of light upon it. The color can be said to be there only if it occupies an area of a certain size, because too small an area is not describable in these terms. Finally, this red would not be the same if it were not the "wooly red" of a carpet. Qualities are inherently meaningful—matter is pregnant with form.

Philosophy, therefore, must move away from the prejudice of a determinate world known through sensations that are clear and discrete. "In other words, ambiguity is of the essence of human existence, and everything we live or think has always several meanings."[78] Because we experience the world as a theme emerging from a vague background, because of phenomena such as the Muller–Lyer illusion where two objectively equal straight lines are not perceived as equal, because I may perceive the shape of a crystal or a familiar face without detailed knowledge of the parts, perceptual experience is essentially ambiguous. "The theory of sensation, which builds up all knowledge out of determinate qualities, offers us objects purged of all ambiguity, pure and absolute, the ideal rather than the real themes of knowledge. . . ."[79]

Wittgenstein moves away from a univocal theory of language as description of objective facts toward the affirmation of a multiplicity of language games, a pluralistic theory of meaning. Merleau-Ponty moves away from the Husserlian ideal of total clarity to an affirmation of many levels of consciousness, each with its own standard of clarity, truth, and value. For Wittgenstein meaning is not only description of actual or possible states of affairs, but many other things as well—for example, questions, commands, prescriptions. None of these is to be judged deficient insofar as it is not descriptive; each is to be accepted on its own terms. For Merleau-Ponty meaning is not simply scientific or intellectualistic, but rather grounded in perception, and perceptual meaning is not reducible to scientific or intellectualistic terms. Perception of a cube is not sensation because I perceive a total gestalt, not a series of isolated qualities. Perception is not the outcome of an intellectual synthesis made according to some ideal geometrical law, because I experience the unseen side of a cube as a presence, as the result of a practical synthesis. The unseen side experienced in perception is not what I think abstractly, but what I can touch with my hand.[80]

For both philosophers the ideal of total clarity and certitude is a myth to be rejected. For Wittgenstein the ideal of exactness, the notion that the use of language must be bounded everywhere by rules removing all ambiguity and all doubt, is a myth. We get along quite well most of the time in ordinary language with some indeterminancy and some vagueness. The attempt to get an absolutely clear explanation devoid of ambiguity leads to an infinite regress of explanations. If I say that by "Moses" I mean the man who led the Israelites out of Egypt, doubts may arise about the meaning of "Egypt," of "Israelites," and so on. An explanation serves only to avert a specific misunderstanding, not to exclude all possible misunderstandings.[81]

If I tell someone "Stand roughly here," this explanation may work perfectly even though it does not conform to some abstract ideal of clarity and exactness. Most of the time in ordinary life we are not in doubt, although it is possible to us to imagine a doubt. It is possible that a person could doubt before she opened her front door whether an abyss did not yawn behind it and would make sure about it before she went through. Most of the time, however, we do not do this because we perceive such precautions to be unnecessary. The purposes of the language game determine the degree of exactness required. "The kind of certainty is the kind of language-game."[82]

Why is it, then, that the ideal of absolute exactness, clarity, and certitude seems to hang on in philosophy? Wittgenstein suggests that the thirst for general explanations is a search for a precisely, clearly defined essence. Show the illusory character of that search and you have at the same time rejected absolute exactness as a universal necessity. As a matter of fact, it is this search for exact explanations that gives rise to most of the puzzles in philosophy. We try to arrive at a universal definition of time and are puzzled when our definition does not cover all the actual uses of the word "time."[83]

For Merleau-Ponty, the Husserlian ideal of apodictic eidetic truth is illusory because a human being is an incarnate consciousness who can never totally thematize all his experience. Incarnate consciousness is a field within which a thematic figure is set off against a vague, indeterminate, implicit background. "This ambiguity is not some imperfection of consciousness or existence, but the definition of them."[84] Also, reflective consciousness has to rely on sedimented presuppositions and assumptions, not all of which can be explicitly criticized and justified at any one time. Consequently reflective thinking about the world presupposes a perceptually known world that reflective thinking itself has not constituted. Prior to thinking about the world scientifically, the perceiver discovers a world that is already there. The free fall that the scientist investigates is initially experienced in perception, not science. Because consciousness is incarnate, therefore, apodictic clarity is impossible. Again we run up against the impossibility of a complete reduction.[85]

Perception itself is a paradox of immanence and transcendence that I cannot dissolve in some non-contradictory thought, but must simply accept. A perceived thing is immanent in the sense that it is always present to the person who perceives it, transcendent in the sense that it is never totally given to the person perceiving. There are always unseen sides, aspects, and so on. Because such is the case, there is no absolute guarantee that a perception is true, and this same tentativeness survives on the level of reflective consciousness itself. For example, later developments have shown the Pythagorean theorem and Euclidean geometry as only partial, not absolute, unconditional truth. There is no guarantee that six months or a year from now I will hold the ideas I do now, and even the best ideas will require additions and qualifications.[86]

To conclude this section, then: I have shown that both philosophers make similar moves away from preconceived views about what experience must be toward experience as it actually occurs. Do not impose some abstract ideal of explanatory clarity on language, Wittgenstein says, but pay close attention to the way language games are played. Do not approach perception with the prejudice that it must be sensation or intellection or a conjunction of the two, Merleau-Ponty advises, but describe perception as it is actually experienced. Do not give in to a thirst for general explanations, despising the particular case; realize, rather, that particular, concrete language games are all there are and that they are enough. Do not approach experience with the intellectualistic prejudice that consciousness must be unsituated and totally clear to itself; phenomenologically reflect on the actual experience of an incarnate consciousness not totally present to itself.[87]

Both thinkers, therefore, move away from meaning as univocal clarity and certainty toward meaning as ambiguity: descriptive, public, expressive, contextualistic, open, partially implicit, pluralistic, and tentative. The search for an absolutely certain, clear foundation for philosophy, whether that be atomic facts or a pure Cartesian subject, is illusory. The goal of philosophy is no longer to exclude all possible error, but to describe actual human experience in all its richness and nuance. Ambiguity, rather than being the bane of philosophy, becomes its glory.

The Limits of the Triumph · Nonetheless, at this point certain disturbing questions arise. Is the job of philosophy simply to celebrate ambiguity and to bring no positive illumination of its own? If so, then the triumph of ambiguity is the negation of philosophy, at least in any traditional sense. And indeed Wittgenstein himself seems to accept this consequence. Philosophical questioning is the result of a misguided search for an exact, clearly defined essence. Once the illusory character of the search is revealed, tortuous philosophical thinking can cease. The fly can find its way out of the fly bottle. Such cessation of philosophical thinking even brings a certain paradoxical clarity, a clarity that comes from the acceptance of ambiguity. "For the clarity that we are aiming at is indeed *complete* clarity. But this simply means that the philosophical problems should *completely* disappear."[88]

If essences are illusory, an objector might ask, how does Wittgenstein explain the use of general words, like "leaf," "cat," "man," and "person"? Wittgenstein's answer is family resemblance. There is no common property that makes people members of a human family. Some people have the same nose; others, the same eyebrows; and others, the same style of walking. These likenesses overlap. Family resemblance, not one property common to all members of a class, grounds the use of general words. The latter is a Platonic hangover that leads to most of our difficulties in philosophy.[89]

Wittgenstein thus rejects the advice Socrates gives Meno to define not just particular kinds of virtue, but virtue itself. Such philosophy has a contempt for the particular case, and what has to be relearned is a reverence for such particulars. One should not reject a definition of number that applies only to finite cardinals, because such a limited definition may be quite illuminating. If we study the grammar of words like "wishing," "thinking," "understanding," and "meaning," we should not be dissatisfied when we have described various cases of wishing, thinking, and so on. For there is not one definite class of features that characterizes all cases of wishing. If a person wanted to give a clear definition of wishing including such a set of features, his definition would never coincide with actual language.[90]

At this point a strong disagreement with Merleau-Ponty emerges. Although he agrees with Wittgenstein about the value of describing particular cases, he still affirms the value of essence in philosophy. These essences are not apart from existence in the life-world, but inseparable from it. Examples of such essences are the notions that all perception is perspectival, that perception is of a figure-on-ground, that reflection must always use either perception or images derived from perception, and that free decisions are motivated.[91]

This affirmation of essence even survives in the thought of the later Merleau-Ponty, in the so-called ontological period. For example, in *The Visible and the Invisible*, he emphasizes that essence is the structure or style of the invisible—the existentials or hinges of the life-world through which persons and things manifest themselves. When I perceive a person, she appears to me a certain way, perspectivally, temporally, as a figure emerging from a ground, and so on. The way a person appears to me ordinarily is not thematic for me—it is invisible. Philosophical reflection makes this mode of appearance thematic. "No longer are there essences above us, like positive objects, offered to a spiritual eye; but there is an essence beneath us, a common nervure of the signifying and the signified, adherence in and reversibility of one another—as the visible things are the secret folds of our flesh, and yet our body is one of the visible things."[92]

The triumph of ambiguity in Merleau-Ponty, therefore, is not unalloyed. What distinguishes the philosopher is his taste for evidence and ambiguity, but there is a bad and a good ambiguity. Bad ambiguity is an equivocation that menaces all certitude and knowledge; good ambiguity contributes to certitude. Good ambiguity consists in that "movement which leads back without ceasing from knowledge to ignorance, from ignorance to knowledge, and a kind of rest in this movement." Sometimes philosophy reaches a point where life is the same to oneself, to others, and to the true, a universality that is not above time but common to all times.[93] Good ambiguity implies an essential knowledge that is neither apodictic nor absolute.

Of the two thinkers, therefore, Wittgenstein is the more radical with respect to the traditional concern for essence. The triumph of ambiguity for him is far more extreme. Whether Wittgenstein is correct or not is another question. For the disagreement between him and Merleau-Ponty concerns the limits of the triumph. Is the search for essence to be consigned to the philosophical dustbin? Is family resemblance or essence the more proper access to meaning in the life-world?

To a phenomenologist who says that one of the universal characteristics of perception is awareness of a particular, embodied figure-on-ground, Wittgenstein would say that "perceive" and "sense" and "see" have uses that cannot be restricted to this narrow sphere. Such words are often used to describe instances more properly intellectual—mathematical or scientific insight, for instance.

Merleau-Ponty's reply would be that, although "perceive," "sense," and "see" can be used to denote intellectual insight, these uses are metaphorical, derivative, and inexact, and that the most proper philosophical use of such words is the one the phenomenologist wishes to give them, external, sensible awareness of an individual gestalt. Such awareness is called perception in an exclusive way because it is primary and because it is essentially different from reflection. It is primary because all other conscious activities presuppose it; mathematical thinking, while directly concerned with the abstract universal, is impossible without using perception or images derived from perception. Perception is essentially different from reflection because the latter knows the universal, whereas the former is concerned with particular individuals. Mathematical thinking knows the universal definition of triangle; perception knows only the individual shaped like a triangle.[94]

The issue here is whether the philosopher has the right to improve on and criticize ordinary, actual usage. Phenomenology says "yes" in order to make clear certain essential differences between kinds of conscious experience such as perception, imagination, reflection, and decision. Wittgenstein seems inconsistent on the point. At times he says that any attempt to make the boundaries sharper and more exact by universal essences is a violation of ordinary, actual usage and, therefore, is more or less arbitrary and incorrect. One must confine oneself to the grammar of particular uses. At other times he talks about the "grammar" of certain expressions like "knowing" in a different way. Such a use of grammar commits him to a universality, in both a negative and a positive sense. It is never correct to use "knowing" for expressions like "knowing one's pain" because such expressions are redundant, and error in such cases is impossible. It is always correct, on the other hand, to use "knowing" in cases where error is conceivable, for instance, in saying that I know the other is in pain. Terms like "knowing" make sense only when their opposites are conceivable. "I can know what someone else is thinking, not what I am thinking. It is correct to say 'I know what you are thinking', and wrong to say 'I know what I am thinking.' (A whole cloud of philosophy condensed into a drop of grammar.)"[95]

In this use of grammar, therefore, Wittgenstein achieves a critical transcendence of ordinary usage that he himself often does not acknowledge. Wittgenstein's ordinary language here is not the ordinary language of the man in the street. Such transcendence is necessary because our ordinary, actual usage covers up those aspects of things that remain most hidden because of their familiarity.[96] In its universality and its distance from the givens of actual usage, such grammar seems to approximate the phenomenological notion of essence. Because Wittgenstein is inconsistent on the issue, phenomenology has the edge in the argument here.

A second argument for family resemblances comes to light in other examples discussed by Wittgenstein. One of these is his analysis of "expecting." To expect someone from 4:00 to 4:30 does not refer to one process but to a great many activities and states of mind. For example, I could look in my appointment book at four, discover the name of the person who is to come, prepare tea, ask myself whether this person smokes, begin to be impatient around 4:30, and imagine how the person will look when she appears. All these activities can be called "expecting B from 4:00 to 4:30," and there are endless variations possible. There is, however, no one activity that is more essential than others, but only a family of activities.[97]

What could a phenomenologist say about such an argument? First of all, the essences with which he is concerned are not of the sort "waiting for B from 4:00 to 4:30." This is merely an empirical, psychological description of consciousness considered as an object in the world. Phenomenology is concerned with the transcendental as opposed to the empirical, with those structures of consciousness and the life-world which make it possible for anything to be learned or done at all. "Waiting for B from 4:00 to 4:30" does presuppose such structures and a certain minimal noematic content as well.

Second, the activity of waiting has a *noema* or object with a certain essential content: "a person who is to come to my room between 4:00 and 4:30." It is true that I do not have to have this content in mind explicitly all the time, but it is present to my consciousness, either implicitly or explicitly, as the purpose of my waiting. I am not waiting for a television program or for the weather to clear, but for a person. I am waiting for this person to appear not at some indefinite time in the next year, but between 4:00 and 4:30. Therefore a certain minimal objective content is necessary.

Third, all the activities Wittgenstein mentioned involve or imply perception and transcendental perceptual structures. Intentionally to wait for a person from 4:00 to 4:30 necessarily involves perception of the time. I perceive when I look in the appointment book around 4 o'clock, when I make tea, and when I begin to be impatient around 4:30. I use prior perceptions, either of B or of other people, when I imagine how B will look.

Finally, one must distinguish between content and form, between what is consciously appropriated or done and how consciousness appropriates that content. I have returned to the notion mentioned earlier of essence as style, as that structure of the life-world and consciousness that makes it possible for any particular "what" or "that" to be known.[98] Even though there is a great deal of empirically discoverable variation possible in what consciousness knows or does, a certain essential "how" is always present, in at least two respects, perceptual and temporal.

First of all, perception has a certain way, which I have already indicated, of relating to any object or person perspectivally, as a figure-on-ground, and so on. Second, waiting for someone has an essentially temporal structure. The structure is of two kinds: the implicit project that consciousness itself is and the explicit project of waiting for someone.

Consciousness is a project because it is temporal. To be conscious is spontaneously and pre-reflectively to anticipate a future in a present flowing out of the past. Past, present, and future are dynamically and internally related aspects of this conscious temporality, none of which makes sense without the other. This level of human temporality is spontaneous and pre-reflective because it is not dependent on freedom or explicit attention to one's own temporality. To listen to a person speak a sentence, for instance, is automatically to anticipate the end of the sentence while retaining what has been said—the end of the sentence makes no sense without the beginning. Consciousness does have an option as to what it will give its attention to. For instance, I could ignore the person who is speaking and listen to music or read a book, but each one of these activities requires the same kind of spontaneous anticipations and retentions.[99]

Besides this most basic level of temporality, inseparable from consciousness itself, there are various explicit projects, determined by choice and reflection. In these projects, time becomes an explicit concern. One of these is the project of waiting for a person. Here on an explicit, thematic level there is a future internally related to a present and a past. My fixing tea in the present anticipates the coming of the person at 4:30 and is motivated because of the past—the person is a good friend, I know she could be influential in getting me a job, and so on. In opposition to Wittgenstein, therefore, the phenomenologist could say that temporality is present in the implicit sense in all conscious activities and in the explicit sense in all activities of "expecting." The psychological contents may vary. I may be afraid of the person, bored by the prospect of spending time with her, or eagerly looking forward to a stimulating conversation with her. Nonetheless the same dynamic "how" is still present, the same structure of internally related anticipations and retentions.

Wittgenstein fails to notice this "how" because he is caught up in the natural attitude, which treats consciousness as an empirical object in the world relating to other objects.[100] Because he considers consciousness as an object, he notices only the multiplicity of psychological contents, not the underlying eidetic "how." Phenomenology moves away from the natural attitude to reflect on the incarnate subject, on the person aware of himself as the source of his conscious activities relating to the world in a certain way.

The move to a phenomenological description of subjectivity does not, therefore, necessarily bring back the non-sensical Cartesian subject so enthusiastically rejected by both Wittgenstein and Merleau-Ponty, a subject that cannot be identified with any particular person in the world.[101] The structures of consciousness are of an incarnate consciousness, essentially expressive and open to the world. As we saw when discussing Merleau-Ponty's analysis of the relation between thought and speech, the "inner" of consciousness is essentially ordered to the "outer" of public expression. The most basic form of human temporality, that which grounds other forms, is perception.

To perceive a chair—moving around it, touching it, seeing it from various angles—is to make use of the same structure of anticipations and retentions already discussed. Also the perceiving subject is aware of herself as a particular person in a particular place and time. She is not an abstract acosmic "anyone" removed from place and time.[102]

CONCLUSION

I have considered both the fact that ambiguity has triumphed and the limits of that triumph. I have judged invalid Wittgenstein's two reasons for family resemblance as opposed to universal essences. Wittgenstein himself at times criticizes and improves on actual usage. Because he does so, the phenomenologist has the same right to say that words like "perception" most properly refer to one kind of activity and not another. Moreover, the psychological multiplicity of conscious experience is grounded in essential eidetic unities Wittgenstein overlooks. The inadequate alternatives of an empirical, psychological world ruled by family resemblance and a Cartesian subject divorced from the world are rejected for an incarnate subject essentially related to the world.

The notion of phenomenology that emerges in this historical reduction is both dialectical and descriptive. Phenomenology is dialectical insofar as it is historically rooted and insofar as it overcomes "either–or" opposition and moves toward a "both–and" mediation. Phenomenology is descriptive in three different senses. First, I describe phenomena of experience with as few presuppositions as possible. Rejecting presuppositionlessness as desirable or possible, I nonetheless attempt to describe human experience as adequately as possible, putting into brackets major, dominant presuppositions—for example, the scientistic presupposition that persons are objective things. In this way I get close to experience in a mediated, not an immediate, immediacy.

Second, I engage in eidetic description whereby I understand and affirm essential structures on each level of human experience, as well as essential relationships between and among levels. Apodicticity in any strong sense, where the possibility of error is excluded, is out because of my rootedness in embodiment, language, tradition, and history. But apodicticity in a weaker sense is possible, where I run up against necessity in my imaginative variation—for example, that perception is perspectival or that perception is embodied. To reach such apodicticity I employ imaginative or eidetic variation, testing my eidetic claims against a judicious selection of counter examples. Yet even this weak sense of apodicticity is not operative in a hermeneutical encounter with tradition or in a hermeneutics of suspicion, two other dimensions of phenomenology I shall explicitly discuss in the last four chapters. Indeed, because eidetic phenomenology is internally qualified by a hermeneutically restorative and suspicious phenomenology, only a weak sense of apodicticity is possible even in the descriptive, eidetic sphere.

Finally, I move into the egological–ontological reduction in which the self in the life-world is the source of meaning in that world, in the sense that for each meaning or level of meaning there is a corresponding conscious act of discovery, creation, choice, and so on. In contrast to Husserl's transcendental ego, mine is embodied, intentionally present in the world to what is not itself, engaged with other things and other people. Nonetheless, because eidetic phenomenology as I practice it uncovers *a priori* noetic and noematic structures, I can legitimately describe this phenomenology as "transcendental method" in a more limited sense.

NOTES

1. See David Carr, *Phenomenology and the Problem of History* (Evanston, Ill.: Northwestern University Press, 1974), pp. 110–20, for a discussion of this move of Husserl's, which Carr describes as an historical reduction. Note, however, that in insisting on a practical as well as a theoretical historical reduction, I have expanded the meaning of this term as it operates in both Carr and Husserl. Note also that the practical historical reduction as it operates in this chapter will not be completed until Chapters 8 and 9. In this chapter, therefore, I describe the experience of alienation that awaits its final, most adequate interpretation in those final chapters.

2. Gabriel Marcel, *Creative Fidelity*, trans. Robert Rosthal (New York: Noonday, 1964), p. 54.

3. First, as the rest of this book will show, these kinds of alienation receive much attention and discussion in the phenomenological literature. Also, there is massive evidence and testimony from different sociological and philosophical traditions about the fact of alienation in this sense and the dominance of the fact. See Max Weber, *Economy and Society*, edd.

Guenther Roth and Claus Wittich, 2 vols. (Berkeley: University of California Press, 1978). Jacques Ellul, *The Technological Society*, trans. John Wilkinson (New York: Vintage, 1964). Herbert Marcuse, *One-Dimensional Man* (Boston: Beacon, 1964). Jürgen Habermas, *Towards a Rational Society*, trans. Jeremy Shapiro (Boston: Beacon, 1970), pp. 81–122. Martin Heidegger, *The Question Concerning Technology, and Other Essays*, trans. William Lovitt (New York: Harper & Row, 1977).

Second, these kinds of alienation are distinctive of the modern era, roughly considered for our purposes here to extend from the time of Descartes to the present. Third, these three kinds of alienation are all-pervasive in Western Europe, England, and the United States, the basic social and historical context I am working out of.

Finally, as I shall show in Chapter 8, because these three kinds of alienation are grounded in and reinforce capitalism, they are dominant over other kinds, such as sexism and racism, which capitalism twists and makes subservient to itself. I do not mean to deny that these ideologies and patterns of domination have an independent origin and relative autonomy in relation to capitalism.

4. Martin Heidegger, *Being and Time*, trans. John Macquarrie and Edward Robinson (New York: Harper & Row, 1962), pp. 210–24.

5. T. S. Eliot, *The Four Quartets* (New York: Harcourt, Brace, & World, 1943), p. 7.

6. Andrew Levison, *The Working-Class Majority* (New York: Coward, McCann & Geoghegan, 1974), pp. 53–69. Harry Braverman, *Labor and Monopoly Capital* (New York: Monthly Review, 1974), pp. 293–356.

7. John Kenneth Galbraith, *The Affluent Society* (New York: Mentor, 1958), pp. 114–30. Stuart Ewen, *Captains of Consciousness: Advertising and the Roots of the Consumer Culture* (New York: McGraw-Hill, 1976).

8. Habermas, *Towards a Rational Society*, pp. 81–122.

9. Jean-Paul Sartre, *The Critique of Dialectical Reason*, ed. Jonathan Ree, trans. Alan Sheridan-Smith (London: New Left Books, 1976), pp. 256–306.

10. A. J. Ayer, *Language, Truth, and Logic* (New York: Dover, 1950), pp. 1–19. Auguste Comte, *Introduction to Positive Philosophy*, ed. and trans. Frederick Ferré, The Library of Liberal Arts (Indianapolis: Bobbs-Merrill, 1970).

11. Ellul, *Technological Society*, pp. 13–19.

12. B. F. Skinner, *Beyond Freedom and Dignity* (New York: Vintage, 1971), pp. 1–24.

13. Edmund Husserl, *Cartesian Meditations*, trans. Dorion Cairns

(The Hague: Nijhoff, 1960), pp. 1–26. Hans-Georg Gadamer, *Truth and Method*, trans. Garrett Barden and John Cumming (New York: Seabury, 1975), pp. 235–74; the phrase is found on p. 240.

14. Edmund Husserl, *The Crisis of European Sciences and Transcendental Phenomenology: An Introduction to Phenomenological Philosophy*, trans. David Carr (Evanston, Ill.: Northwestern University Press, 1970), pp. 3–100.

15. Ibid., pp. 1–19, 60–62; and *Cartesian Meditations*, pp. 1–6.

16. René Descartes, *Meditations on First Philosophy*, in *Philosophers Speak for Themselves: From Descartes to Locke*, edd. T. V. Smith and Marjorie Grene (Chicago: The University of Chicago Press, 1940), pp. 49–69 (the quotation is found on p. 64).

17. Ibid., pp. 69–83. For the definitions of "clear" and "distinct," see p. 70*n.*

18. Ibid., pp. 94–97.

19. Ibid., pp. 102–106.

20. Ibid., p. 112.

21. Ibid., p. 106.

22. Husserl, *Cartesian Meditations*, p. 2.

23. Ibid., pp. 3–6.

24. Ibid., pp. 7–9.

25. Ibid., p. 10.

26. Ibid., pp. 10–11.

27. Ibid., p. 12.

28. Ibid., p. 13.

29. Ibid., pp. 14–15.

30. Ibid., pp. 15–16.

31. Ibid., pp. 17–18.

32. Ibid., pp. 18–19.

33. Ibid., pp. 19–20.

34. Ibid., pp. 20–26.

35. Ibid., p. 8.

36. Husserl, *Crisis*, pp. 14–15, 15–16.

37. Ibid., p. 6.

38. Ibid., pp. 17–18.

39. Ibid., p. 17.

40. Ibid., pp. 23–24.

41. Ibid., pp. 24–28.

42. Ibid., pp. 28–29; the quotation is found on p. 40.

43. Ibid., pp. 28–40, 53.

44. See Alfred North Whitehead, *Process and Reality* (New York: Macmillan, 1929), p. 11, for a definition of this term.

45. Husserl, *Crisis*, 34–51; the quotation is found on p. 51.

46. Ibid., p. 49; the quotation is found on p. 111.

47. Ibid., pp. 73–82.

48. Ibid., pp. 60–65.

49. Ibid., pp. 84–86; the quotation is found on p. 86.

50. Ibid., pp. 86–87; the quotation is found on p. 87.

51. Ibid., pp. 86–88.

52. Ibid., pp. 88–90.

53. Ibid., pp. 91–93.

54. Ibid., p. 70.

55. Edmund Husserl, *Ideas*, trans. W. Boyce Gibson (London: Allen & Unwin; New York: Macmillan, 1931), p. 86.

56. Husserl, *Crisis*, pp. 125–29; the quotation is from pp. 125–26.

57. Ibid., pp. 129–32.

58. Ibid., pp. 132–35. Maurice Merleau-Ponty, *Phenomenology of Perception*, trans. Colin Smith (New York: Humanities, 1962), p. xiv.

59. Husserl, *Crisis*, pp. 182–83.

60. See, for example, Paul Ricoeur, "Husserl and Wittgenstein on Language," in *Phenomenology and Existentialism*, edd. E. N. Lee and M. Mandelbaum (Baltimore: The Johns Hopkins University Press, 1967), pp. 207–17. Eugene TeHennepe, "The Life-World and the World of Ordinary Language," in *An Invitation to Phenomenology*, ed. James Edie (Chicago: Quadrangle, 1965), pp. 133–46.

61. Ludwig Wittgenstein, *Philosophical Investigations*, 2nd ed., trans. G. E. M. Anscombe (New York: Macmillan, 1958), pp. 31, 45, 49, 50; the quotation is found on p. 31.

62. Merleau-Ponty, *Phenomenology of Perception*, pp. viii–xi.

63. Ibid., pp. viii–xxi. Ludwig Wittgenstein, *The Blue and Brown Books* (New York: Harper & Bros., 1958), pp. 25–26; and *Investigations*, 38.

64. Wittgenstein, *Investigations*, p. 48.

65. Maurice Merleau-Ponty, "The Primacy of Perception and Its Philosophical Consequences," in *The Essential Writings of Merleau-Ponty*, ed. Alden L. Fisher (New York: Harcourt, Brace & World, 1969), p. 48.

66. Wittgenstein, *Blue and Brown Books*, pp. 4–5; Maurice Merleau-Ponty, "On the Phenomenology of Language," in *Essential Writings of Merleau-Ponty*, ed. Fisher, pp. 214–23.

67. Wittgenstein, *Blue and Brown Books*, pp. 41–65; the quotation is found on p. 41.

68. Ibid., p. 41. Ludwig Wittgenstein, *Zettel*, edd. G. E. M. Anscombe and G. H. von Wright, trans. G. E. M. Anscombe (Berkeley: University of California Press, 1967), p. 33.

69. Merleau-Ponty, *Phenomenology of Perception*, p. 198.

70. Ibid., pp. 90–92.

71. Ibid., p. 180. Merleau-Ponty, "On the Phenomenology of Language," p. 221. Maurice Merleau-Ponty, *The Prose of the World*, ed. Claude Lefort, trans. John O'Neill (Evanston, Ill.: Northwestern University Press, 1973), p. 114; and *Consciousness and the Acquisition of Language*, trans. Hugh Silverman (Evanston, Ill.: Northwestern University Press, 1973), pp. 4, 6.

72. Wittgenstein, *Blue and Brown Books*, pp. 39, 77–84; the quotation is found on p. 78.

73. Merleau-Ponty, "On the Phenomenology of Language," pp. 217–23 (the quotation is found on p. 217); *Prose of the World*, pp. 26–28, 89; *Consciousness and the Acquisition of Language*, pp. 52, 80, 89, 92.

74. Wittgenstein, *Investigations*, p. 21.

75. Ibid., pp. 22–24.

76. Ibid., pp. 194–95, 199; *Blue and Brown Books*, pp. 163–69; *Zettel*, pp. 37–41.

77. Merleau-Ponty, *Phenomenology of Perception*, p. 166.

78. Ibid., p. 169.

79. Ibid., pp. 3–11 (the quotation is found on p. 11); Merleau-Ponty, "Primacy of Perception," p. 47.

80. Wittgenstein, *Investigations*, pp. 11–12, 20–21; *Zettel*, p. 9. Merleau-Ponty, "Primacy of Perception," pp. 47–49.

81. Wittgenstein, *Investigations*, pp. 39–41.

82. Ibid., pp. 39, 41, 224; the quotation is found on p. 224.

83. Ibid., pp. 42–43; *Blue and Brown Books*, pp. 17–19, 25–27.

84. Merleau-Ponty, *Phenomenology of Perception*, p. 332.

85. Ibid., pp. xi–xiv; the quotation is found on p. xiv.

86. Merleau-Ponty, "Primacy of Perception," pp. 51–57.

87. Wittgenstein, *Blue and Brown Books*, pp. 17–20. Merleau-Ponty, *Phenomenology of Perception*, pp. viii–xvii. In addition to passages I have explicitly quoted or to which I have referred, there are many other discussions in *Phenomenology of Perception* devoted to the theme of ambiguity; see, for example, pp. 227–28, 238, 333, 345, 364–65, 379, 381, 394.

88. Wittgenstein, *Investigations*, pp. 51, 103; the quotation is found on p. 51.

89. Ibid., pp. 31–35; Wittgenstein, *Blue and Brown Books*, p. 17.

90. Wittgenstein, *Blue and Brown Books*, pp. 17–21.

91. Merleau-Ponty, *Phenomenology of Perception*, pp. xiv–xvii, 3–6, 90–92, 383–92, 444–48.

92. Maurice Merleau-Ponty, *The Visible and the Invisible*, trans. Al-

phonso Lingis (Evanston, Ill.: Northwestern University Press, 1968), pp. 118–19, 180, 204, 236, 237, 247, 257; the quotation is found on p. 118.

93. Maurice Merleau-Ponty, "In Praise of Philosophy," in *Essential Writings of Merleau-Ponty*, ed. Fisher, pp. 17–18 (the quotation is found on p. 18); and "Phenomenology and the Sciences of Man," in *The Primacy of Perception*, ed. James Edie (Evanston, Ill.: Northwestern University Press, 1964), pp. 49–50.

94. Merleau-Ponty, "Primacy of Perception," pp. 50–52; and "The Relations of Soul and Body and the Problems of Perceptual Consciousness," in *Essential Writings of Merleau-Ponty*, ed. Fisher, p. 168.

95. Wittgenstein, *Blue and Brown Books*, pp. 15, 53–54, 78; *Investigations*, pp. 89, 221, 222 (the quotation is found on p. 222); and *On Certainty*, trans. Denis Paul and G. E. M. Anscombe (New York: Harper Torchbooks, 1969), pp. 6, 9, 10, 66.

96. Wittgenstein, *Investigations*, pp. 47, 50.

97. Wittgenstein, *Blue and Brown Books*, p. 20.

98. See above, pp. 33, and Merleau-Ponty, *Visible and Invisible*, pp. 118–19, 180, 204, 236, 237, 247, 257. This distinction is made explicitly by Husserl in *Crisis*, pp. 143–45, a work which influenced Merleau-Ponty very much.

99. Merleau-Ponty, *Phenomenology of Perception*, pp. 415–42.

100. Wittgenstein, *Blue and Brown Books*, pp. 67–70. Here he distinguishes between the illegitimate use of "I" as subject and the legitimate use of "I" as object.

101. Ibid.

102. Merleau-Ponty, *Phenomenology of Perception*, pp. xi–xiii, 69–70, 428–33.

2

Perception, Expression, and Reflection

IN THIS CHAPTER we begin with a relative, not an absolute, beginning, with a perception that is already mediated by language and by personal and social history. Perception, nonetheless, is a relative *beginning* because it founds all other levels of conscious experience. Without perception, there is no science, art, morality, philosophy, or religion. From perception we shift in this chapter to expression, which moves from the immediacy of sheer perceiving to expressing meanings, and to reflection, which is a still higher level of mediation and is nonetheless related to perception and expression. The movement in this chapter, therefore, is a movement from immediacy to mediation, from perception to reflection.

THE PARADOX OF PERCEPTION

Phenomenology rests on a paradox: the constitution of objectivity through subjectivity. Every meaning is related to a certain conscious act and is discovered or created by that act. All meanings are in experience; nonetheless no meaning is reducible to or identical with the act by which it is constituted. All objects of conscious acts are given within experience itself as transcendent to these acts. The task of phenomenology is to lay aside prejudices about what conscious experience must be and to discover, through patient reflection on such experience, the *a priori* structures of consciousness and of the various kinds of objectivity.

An important issue concerning phenomenology is whether the above paradox is fruitful or vicious. One way of beginning to answer this question is to examine one example of constitution, perception, understood here as external, sensible awareness of individual material objects or persons. This is a crucial test case because perception is the primary act of constitution, that upon which all other conscious acts are founded. Even logical truths have certain presuppositions deriving from perception, such as their identity over time, intersubjective validity, and so on.[1]

One objection to a phenomenology of perception is that to begin with an analysis of subjective experience is to preclude the possibility of establishing objectivity. I become locked within my own consciousness, unable to reach beyond my own impressions and ideas. The inevitable result of such reflection on subjectivity is idealism in the bad sense, a philosophy that can no longer account for objectivity.

Yet a phenomenologist could say in reply that such an objection misconceives the relationship between objectivity and subjectivity by divorcing them, and that such a divorce makes no sense. The meaning "objective thing" is a sense established in conscious experience. Either the affirmation of objective things is arbitrary, or it is not. If it is arbitrary, what is arbitrarily asserted can be arbitrarily denied. If it is not, then there is evidence for such knowledge, evidence that itself is known through conscious experience. The affirmation of objective being, therefore, implies subjectivity.

But subjectivity does not equal subjectivism. True objectivity implies subjectivity, and true subjectivity implies objectivity. To conceive consciousness as locked up inside itself and aware only of its own representations is to ignore the experience of intentionality, the awareness that I have of already being oriented outside myself to what is not myself, the wall that I am looking at "there" as opposed to where I am sitting here, the person over there in contrast to my own presence here. My consciousness is already stretched outside myself, present to what is experienced as not myself.

I do not experience representations as a third reality, intermediate between myself and the perceived thing. To think of representations as simulacra, as mere images or pictures of something outside myself to which I do not have immediate access, is to forget that "image" or "picture" has its meaning only in relation to a content of immediacy. An image of someone in my imagination is an image only in relation to the perceived, real presence of that person. A picture is an accurate or inaccurate likeness only in relation to veridical, real perceptions of the person. "Image" has meaning as a reality and concept only in relation to that with which it contrasts in perception; "picture" has meaning only in relation to that which is not a picture in perceptual experience.

The task for the phenomenologist is to explicate the evidence for objectivity, which for the most part is implicit and inarticulate for the normal perceiving consciousness caught up in common sense or the natural attitude. Careful reflection on perception reveals, first of all, a unified object known through a multiplicity of conscious acts. When I perceive a table, for example, the table remains the same table as I move around it, touch it, look at it, focus on its roughness or smoothness, and so on. When I leave the room and return, the table is still given as the same individual table in the same place. Its various qualities, such as color, roughness, and shape, are given as dependent aspects of the table, discoverable through successive acts of perception. There is an experienced difference between the unified object and the multiplicity of conscious acts, a difference functioning as a motive for our belief in objective things. Because the object is one and the acts many, the object transcends these acts and is not reducible to them.[2]

Such a difference is evidence of intentionality, the essential relation of conscious acts to their correlative objects. Intentionality includes act and object as certain distinct moments or aspects of experience, each one implying the other. Because philosophers in the past have overlooked intentionality, they were led into idealism or skepticism concerning the objective world. Two distinct but related meanings were confused in discussions of "impression" and "idea": the object known and the act by which it is known. Because these meanings were not distinguished, philosophers were led to the conclusion that all I can know through reflection on my knowing is my own impressions and ideas.[3]

Besides the experienced difference between the multiplicity of conscious acts and the unity of the object, there is the distinction between the object as detachable, as "there," and thematic and my own body as inseparable from me, "here," and implicit. The external thing is given as an explicit theme on which I intentionally focus. It is given at a distance, as "there," in opposition to the absolute "here" of my body. My body is given to me implicitly as subject, as that "I" perceiving and relating to the world. When I perceive the table, I am not at the same time perceiving my acts of perceiving the table, but I am prethematically and vaguely aware of these acts. Because of such awareness, I can later remember and describe to someone what I was doing at the time. Without such awareness such remembering would be impossible.

My body is not an instrument; if it were, I would need a second body in order to use the first as an instrument, and an infinite regress would follow. My body is not detachable from me or distinct from me. I can lose or forget a book, but I cannot lose or forget my body. I can leave the table behind when I leave the room, but I cannot leave my body.[4] Indeed, I can only "lose," "forget," or "leave" because I am embodied. My body is not an instrument, but the condition of the possibility of my having instruments.

It is true that I can objectify parts of my body; I can, for example, touch one hand with the other or scratch my back. But such actions presuppose the touching or scratching body as subject. Moreover, when I do objectify one part of my body, I retain an awareness that it is a part of "my body" that is being objectified; it is the "body-subject-become-object." There thus remains an irreducible difference between this kind of object and things in the external world, which never have been and never could be parts of my body.

Third, there is the difference between the perspectival presence of the external thing, subject to continuous synthesis, and the non-perspectival presence of the perceiving body. The thing is given to me from a point of view; not all its sides or aspects are present in the strict sense. The back side of the table is co-given with the front, but not literally seen. The perceiving subject spontaneously anticipates the hidden side. Because of such anticipation, perception is essentially temporal. The thing is given as something that I can temporally, indefinitely explore. Because the thing is not totally given, it reveals itself as transcendent in each perceptual act or series of acts. There are always aspects or sides that transcend perception because they are not present in the full, literal sense.[5]

Since the thing is only partially given, I can be deceived about it. That the thing is never adequately given and is subject to a continuous process of confirmation and synthesis is a universal, eidetic *a priori* law of perception. I am continually relating past perspectives to present viewpoints; I can either confirm or nullify present interpretations by future perceptions. Someone in a department store window, who looks like a woman, could turn out to be a mannequin. The noise of records playing, which appears to be coming from the apartment below me, might indeed be coming from the adjacent apartment building. An external thing is real, therefore, insofar as future perceptions confirm and corroborate past and present perceptions. Such objectivity is always only presumptive.

The perspectival presence of the thing is different from the massive, non-perspectival, certain presence of my perceiving body. My body subject is the agent or source of perceptual activity. I cannot, therefore, legitimately doubt my body. My body is the necessary condition for resolving perceptual doubt because any doubt, perceptual or otherwise, concerning the existence of the body seems to be illegitimate in principle. I cannot in principle doubt my body without presupposing the existence of the body as motive for my doubting. For similar reasons, as I shall argue more fully later on in this chapter, I should not in principle doubt the world as context or background in which individual objects appear. I can doubt or try to doubt both body and world as both Descartes and Husserl did, but such doubt reveals itself to be self-refuting; any doubt concerning the existence of body and world as a whole implicitly presupposes the existence of body and world.

If the inadequate, perspectival, progressively synthetic character of perception is an eidetic law, radical Cartesian doubt, motivated by this inadequate givenness, concerning the existence of external things or of the external world as a whole is mistaken. We can demand of a level of conscious experience only the kind of certainty appropriate to it. Otherwise we arbitrarily impose criteria of exactness on experience without conducting a prior descriptive inquiry concerning the fit between these criteria and the experience in question. We do what Husserl calls "philosophizing from on high."[6] If external things cannot be adequately given, then it makes no sense to doubt them because they are not adequately given. Descartes uncritically used a criterion of absolute certainty derived from mathematics without first asking whether it was appropriate for perception.

A defender of Descartes might object here that perception is uncertain and inexact, and that one should seek a philosophical science not subject to the limitations of perception and possessing a source of certainty other than perception. I do not wish to deny that there are levels of reflection—mathematics, formal logic, science, and philosophy—not reducible to perception. What I do wish to assert and shall argue fully in the last part of this chapter is that these other levels, though not reducible to perception, are founded on it; reflection requires perception as a necessary condition for its own activity. Because of that relation of dependence, perception cannot be rejected without undercutting the truth of reflection itself. If perceptual contact with things is a necessary condition for the truth of science itself, then the truth of perception cannot be denied without denying the truth of science. Also, as I shall show later in this chapter, because reflection is founded on perception, the body, and language, total apodictic certainty is impossible. What the reduction shows is the impossibility of a complete reduction.

A fourth characteristic of perceived objects is that their content is given as "not-dependent-on-me," in contrast to my own acts of perceiving, which are dependent on me. When I look at the table from this point of view, its shape, color, and size are what they are. I might like them to be different; nonetheless they remain what they are whenever I look at the table and no matter how often I look at it. My acts of perception, on the other hand, are dependent on me. It is up to me whether I see or touch, look at this object or that object, focus on the shape of the table or on its color. This experienced difference between what depends on me and what does not is crucial.

Yet this difference is not sufficient to establish the objectivity of external things because at times I experience contents in my body, stomach-aches or headaches, that are not dependent on my choice or perception. However, I still experience these vicissitudes as contents of the subject body, irreducibly different from the content of objects that are "there" and removable. I cannot be in doubt about whether I am in pain, but I can be in doubt about whether someone else is in pain. Although this independence of content is an important aspect of perceptual objectivity, I must take such independence in conjunction with the aspects already mentioned.

There are two other mistakes that we must avoid. Discussion of these will reveal the fifth aspect of perceptual objectivity. The first is saying that perception is purely passive. Perception is not passive; it is receptive, uniting aspects of passivity and activity. It is passive in that there is awareness of content not dependent on perception itself; it is active in the sense that it is attentive, able to focus on this object rather than that. It is also interpretative, as my examples of the mannequin and the noise next door have already indicated. Another example is the figure dear to psychologists that can be seen as either a duck or a rabbit. In rectifying a misinterpretation, I always have recourse to contents in the object not dependent on me. When I see that the figure in a department store window is a mannequin and not a woman, I have perceived that it cannot move itself, that it is made of wood, and so on. Activity and passivity are essentially related moments or aspects of perception that I cannot divorce from one another. This notion of an active receptivity will be present on other levels of conscious experience as well.

A second mistake is the myth of the given, something of which phenomenology is often mistakenly accused. Five considerations indicate the mistaken character of this belief. (*a*) The thing in perceptual experience is not totally, but only inadequately, imperfectly given.

(*b*) Because perception is temporal there is not an immediate present divorced from past and future. In my search for a pure present instant, I always discover aspects of past and future, no matter how far I break my perceptions down. Whether the proposed present is this hour or this minute or this second, I can always break it down further. The perceptual present is dynamically related to past and future. When I hear a person utter a sentence, I anticipate the ending of the sentence while automatically retaining what that person has said; only in this way do I understand what is said. When I perceive a chair in my room, I am drawing on past perceptions of the chair. When I come into my study, I expect to see a certain kind of chair with a certain color, shape, and so on in a certain place.

(*c*) What is given is not a mass of uninterpreted sense data, but a structure or gestalt within a field. The table is given as a figure-on-ground, as a meaning within a context. I am explicitly aware of the table, but I am implicitly, vaguely, prethematically aware of the room, of the apartment in which I live, of the outdoors, of the city, and so on. This context is the life-world, the horizon in which objects and persons appear.

The figure of the table has its own particular physiognomy or structure, each part of which is essentially related to other parts and to the whole. The leg of the table is a leg only in relation to the whole; the top can be perceived only in relation to the bottom, the front only in relation to the back, color only through extension, and extension only through color. "Figure" and "ground" are internally related meanings, neither understandable without the other. The green of the table appears as a particular kind of green because of the grain and texture of the wood and because of the kind of lighting in the room.[7]

The objective gestalt of the thing appearing against a background corresponds to the subjective gestalt of the lived body as my lived, incarnate presence to the world. Because my body is available to me prethematically as a gestalt in which all parts are spontaneously co-ordinated with each other, I do not have to think about what I am doing when I move. My body is spontaneously available to me as an organ of movement as I walk to the kitchen, get a cup of coffee while thinking about philosophy, and return to my study. As I walk, pick up a cup, and shift the cup from one hand to the other when I pick up the coffee pot, I experience my body as spontaneously, almost impersonally coordinating these movements one with the other.

The experienced contrast between the objective and the subjective gestalt, therefore, is that between immediate organ of movement and that toward which I move, between a gestalt that I see and explore and a gestalt that sees and explores. My body is the absolute "here" that "moves toward"; the thing is the "there" toward which I move. Even learning new behavior such as shooting a basketball, playing a piano, or driving a car presupposes the prior, implicit presence of the body as organ of behavior. I can learn to shoot a basketball only because I am able to move, pick up things, bend, and run.[8]

(d) When I look at one figure rather than another, at the table rather than the chair or at the coffee cup rather than the book, I am motivated by interest. I need to use the table for piling up books, or I wish to refill my coffee cup. Perceptual figures, therefore, have a value for me to which I relate practically. To perceive is to act practically. Perception as it occurs prescientifically and common-sensically is a kind of rudimentary praxis, and no perception is value-free.

Finally, (e) perception, as I shall develop more fully in the next section, is mediated by language. Sedimented language is an aspect of the past that influences the perceptual present. Even to recognize something as "red" presupposes a language, in which red has its meaning in contrast to "blue," "white," "green," and so on. I know the rectangular shape of the table as such in contrast to other shapes such as "triangle" and "hexagon." I recognize the table as a table because of its relation to my purposes, articulated through language.[9]

The immediacy to which phenomenology returns, therefore, in its reflection on perception is a mediated immediacy; the given is an interpreted, structured given. There is no "seeing" apart from "seeing as." This gestalt within a context of world and language constitutes a fifth important characteristic of real perceptual things. What I perceive as "there" are not isolated sense data, but structured, organized wholes in a context. This gestalt character, taken in conjunction with the other four motives, constitutes the meaning of "objective, external thing." None of the five is sufficient by itself, but all must be together and function together in perceptual experience. Even though phenomenologists have discussed one or other of these aspects, no phenomenologist has synthesized them the way I have here.

This analysis of perception has four important consequences. The first is that we see the mistake of trying to prove or infer the existence of the external world. It is a fallacy because all inferences are judgments, and access to the world is initially perceptual and pre-judgmental. Certain objects within the world can be proved or doubted only because the world itself as the totality of objects is indubitable. Any attempt to prove the world empirically must implicitly presuppose the validity of the life-world as that in which all proof goes on. I can know certain perceptions as erroneous only because I have veridical perceptions. I can correct the illusion that the stick in the water is bent only because of trust in touch as veridical. But I cannot prove or verify anything while doubting the totality of perception and its method of continuous synthesis within the life-world. Because the life-world is the essential presupposition of all doubt and proof, I cannot prove that it exists; I can only describe it.

A second consequence is that within transcendental philosophy the burden of objectivity moves from understanding and judgment in the Kantian sense to perceptual experience. Unless the objective world is given in experience, I will never know it as such. I will be left with the impossible task of inferring from objective impressions and ideas to something outside them without being able to compare these impressions and ideas with the thing. In order to know that these impressions and ideas are similar to the thing, I would have to leap outside my knowledge in order to know the thing—a manifest absurdity. Also, if I am not arbitrarily to impose categories on sensible experience, there must be a structure within that experience given prior to understanding. If "cause" is the appropriate category to use in a certain experience, this use is legitimate because this experience has a certain structure, distinguishing it from certain experiences for which "cause" is not applicable.

A third consequence—and here I am anticipating later parts of the book—is that the gestalt is a totality of internal relations. I shall show such a totality to be present in language, abstract reflection, intersubjectivity, and the individual psyche, and finally in the concrete social whole of capitalism.

A fourth consequence is that phenomenology retains the truth of common-sense belief in the reality of the external world while moving beyond such belief. By articulating the implicit motivations of the natural attitude or common sense, phenomenology supplies a critical foundation for such belief. By successfully relating objectivity to subjectivity, phenomenology becomes a fruitful paradox, an idealism that is true.

EXPRESSION

As I conclude my description of the perceiving consciousness, I must also realize the partial and abstract character of this description. Consciousness not only perceives the world cognitively, but acts in the world practically and expressively. In expression, therefore, there is a break with the immediacy of sheer perceptual experience and an attempt to say and objectify what I have perceived or wish to achieve practically.

When I reflect on my experience of expressing myself, expression begins to seem paradoxical. For example, I am trying to articulate my impressions about a person, several incorrect expressions come to mind, and finally I hit upon one as the correct expression. "Yes, that is it. That is what I was trying to say." In the process of trying to work out a proof about a geometrical figure, I end up knowing more about the figure after the proof than before. In writing a poem or painting a picture, I move from an initially vague and incomplete idea to one that is finally realized definitely in the external product. In putting in the final word or adding the final brush stroke, I see that this is indeed what I wanted to say.

What all these experiences have in common is that something is expressed. The basic proposition of this section is that the notion expressed is internally related to expression, and that consciousness implies expression. In a sense, I already know what I want to say; otherwise I would not attempt to express anything. In a sense too, I do not know what I want to say until I have said it; otherwise I would experience no inner necessity for expression.

In the above examples of expression, I experience an idea initially vague, incomplete, and indefinite struggling to become precise, complete, and definite through expression. My struggle for expression is the struggle for understanding, for the full realization of the idea. My movement from an initially indistinct and unclear idea to one that is relatively distinct and clear is a movement from the empty to the full, from inadequate to adequate understanding.[10] There is a teleology built into the process of expression. With the first glimmering of an insight, there is the anticipation of the complete, clear articulation of that insight.

Consciousness, my awareness of myself as actively present in the world, is essentially related to expression, and vice versa. This account of the consciousness–expression relation differs from two others, the behaviorist and the intellectualist.[11] My account differs from the behaviorist's in that there is an inner, private aspect essentially related to the outer domain of expression. This inner aspect is a moment in the Husserlian sense, an aspect internally mediated by other aspects.[12] The initial, incomplete insight finds its completion in expression. Wittgenstein's behaviorism of meaning, which does not deny that there are private mental events but does deny that they are essential for meaning, is inadequate.[13] Meaning is neither merely inner nor merely outer but both, because it is both conscious and expressive. My account differs from the intellectualist's in that the relationship between consciousness and expression is internal, not external. Expression is not mere external clothing draped over a thought complete in itself.

Dialectically this internal relationship between consciousness and expression emerges when I realize the one-sidedness of both behaviorism and intellectualism. Behaviorism cannot account for the privacy that we experience at all times and that at certain times becomes specially salient—for example, when I experience myself or others withholding information or lying. Behaviorism cannot account for the difference I sense at times between what I am trying to say and what I actually say. The struggle to say something presupposes the inchoate, relatively private idea governing the expression, allowing me to distinguish between words or expressions that say what I mean and others that do not. Also, behaviorism cannot account for the difference between really convincing someone that something is so and physically torturing that person into the appropriate public behavior.

Intellectualism, on the other hand, does not do justice to the experience I have of expression completing the thought, of my not knowing what I want to say until I have said it. The painter, for example, does not have a fully determinate idea of what to paint when initially confronting the blank canvas. Rather through interaction with the canvas, with the paint, with the subject being painted, a nude or landscape, or a still life, the painter's vision evolves. The subject reciprocally interacts with the object, and each changes in the course of the encounter. A *Mt. St. Victorie* or a *Mademoiselles d'Avignon* or a *Red Studio* is neither initially present in fully determinate form in the painter's mind nor full blown in reality. Rather, paintings are the results of a process that unites inner and outer, subject and object, person and world.

An apparent counter-example seemingly justifying the intellectualist is the experience of thinking to myself. I can sit in my study and reflect philosophically without expressing anything externally. There are two important points about such solitary reflection. First of all, such thinking to myself presupposes that I have learned a language, and learning a language presupposes a public, intersubjective world in which I learn which expressions are correct. Correctness and incorrectness make no sense in a purely private language because no distinction can be made between what seems correct and what is correct.[14] Private, solitary reflection, therefore, is founded on the public, intersubjective context of shared, expressed meanings. Second, thinking to myself is a saying to myself whereby I mentally, imaginatively put into words what was previously vague, incomplete, and tentative.

I cannot think to myself without language. Wittgenstein's experiments here are decisive. For example, he suggests that I say and mean the sentence "It will probably rain tomorrow." Then he suggests that I think the same thought, but without saying anything, either to myself or aloud. The impossibility of doing this suggests that thought requires language.[15]

Expression can take various forms. It can take the form of prescientific, ethical linguistic interaction in the world with other people for the purpose of realizing political goals in the community, symbolic interaction, or the form of work producing an object such as an automobile or an airplane according to a technical design, purposive rational action.[16]

Symbolic interaction is governed by intersubjectively shared norms and is ordered toward a communication free from domination; purposive rational action is governed by technical rules and is ordered toward technical control. The sanctions against failure are punishment on the basis of institutional sanctions, in the one instance, and inefficiency, failure to produce a good product or perform a good experiment, in the other. In symbolic interaction the kind of definition that operates is reciprocal expectations about behavior; in purposive rational action the type of definition is a conditional prediction. Symbolic interaction is ordered toward other subjects in an "I–thou" relationship; purposive rational action is ordered toward objects in an "I–it" relationship. When purposive rational action relates to other subjects in an instrumental, utilitarian manner, strategic action, it tries to manipulate and control them, not communicate with them through a dialogue free of domination.

I do not wish to make the mistake, as Habermas seems to have done at times, of talking about purposive rational action and symbolic interaction as totally separate realms. There are many situations, such as workers conversing together as they construct an automobile or a Senate committee interviewing a weapons expert from the Pentagon, in which the two kinds of action intermingle. But usually one of the forms of action is dominant—purposive rational action in the automobile plant and symbolic interaction in the Senate—and each has a distinct structure or logic. When I perform a successful experiment, moral praise or blame is irrelevant; when a community publicly criticizes the justice of a war, thoughts about the technically best means of waging such a war are irrelevant.[17]

Artistic creation is still another form of expression, in which the artist can use not only language but various non-linguistic media such as sound or color or physical movement to produce an object worthy of contemplation for its own sake. It has in common with work and interaction the property of being a practical activity in the world. It differs from them in being oriented to disinterested contemplation rather than political changing of the world or technical transformation of it. When I contemplate a Matisse at the local art museum, the immediate point of that activity is not moral improvement or economic profit, but an aesthetic contemplation that is sensuous, emotional, and reflective.[18]

Finally, expression can take the form of theory as that is expressed in science, mathematics, formal logic, or philosophy. All these kinds of expression, moral, economic, aesthetic, and theoretical, have in common the movement from prethematic to thematic, inner to outer, incomplete to complete, vague to precise. Expression in all its range, therefore, is an activity or praxis in which human beings realize themselves in the world.

Expression involves a reference of the present, vague, unexpressed insight to a sedimented past of habitual meanings and to a future articulation. Past, present, and future are dynamically linked moments or aspects essentially related to one another and unthinkable without one other. In expression, I make use of what has been said in order to say what is new, at least to me.

Is there nothing in conscious experience that is inexpressible? In a sense everything is expressible and in a sense not. There is nothing in consciousness that is totally inexpressible. We are aware of this fact because the very attempt to indicate such a phenomenon is to express it. But in another sense, we constantly have the experience of meaning more than we say, of being conscious of more than we express. If someone asks whether the road was crowded when I was driving home from work an hour ago, I can answer the question even though I did not explicitly note or express the fact at the time. The reason I can answer the question is that I was implicitly, prethematically aware of the relative number of cars on the road.

Expression is always related to unexpressed, tacit awareness. Expressed and unexpressed, figure and ground, explicit and implicit stand in dialectical relation to one another because they imply each other. Explicitly articulating my awareness of another person presupposes an objective background from which that person emerges and which remains unexpressed. Describing something as "white" implies reference to an entire unexpressed scheme of colors and color contrasts that gives "white" its meaning. "White" is "white" only in contrast to "black," "red," "green," and so on.

Saying that consciousness is essentially expressive, therefore, means, not that there is no tacit dimension to consciousness, but that this tacit dimension always is complemented by a thematic dimension. Thematization, synonymous with "thinking" as I am using the terms here, requires expression because thematization is interpretation, a transcending of the given in order to express an insight into the given. Even perception, as we have seen, does not have a "seeing" without a "seeing as." To see a red figure as "red" is to perceive it in the light of previously articulated color contrasts. Perceiving the duck–rabbit figure as either a duck or a rabbit requires either a past or a present articulation of meaning.

This "past or present" qualification is important because the unexpressed–expressed relation is a temporal relation as well. There seem to be some acts of perception that are not expressed at the time, but presuppose a relation to past expression. When I am driving, approach an intersection, see a red light, and stop, it is not necessarily true that I say, either out loud or to myself, "There is a red light; therefore, I must stop," or "My gosh, there's a red light." Often what happens is a wordless perception in the present, but one that is essentially mediated by past sedimented expressions. The meaning the red light has for me presupposes past expressed insights about the meaning of red in the whole scheme of colors, the connection between red and the action of stopping one's automobile, and so on. Otherwise, the red light would mean nothing to me, and I would simply drive through the intersection.

What I have said before now needs qualifying. Not all notions have to be expressed at the time I have them. If a notion is new, then it requires expression, either external or internal, in order to realize itself as a notion. If it is not new, then present expression need not take place, and all that is required is a relation to sedimented past expressions. The unexpressed and expressed are internally related as present and past.

A person listening to a symphony, for example, does not have to express, either out loud or silently, what is going on at the time. However, one's very awareness of the music as a symphony, with four movements, each with a different musical form, presupposes a sedimented past of expressed linguistic meaning. One's appreciation of the piece being played will be deeper and more profound insofar as expression of articulated judgments occurs before, during, and after the performance. Never to express an idea about music is to condemn oneself to a primitive appreciation of music. Expression is a matter not simply of language, but of bodily action and gesture as well. The physical act of going to the concert hall, the quiet posture of sitting during the performance, and the attentive look directed toward the musicians—all are expressions of one's intention to listen to the symphony.

The full reality, therefore, is hyphenated, "consciousness-expression," two moments that are essential to one another but that cannot be reduced to one another. In at least four senses, there is a pre-linguistic and pre-expressive aspect to consciousness, correlative to an expressed, thematic aspect: (a) the initially unexpressed insight striving to be expressed, (b) the figure–background relation present in all expression, (c) the unexpressed, habitual linguistic context, and (d) the agent's implicit awareness of herself as the one who is doing the expressing.

If consciousness is essentially expressive, then consciousness is essentially embodied because the body-subject is necessary for expression. Try to imagine expression without the gestures of the lover, the verbal expression of the poet, the sharp, deft strokes of the painter. The expressing or subject body is not an object or instrument. If it were, then a second body would be necessary in order to use it as an instrument, and an infinite regress would follow. A necessary consequence of this view of expression, therefore, is the impossibility of the transcendental reduction in Husserl's sense, in which the transcendental ego is distinct from the empirical ego. Consciousness is essentially incarnate and open to a world.

There is one final possible counter-example that might be considered: mysticism. Is a mystic engaged in a kind of activity for which expression is not essential, only the silent, wordless adoration of one's God? I think not, for there are at least three different levels of expressiveness involved. First, there is the bodily posture of the mystic expressing reverence for God. Second, there is the sedimented religious tradition, which is necessary for the recognition, either at the time of the experience or afterward, that it was indeed "Christ" or "God" the mystic was experiencing. Without such recognition giving a meaning to what is experienced, religious experiences would remain indistinguishable from other peak experiences. Third, there is the subsequent interpretation and criticism of the experience. Was it indeed God the person was experiencing? If so, what is God's will? How does this experience compare with other past experiences? These and other questions are considered in such reflection.

The phenomenon of expression reveals consciousness as a unity of opposites: inner and outer, private and public, past and future, implicit and explicit. The error made by both the behavioristic and the intellectualistic traditions is reductionist: reducing expression to one of its opposites and excluding the other. An adequate phenomenological account of expression reveals this reductionism to be a mistake.

REFLECTION

Already within perceptual experience and expression, there is some reflectivity, some thoughtfulness, some mediation. To grasp the gestalt of a triangular thing is to grasp it as meaningful and to be aware of myself as different from the thing. To express myself through language or symbols in a painting or a poem, a conversation or a piece of sculpture, is to do so thoughtfully, mindfully. However, I move to a qualitatively different kind of mediation when I move to abstract reflection, the kind of thinking that goes on in science, mathematics, formal logic, and philosophy.

One of the oldest problems in philosophy is that of the relation between sensing and thinking, perception and abstract reflection. How are these kinds of activity distinct? How are they related? One can try to adopt an empiricist strategy of saying that the basic model for reflection is taking a good look at a concrete particular. Reflection then becomes simply a form of imagining, a pale impoverishment of the original, rich sensuous experience. The difficulty with such an account is that reflection seems to transcend the sensuous particular in some respects. I can think the difference between a 984- and a 985-sided figure without imagining the difference. I can also think perfect equality or justice or triangularity, but the sensible particular, whether perceived or imagined, can only approximate such perfection. Finally, intellectual insight seems to be enriching, not impoverishing;[19] a definition of a circle enables me to know more about the circle than I did before. I move from a merely nominal definition of the circle and its mere immediate, sensuous presence to an understanding of it as a closed, plane figure equaling 360 degrees with all points equidistant from the center.

On the other hand, one can try to reduce perception to reflection, to say that all sensation is merely disguised intellection. The difficulty with this conception is that the reality of perception is overlooked. For the triangular object that I see from a point of view is not thought according to a definition, is not abstract, is not universal. I do not need a physical definition of force in order to lift a box onto a shelf in my apartment, or a scientifically measured and formulated abstract conception of distance to know that the train is receding into the distance. There is a lived, perceived awareness of shapes, forces, and distances that cannot be reduced to reflection in the abstract sense without distorting and explaining away this experience. Moreover, the abstract reflection of a discipline like mathematics, while not reducible to perception, seems dependent on perceptions or images of concrete individuals. To generate definitions and proofs the mathematician needs images of particular triangles, rectangles, or circles.[20]

The relation between perception and reflection, therefore, seems to be a unity in duality, and the phenomenological task is to do justice to both the identity and the difference. Human knowing is a limited whole to which both perception and reflection contribute, but which cannot be reduced to either perception or reflection. Consequently, this section will discuss reflection first, then the relationship between perception and reflection, and finally some consequences in the conclusion.

The Emergence of Reflection

Perception, initially understood as external sensible awareness of material individuals, gives us a world. To perceive is to be aware of sensible things against a background. For example, to see a tree is to perceive it against the background of the neighborhood, city, environment, in which it exists. This ultimate horizon is "world" in the phenomenological sense, the ground out of which the perceptual figure emerges. Because, as I have already shown, I am in the world as embodied perceiver, there is a second, broader meaning of world: world as life-world, as unity of perceiver and perceived. Because the life-world functions as the context of contexts, it makes sense to describe it initially as "being."

Because perception is interpretative, mistaken perceptions can occur. I can think that a mannequin in a department store window is a person, that the blow-out of a tire is a gunshot, that the footsteps of Mary in the hall are really those of John. Even on the perceptual level, there is a break with immediacy in the sense that certain perceptions become questionable because of a conflict between them. I thought it was the footsteps of John in the hall, but I hear the voice of Mary. Consequently, perceptual judgments have to be made. "Yes, it is Mary in the hall, not John."

Not all perceptions are judgments; indeed, most are not. Judgments occur only when there is conflict between perceptions, questions arise, and explicit articulation occurs. Most of the time perceiving is continuous and unquestioning. When I get up in the morning, stumble in a daze to the refrigerator, get the milk, and make the coffee, much perceiving is going on, very little judging. If I discover that the milk is sour or that I am out of coffee, then judgment occurs.

"Perception," therefore, has three different meanings: (a) the sensuous presence of the individual thing; (b) the meaning that it has for me, "tree" or "chair" or "Mary" or "John"; (c) the judgment made when meanings conflict. The first and second senses are never disjoined; there is no "seeing" without a "seeing as."[21] The third sense is founded or dependent on the first two. To judge that something is true, I have to have access to certain perceptual gestalts, "the straightness of the stick," "the voice of Mary," "the wood of the mannequin." If this were not so, there would be no way of distinguishing true from false judgments. All judgments would be imposed, equally true and equally arbitrary.

Even perception at the most primitive level, therefore, is never totally immediate because of the role of interpretation and judgment. There are no strictly given sense data, only organized wholes in a context, such as the "refrigerator," "milk," and "coffee." Even perceptions in which I do not judge but only interpret passively, such as my seeing the milk in the refrigerator in the morning, presuppose previous perceptions in all three senses of the word. Perceiving anything, therefore, involves a sedimented or habitual context of meaning built up through time.

Perception, because it is interpretative and critical, is already re-flective in a limited sense. There is no absolute given, only a relative, interpreted given. What is usually contrasted with perception is re-flection in the full, explicit sense, abstract reflection, examples of which are science, mathematics, logic, and philosophy. From Des-cartes through Kant, this kind of reflection carried a heavy burden: that of giving us a world. The present analysis liberates abstract reflection from that burden. Perception supplies us with a world; re-flection has only to interpret it.

Even this contrast is not strictly accurate because the perceived world is already interpreted. Abstract reflection is one kind of inter-pretation, dependent on and yet transcendent to the interpreted life-world. The noetic link between perception and abstract reflection is questioning. Perception, lift to its own devices, is not able to answer certain questions. Perceiving a tree does not enable me to answer the question "What is the nature of a tree?" Perceiving a triangular-shaped object will never enable me to answer the question "What is the nature of a triangle?" These questions motivate me to move to the abstract reflection of biology and mathematics.

Questions are expressions of a desire to know that is disinterested and unrestricted. It is disinterested in that it is oriented to what is true, not to what pleases, edifies, or uplifts. Such disinterestedness is the obverse side of a passionate interest in the truth. The scientist operating on the basis of the desire to know is detached from the nar-rowness of bias, the whim of fancy, and the force of passion, but pas-sionately interested in the comprehensiveness of a theory, the con-sistency of formulations, and the cogency of evidence.

The desire to know is unrestricted in both an experiential and a logical sense. Experientially the scientist, mathematician, or philos-opher is always aware of a gap between the known and the unknown, between answered and unanswered questions. Logically to assert that there is something outside the range of the desire to know is self-refuting. For I make such a claim either without sufficient evi-dence or with sufficient evidence. If I make the claim without suffi-cient evidence, what I arbitrarily assert can be rationally questioned or denied. If I make the claim with evidence, what supposedly lies outside the range of the desire to know becomes something known, argued for, and understood.[22]

This reflection is "abstract" because its object is different from that of perception. First of all, the object of reflection is universal as opposed to the individual, perceived thing, the universal definition of triangle as opposed to the individual, sensuous gestalt.[23] This universal is non-perspectival as opposed to perspectival, true not simply from my point of view but from all points of view.

Were one to claim that the universal is merely a name conjoined to a particular idea and applying to similar individuals,[24] I could ask a counter-question about how such similarity is grasped. If the claim to grasp certain individuals as similar is not arbitrary but true, then one would have to know the property in light of which the individuals are seen as similar—for example, "redness," "triangularity," or "bitterness." But such a property, grasped as one in the mind and as many in the individuals instantiating it, is precisely what we mean by the universal. When I say "the table is red" and "the house is red" and intend to express similarity, there is an identical intelligibility, "red," expressed in both sentences. Otherwise, I could not affirm the similarity. Understanding of similarity in things, therefore, presupposes understanding of the universal. If, on the other hand, the claim about similarity is arbitrary, then such an affirmation implicitly contradicts its claim to truth, and what is arbitrarily asserted can be rationally questioned or denied.

Second, at times the object of abstract reflection will be necessary as opposed to the contingent existence of the individual, perceived thing. "Necessary" here means that the proposition in question cannot not be true, that its falsity is logically unthinkable. Although the propositions of modern science are not necessary, those of symbolic logic, mathematics, and phenomenology are. Mathematics and formal logic are formally analytic, resting on the principle of contradiction. The propositions of phenomenology are materially analytic because they arise, not out of mere linguistic definition or postulation, but from reflection on experience. One discovers that certain properties are internal or essential to certain types of experience, such as "perspectival" to perception, or "universal" to reflection. Neither perception nor reflection can be what it is without its peculiar property.

Finally, the object of reflection, as opposed to the object of perception, is non-imaginable. I can bring to mind the picture of an individual triangle when it is no longer perceptually present. I cannot picture a defined, abstractly conceived triangle, however, because it is not individual and all images are individual. Also, the lines of such an abstractly conceived triangle have no width, thickness, or depth, but the lines of an imagined triangle do have such properties. If the Humean or Berkeleyan skeptic is still not convinced, one can ask such a skeptic to consider many-sided figures. For example, I can conceive the difference in an instant between a 987-sided figure and a 986-sided figure without imagining or picturing such a difference. If conception were the same as imagining, such a feat would be impossible.

There are two kinds of abstract reflection, understanding and judgment.[25] Similar to the second moment of perception are the questions posed by understanding: "What is it?" "Why is it?" or "How is it?" These questions intend the intelligible structure or pattern of a phenomenon. What is the nature of a circle? What is the meaning of a free fall? What is force? What is the general law of biological development?

By itself, such an intelligibility is incomplete because it is merely possible. Consequently, a second kind of question becomes necessary, similar to the third moment of perception: "Is it true?" or "Is it so?" This is the moment of judgment, of ascertaining what the evidence is for a particular hypothesis. This second moment is essential if ideas are not to remain merely bright ideas.

From perception through understanding to judgment, there is a progressive movement from empty to full,[26] from no intelligibility to possible intelligibility to actual intelligibility. The question for understanding is expressed as an empty anticipation of an answer that would fulfill it. The question for critical reflection is an empty anticipation of evidence determining the truth or falsity of what is understood. My desire to know moves me from perception to understanding to judgment, and constitutes the unity of the process. Dissatisfied with the merely contingent, perspectival meanings offered by perception, I ask questions for understanding. Dissatisfied with merely bright ideas, I ask the further critical question. Understanding and judgment, therefore, are essentially related. Judgment presupposes understanding as the source of an hypothesis that may or may not be true. Judgment completes understanding by adding the moment of truth.

Judgments, whether they are the materially analytic judgments of phenomenology or the empirical, probable judgments of science or common sense, are virtually unconditioned in that they are judgments with conditions that happen to be fulfilled. In phenomenology, the fulfillment of the conditions for making a virtually unconditioned judgment—for example, "all perception is perspectival"—occurs in reflection on that experience. The conditions for such a judgment include experience of perception, imaginative variation in which I reflect on various actual and possible counter-examples, and my running up against the impossibility in reflection that perception could occur without being perspectival. On a common-sense level, the conditions for the judgment "the chicken dinner is on the table" are the five aspects of perceptual objectivity discussed earlier in this chapter.

In all virtually unconditioned judgments, there is a conditioned, a link between the conditioned and what it conditions, and the fulfillment of the conditions. For example, in the above common-sense example, the conditioned is the judgment "the chicken dinner is on the table," the link is the cognitional process moving from experience through understanding to judgment, and the fulfilling conditions are the aspects of perceptual objectivity. Judgment flows from the reflective grasp of the virtually unconditioned. Just as the concept flows from insight on the level of understanding, so the judgment expressed in propositions flows from the reflective grasp of the virtually unconditioned. On the levels of both understanding and judgment there is a preconceptual moment that precedes, leads into, and completes itself in the conceptual moment.[27]

The Relation of Perception to Reflection

Even though abstract reflection differs essentially from perception, such reflection does not leave perception totally behind. Such reflection is founded on perception in three different ways. First, perception gives reflection objects to think about in order to conceive its own proper objects, and supplies the social context within which reflection goes on. In the sciences questions arise about perceived objects in the world such as falling apples, light, animals, or the sun; hypotheses arise to explain these phenomena, and are verified in these phenomena. The perceived world functions as the initial basis for such questions and as the source of evidence for answering such questions. Also hypotheses are verified intersubjectively. Einstein makes use of the Michelson experiments and hypotheses, but he is not using a theoretical construction of the being of Mr. Michelson or other researchers. Rather, Michelson is accessible to Einstein only through the prescientific life-world as an object of perception.[28]

Such dependence on perception is true not just of physical science, but also of more abstract disciplines such as mathematics or symbolic logic. Even here one needs the sensuous image of the triangle in order to work out a proof about the triangle, or the symbols of symbolic logic in order to work out a proof in that discipline. Linguistic symbols function here not simply as expressions for concepts, but as objects that reflection thinks about in order to conceive its own proper objects.

Second, abstract reflection is founded on perception because language is essential for such reflection, both to express one's insights and to constitute them as fixed and abiding. In the process of expressing, as we have seen, there is a movement from empty to full, from the initial, vague, preconceptual understanding to one that is complete and articulated. In defining the essence of a triangle, for example, I experience the following moments: (*a*) I perceive or imagine a triangular figure; (*b*) I ask the question about the nature of a triangle; (*c*) I move from preconceptual insight to conceptual insight, when I begin to get hints or intimations of the answer, draw lines perpendicular to the base, and begin to suspect the connection in number of degrees, number of angles, and the essence of triangle. Finally, I arrive at the linguistically expressed definition that a triangle is a closed plane figure with three angles totaling 180 degrees. These moments are qualitatively, not necessarily temporally, distinct.

The sensuous expression in language is not mere external clothing on a thought complete in itself, but rather helps to realize it. As the example of the triangle shows, I really do not fully know what I want to say until I have said it. Also without language, reflection would be a momentary affair in which meaning could never be clearly, permanently captured. Reflection would never be able to transcend the present moment and would be at the mercy of a vague, unarticulated flux of meanings.

Third, reflection is founded on perception because the former contains presuppositions derived from the latter. The objectivity so important for science and logic is an objectivity that is intersubjective, valid for all observers or thinkers. As I have already shown, other persons are initially accessible not as objects of reflection, but as perceived in the prescientific life-world.

To talk about what is universally or generally true implicitly presupposes a group of individuals covered by the proposition. For example, to talk about a law of force presupposes a multiplicity of individual forces known through perception. To say "Some X is Y" in symbolic logic presupposes at least one individual "X" of which the proposition is true. Since perception initially gives us access to individual things and persons, the language of perception founds the language of abstract reflection.

The mere possibility of formal sense in logic implicitly presupposes content, the material compatibility of subject and predicate. A proposition such as "2 + 2 = red" literally makes no sense because subject and predicate are materially irrelevant to one another. The ultimate basis of material relevance, however, is the perceived life-world, which supplies evidence for such relevance. The above proposition is senseless because number is different from color, and this difference is initially known through perception. The number of perceived objects has nothing to do with the color of these objects.[29]

The paradoxical relation between perception and reflection is that such reflection is distinct from perception and yet dependent on it. Such dependence does not imply the empiricist proposition that abstract reflection is a mere impoverished replica of perception. No, abstraction is enriching in that it gives us intelligibilities that perception could not give us. These intelligibilities, once discovered, paradoxically become a part of the life-world. My world is a world that is subject to evolution and to the theory of relativity. My solar system is sun-, not earth-centered. Also, scientific discoveries influence my everyday conduct. I do not use an electric shaver while standing in a pool of water; nor with a heart condition do I eat many fat foods. Because of abstract reflection, my life-world is a more interesting, richer world.

It is perhaps for the above reasons that Husserl at times says that the life-world is distinct from the objects known by science and at other times says that the life-world includes these objects.[30] The life-world is both ground and consequent. As ground, it is the foundation and basis of abstract reflection. As consequent, it is a whole that includes the intelligibilities discovered by abstract reflection. Such reflection is, therefore, founded on the life-world in two senses: as dependent on a perceived whole from which it is distinct, and as part of a whole which includes this reflection as one project among many. In neither sense is abstract reflection sufficient unto itself.

Finally, because of this foundation on perception in the above senses, eidetic claims are apodictic only in a weak, not a strong, sense. Because the body, the life-world, and language are a sedimented context from which thematic thinking emerges and on which it depends, no thematization can be total. Consequently there is always the possibility that in my reflection I have not considered relevant counterexamples, explored crucial presuppositions, and so on.

CONCLUSION

The tendency of intellectualism from Descartes through Leibniz is to make abstract reflection a necessary and sufficient condition for intelligibility and truth. Kant tries to remedy the situation by joining sensuous intuition to thought, but his intuition remains too impoverished, devoid of structure, and subservient to science and mathematics. Kant gives insufficient attention to the prescientific life-world. As a result, abstract reflection still carries too great a burden and lands in a vicious idealism. Freed from such a burden, abstract reflection can perform its own proper role of interpreting and enriching our life-world. Abstract reflection is not sufficient unto itself, but is founded on perception. Reality is not initially known through such reflection, but perceived as the life-world context of individual gestalts. The intelligibilities intended, understood, and judged by the desire to know are founded on this life-world context.

One consequence of such an analysis is the falsity of scientism and logicism because they are self-refuting and arbitrary. If abstract reflection is founded on perception, then abstract reflection cannot deny its roots in perception without undermining its own claim to truth. If perception is essential for scientific truth and yet proclaimed by scientism as illusory and merely subjective, then scientific truth rests on an illusion and is itself an illusion.

Scientism and logicism are arbitrary because they assume as universal and fundamental a standard of truth that is merely particular and founded. To say that perceptual claims are false because they do not conform to scientific or logical norms of exactness and rigor assumes that such norms are appropriate for perception. In such an assumption, scientism and logicism reveal themselves, contrary to their explicit claims about themselves, to be arbitrary and irrational. In Chapter 8 this argument will be an important part of my criticism of scientism and logicism as ideologies for late capitalism.

Another consequence of my analysis is that both perception and reflection have a common cognitional structure of experience, understanding, and judgment. In both there is a given sensuous presence, interpretation of the given, and judgment about the truth or falsity of the interpretation. Perception as prescientific and common-sensical, then, is a *pattern of experience*, with its own criteria of truth and value; so too is reflection, which operates in the strictly intellectual pattern of experience.[31] Whereas perception in its common-sense orientation is pragmatic, inexact, and uncritical, reflection as it operates in science, logic, and philosophy is interested in knowing for its own sake, exact, and critical. "Don't put off until tomorrow what you can do today" and "A stitch in time saves nine" are satisfactory as common-sense maxims, but not as reflective, scientific claims concerned with evidence.

Phenomenologists such as Merleau-Ponty have done a good job of restoring a richness and intelligibility to accounts of perceptual experience, thus overcoming empiricist and rationalist distortions. Where Merleau-Ponty is less adequate is in distinguishing between perception as cognitional structure and perception as pattern of experience and among the elements of that structure, experience, understanding, and judgment. Nor does he adequately distinguish between reflection as a pattern of experience and reflection as a cognitional structure, or among the different elements of that structure.[32]

My account attempts to go beyond Merleau-Ponty in making the above distinctions and at the same time in bringing reflection and perception closer together. All perception is reflection, in the sense of the cognitional structure of experience, understanding, and judgment. All reflection involves perception in the sense of being founded on it. Perception functions as the experiential component of reflection and supplies the objects, intersubjective context, language, and presuppositions without which such intellection could not occur. This account avoids the facile "either–or" of reducing perception to reflection or vice versa, recognizes their distinctiveness, and relates them. Human knowledge (and indeed human life) reveals itself as a lived, fruitful, intelligible tension and collaboration between immediacy and mediation, the sensuous and the intellectual, perception and reflection.

Thinkers such as Habermas have done a good job in distinguishing various patterns of experience from one another. As we saw earlier in this chapter, Habermas distinguishes symbolic interaction, prescientific ethical action of human beings in the world for the purpose of realizing political goals in the community, from purposive rational action, labor carried out according to technical rules to produce an object of consumption. From my perspective, Habermas is distinguishing between two patterns of experience. He has not adequately shown, however, the unity between and among these patterns insofar as cognitional structure is present in both. To judge through interaction that I should do X presupposes an experience of the context and an understanding of the various possibilities. Likewise, to judge that I should or should not make a certain product presupposes an experience of using or consuming products and an understanding of the differences between and among them.

NOTES

1. Edmund Husserl, *Formal and Transcendental Logic*, trans. Dorion Cairns (The Hague: Nijhoff, 1969), pp. 162–67, 23–37, 188–91, 194–95, 202–209, and *Experience and Judgement*, ed. Ludwig Landgrebe, trans. James S. Churchill and Karl Ameriks (Evanston, Ill.: Northwestern University Press, 1973), pp. 25–28.

2. Husserl, *Formal and Transcendental Logic*, pp. 162–66, and *Experience and Judgement*, pp. 50–60, 113–16.

3. Edmund Husserl, *Logical Investigations*, trans. J. N. Findlay, 2 vols. (New York: Humanities Press, 1970), II 620–21, 652–59, 593–96.

4. Husserl, *Cartesian Meditations*, pp. 96–97, 116–17. Merleau-Ponty, *Phenomenology of Perception*, pp. 90–97.

5. Husserl, *Formal and Transcendental Logic*, p. 233.

6. Ibid., p. 280; emphasis deleted.

7. Husserl, *Crisis*, pp. 142–48. Merleau-Ponty, *Phenomenology of Perception*, pp. 3–6.

8. Merleau-Ponty, *Phenomenology of Perception*, pp. 98–153.

9. Wittgenstein, *Blue and Brown Books*, pp. 77–79. Merleau-Ponty,

"On the Phenomenology of Language," pp. 216–23, and *Visible and Invisible*, pp. 121–29.

10. Husserl, *Logical Investigations*, II 694–702, 710–13, 728–29, and *Formal and Transcendental Logic*, pp. 56–62.

11. The term "intellectualist" is borrowed from Merleau-Ponty, *Phenomenology of Perception*, pp. 176–80.

12. Husserl, *Logical Investigations*, II 467–69.

13. Wittgenstein, *Blue and Brown Books*, pp. 32–43, and *Philosophical Investigations*, pp. 60–61, 102–105, 115, 120, 150, 165, 172, 217–20.

14. Wittgenstein, *Philosophical Investigations*, pp. 92–97.

15. Wittgenstein, *Blue and Brown Books*, p. 42.

16. Habermas, *Towards a Rational Society*, pp. 91–94.

17. Thomas McCarthy, *The Critical Theory of Jürgen Habermas* (Cambridge: MIT Press, 1978), pp. 23–30.

18. Readers of Hannah Arendt will see in my distinction among work, art, and symbolic interaction her distinction among labor, work, and action as three different forms of practical reason or praxis. See her *The Human Condition* (Garden City, N.Y.: Doubleday Anchor, 1959). As I shall argue in Chapters 6 and 8, theoretical reason, when used primarily to criticize oppressive psychological and social structures, can also be a form of praxis in an indirect sense.

19. See Bernard Lonergan, *Insight: A Study of Human Understanding* (New York: Longmans, Green, 1957), pp. 88–89, for a discussion of insight as enriching.

20. Merleau-Ponty, *Phenomenology of Perception*, pp. 383–88.

21. Wittgenstein, *Philosophical Investigations*, pp. 190–214.

22. Lonergan, *Insight*, pp. 348–52.

23. In a sense, the universal is already present on the level of perception itself. When I recognize an individual thing as red, I am using a universal notion but not explicitly adverting to it. In abstract reflection this universal becomes explicit, and the object of reflection is itself universal, abstracted from the individual instances in which it was initially encountered.

24. See David Hume, *A Treatise on Human Nature*, ed. L. A. Selby-Bigge (Oxford: Clarendon, 1888), pp. 21–25, for a version of this argument.

25. Lonergan, *Insight*, pp. 272–78, 322–24.

26. Husserl, *Logical Investigations*, II 694–702, 710–13, 728–29.

27. Lonergan, *Insight*, pp. 280–81.

28. Husserl, *Crisis*, pp. 125–26.

29. Husserl, *Formal and Transcendental Logic*, pp. 205–16.

30. Husserl, *Crisis*, pp. 129–32.

31. See Lonergan, *Insight*, pp. 173–206, for a definition of pattern of experience and for the distinction between the common-sense and the intellectual patterns.

32. For example, see Merleau-Ponty, *Phenomenology of Perception*, pp. 26–51, 207–42.

3

Objectivity, Alienation, and Reflection

WITH THE PHENOMENOLOGICAL describing, defining, and relating of perception, expression, and reflection, we have made a significant advance in our inquiry into the self. At this point a crucial issue arises for phenomenology, the meaning and significance of the objective knowledge that reflection claims to achieve. Does such objective knowledge have positivist, objectivist, value-free implications as some have claimed? Is there a necessary connection between objectivity and alienation as some within the traditions of existentialism and phenomenology have claimed?

DIALECTICAL CONSIDERATIONS

One of the dominant trends of the time is objectivism, the idea that one can achieve a value-free, immediate knowledge of things with no contamination by subjectivity. To such a view there are significant objections, some of which are grounded in evidence already uncovered in this book.

First of all, I have shown that even on the most immediate level, the perceptual, there is interpretation. There is no seeing without a "seeing as." Perception is mediated through language, and language is interpretative. Not even on a perceptual level is knowing a mere immediate looking or touching.

Second, perception is not only interpretative but value-laden. I look toward this and away from that because of attractions and repulsions, values and counter-values. I focus on the milkshake now in this hot weather because I am thirsty, the book by Husserl because I am writing a book on phenomenology, the writing table because that is essential for my project as a writer. Everything I encounter in the world is in a value-laden context of concern, a totality of means–ends relationships in the context of my work as a writer and thinker. I need this writing paper to type on, I need to type this chapter for my book, I need to write this book as the first volume of a multi-volume project in philosophy, and so on.[1]

Third, if all perceptions are interpretations and all interpretations involve or imply values or interests, then all perceptions are value-laden. Fourth, I can generalize the preceding claim about perception to include all knowledge, even that of science itself. For science is founded on perception, certainly does interpret sensible phenomena, and is governed by criteria, norms, and values of truth such as parsimony and comprehensiveness. Science as a form of reflective activity is interested in a project of prediction and control. Science rejects as untrue and uninteresting any hypotheses not allowing it to do that. Science, therefore, is interest-laden, and such interest constitutes internally the kind of project and kind of objective knowledge that science is. Without the orientation to prediction and control and the preference for empirically verifiable knowledge over other kinds, science would not be science.[2]

Fifth, scientific inquiry is an inquiry carried on in a community of investigators. As such a community, however, it presupposes certain norms or values: comprehensibility, truth, sincerity, and appropriateness. Claims should be clear, should be experimentally verified, should be accurately reported, and should be verified without any dogmatic recourse to authority. Any obfuscation of meaning, inadequate verification, lying, or dogmatic imposition of authority is a violation of such norms. Because such norms are internally necessary for the practice of science, science itself is inherently informed by moral values.[3]

Sixth, even if science tried to achieve a totally value-free knowledge, and many scientists and philosophers of science so misinterpret science, the effort is self-contradictory. For the effort to be value-free implies striving and choosing to be value-free; being value-free is better than not being value-free. Being value-free, therefore, is a value for science and scientists.

The attempt at a totally value-free objectivity divorced from all subjectivity, therefore, negates itself. Perhaps, as Kierkegaard and Nietzsche argue, subjectivity is the truth. The arch-villain for Kierkegaard in the *Concluding Unscientific Postscript* is the objective thinker, the most outstanding instance of whom is Hegel. Such a thinker ignores the fact that systematic, objective truth is possible for God, not for finite man. The error of trying to think objectively is that, in the pursuit of universal, speculative, conceptual truth, I ignore my own limited existence as an individual in the process of becoming and lapse into comic self-forgetfulness. In my quest for certitude, I forget the passionate desire that motivates the quest. In the search for universal truth I become a philosophical Hamlet, bewitched by possibility and unable to commit myself to a definite course of action.[4]

For genuine existential truth, the presence of passionate freedom is decisive. It is not the objective content that is important but how I appropriate that content. "The objective accent falls on what is said, the subjective accent on how it is said." For this reason, something true in itself may become, in the mouth of the one uttering it, untrue because I express it inauthentically. If my relationship to that content is one of infinite passion, where commitment is total and where this commitment governs and unifies my life, then I am in the truth. Such truth is "an objective uncertainty held fast in an appropriation process of the most passionate inwardness." Objective knowledge, although vital and important in other spheres, is not decisive for ethico-religious truth.[5]

As an example of what he means by existential truth, Kierkegaard considers the knowledge of God. Objectively, reflection is concerned with whether or not the individual is knowing the true God. Subjectively, reflection is concerned with whether the individual is related to something in such a manner that the relationship is worthy of God. For this reason, one who objectively worships an idol could be more in the truth than the tepid Sunday Christian who believes the correct doctrines. The passionate intensity of one's commitment constitutes the existential truth of that commitment. Nor can "what" and "how" be related or mediated, for to be in a state of mediation is to be finished and complete, whereas the existing individual is constantly becoming.[6]

For Kierkegaard existential truth is individual, not universal. Abraham in *Fear and Trembling* is an example of existential, religious freedom cut off from the universal. Abraham is told by God to sacrifice his son, Isaac, and cannot explain himself to anyone. There is not a universal reason that he could give, such as the tragic hero Agamemnon gave for sacrificing Iphigenia. Abraham's faith is one of passion, and the only justification is his passion itself. Because he is on the level of individual passion, he has to bear the burden of an incommunicable solitude and be willing to commit what, from an ethical point of view, is murder.[7]

Rather than reasonable transitions from one stage of existence to another, there is a series of leaps, in which the degree of commitment goes beyond any possible reason for making the leap. Absolute certitude on a venture is impossible; to ask for such is to ask that it cease to be a venture.[8] Often the situation is that one must act where there are as many reasons pro as con. "The absurd is that I must act where my powers of reflection tell me: you can just as well do one thing as the other." For this reason, "there is nothing more impossible or more self-contradictory than to act (decisively, infinitely) by virtue or reflection."[9]

Because of this discontinuity between reason and freedom, Kierkegaard often talks as though motives and reasons are unnecessary. A Christian does not require objective, historical proof of the truth of the Scriptures, any more than one in love needs external marks of excellence in the loved one. Even if the Scriptures were proved to be false, the Christian should go on believing. Even if it is shown convincingly that the books were not written by their reputed authors, were not authentic, were not in integral condition, and were not inspired, it does not follow that these authors and Christ have not existed. The believer is equally free and obliged to assume the opposite.[10]

For Nietzsche too the attack on objective truth often takes the form of an attack on metaphysics. For Nietzsche, however, the deepest reason for the impossibility of metaphysics lies in the death of God. Because God has functioned as the ground of objective truth and value, the death of God means the death of objective truth and value. The scientist, researcher, and scholar, absorbed in the pursuit of the universally valid and forgetful of self, are the last sick hangovers of such a belief in metaphysics. Because there is now no truth or value existing independently of man, human beings should create value. Human beings as they exist ordinarily, believing in objective truth, must give way to the "over man," the creator of truth and value.[11]

The over man is described in Neitzsche's parable of the camel, the lion, and the child. The camel is the human being who has existed up to now, burdened down and alienated by belief in objective truth and value, by moral rules imposed from without and ultimately grounded in God. The lion is the person who says "no" to all this and throws off the shackles of the Christian slave morality, alienating that person from her own sexuality and freedom. The child is the triumphant new person, able to affirm himself and the world and to create value.[12]

What follows from the denial of objective truth is the doctrine of perspectivism; all truth is relative to the will-to-power of the individual, the drive of the organism toward self-affirmation. Because there is no objective truth, everything is a lie. There are, however, unnatural, sick lies and natural, healthy lies. An example of the former is the slave morality of Christianity; an example of the latter is the notion of the over man.[13]

The attack on objective truth, then, for both Kierkegaard and Nietzsche is an attack on a one-sided notion of objectivity, unrelated to and forgetful of subjectivity. There is a tension, first, between this negation of objectivity and a deeper, more implicit notion of objectivity. For example, in Kierkegaard there is a conflict between the contention that the "how" of passionate freedom is important for ethico-religious truth and cannot be mediated with the "what" of objective content, and the contention that one should not love something finite with infinite passion, at the price of becoming comical and ridiculous. The latter affirmation necessarily implies the importance of objective content as a way of distinguishing between a finite and an infinite object of one's passion.[14]

Second, there is a contradiction between Kierkegaard's defense of the isolated religious individual, cut off from the universal, and his notion that the authentic individual not merely is eccentric but embodies and realizes possibilities that are universal, that is, common to all human beings. The highest essential human possibility is religious commitment to an infinite God.[15] Third, this isolated individual turns out to be describable in universal terms. "Faith," "love," "commitment" are not merely individual but universal; otherwise Kierkegaard's descriptions would mean nothing to us.

Finally, Kierkegaard argues in universal terms for the superiority of the ethical level of existence, living according to universal moral rules, over the aesthetic level of existence, the level of uncommitted pleasure-seeking; and for the superiority of the religious level of existence over the ethical. Moreover, Kierkegaard gives us reasons for moving from one level to another. Why should one be dissatisfied with the aesthetic level and be willing to move to the ethical level? The reason is that the search for pleasure ceases to be pleasurable, and the self is tempted to melancholy and despair. Why should a person move beyond the ethical level to faith? The reason is that the one-sidedness, sin, and despair endemic to the ethical level are overcome only on the level of faith. Kierkegaard's reflective description and criticism of the three kinds of human existence belie his rejection of objective truth.[16]

This same tension between an explicit rejection of objective truth and a covert notion of objective truth is also present in Nietzsche. First of all, in a self-contradictory way he affirms that all truth is perspectival. Either this statement itself is non-perspectival and consequently an implicit denial of the explicit claim, or it is perspectival and, therefore, not to be taken seriously. Second, the distinction between the sick and the healthy lie presupposes an objective criterion of health. Third, the parable of the camel, the lion, and the child presupposes a standard by which the lion is judged to be *better* than the camel, and the child *superior* to the lion. Finally, the previously mentioned standards seem to be grounded in a metaphysical affirmation that everything is characterized by the will-to-power, an affirmation contradicting the attempt to deny all metaphysics and all objective truth.[17]

Nietzsche does say, of course, in responding to this kind of objection that the doctrine of the will-to-power is his perspective, his fruitful fiction. But the problem with such a reply is, first, that the claims about the will-to-power do not seem to function that way in all contexts, but seem to be intended at times as truth claims. Second, as I indicated above, an objective criterion of truth seems to be present in his account of the difference between a fruitful, healthy lie and one that is not, and in the doctrine of perspectivism. It is hard not to conclude, as Jaspers argues, that Nietzsche's thought is a will to truth and objective knowledge that is at odds with itself.[18]

In spite of their criticism and apparent rejection of objective knowing, therefore, Kierkegaard and Nietzsche seem tacitly to endorse and at times to use objective knowing. Too often, although not always,[19] existentialism and phenomenology have slighted objectivity in favor of subjectivity. Whereas in the nineteenth century the academic and cultural bias was in favor of objective, conceptual thinking, now in some versions of existentialism and phenomenology the bias has shifted away from objectivity toward a passionate, non-conceptual, non-scientific thinking and willing: for example, Kierkegaard's passionate inwardness, Nietzsche's will-to-power, Sartre's negative freedom, and Heidegger's meditative thinking. Is it true that any thematic knowledge of the other person necessarily degrades the other?[20] Does objective knowledge necessarily alienate one from oneself?[21] Is a conceptual, metaphysical knowledge of being necessarily "murderous," as Heidegger claims?[22] These and other related questions cry out for more balanced, systematic treatment.

PHENOMENOLOGICAL DESCRIPTION OF OBJECTIVITY

The result of the preceding dialectic is that objectivity implies subjectivity and vice versa. Just as a one-sided subjectivism negates itself, so also a one-sided objectivism. We must now consider the content of such a necessary interaction between subjectivity and objectivity. In this part I first distinguish phenomenologically various kinds of objectification, then establish fundamental relationships between kinds, and finally argue for certain consequences. What I show negatively is that, in a sense somewhat the same and somewhat different from Marx's critique of Hegel, there has been in some versions of existentialism and phenomenology a confused, mistaken identification of objectification with alienation.[23] What emerges positively from such an analysis is a limited phenomenological rehabilitation of objectivity. It is limited because no objective knowledge can be total, but rather presupposes a prethematic context that can never be fully articulated. "Objectivity" is understood here as the noematic or objective pole of a conscious act; "objectification," as the noetic or intentional pole of that same act. "Reflection" as understood and practiced in this chapter is the kind of thinking done in the intellectual pattern of experience by such disciplines as science, formal logic, and philosophy, with philosophy playing a privileged role.

The Eight Kinds of Objectivity

The first, most obvious, kind of objectivity is perceptual, the presence of a concrete, sensuous thing to a perceiving, embodied subject. As

I have already shown in Chapter 2, the objectivity of the object has at least five different aspects, all of which taken together constitute the thing as distinct and independent from me. Although the thing is distinct from me, it is nonetheless related to me because it is present to my consciousness. The real table is not something hidden behind the phenomena of perception, but present in and through these phenomena. Consequently there is a basic paradox in perceptual objectivity shared by all other kinds as well. The thing is known as independent of consciousness only because of evidence present to consciousness. Perception is perception of an object distinct from the perceiver and yet present in the perceiver's conscious experience. Corresponding to the thing perceived is the subject perceiving through his body, in the terms of the last chapter, a perceiving as opposed to a reflecting subject.

A second kind of objectivity is that of the universal, present in such disciplines as science, mathematics, formal logic, and philosophy. The object here, in contrast to the perceived object, is universal, applicable to many different particulars. The scientific law $f = ma$ or the mathematical definition of a triangle are true not just of one force or one triangle, but of all forces and all triangles. Because the object of such thinking is universal, it is also non-perspectival and non-imaginable. In contrast to perception, which occurs always from a point of view, the definition of force or triangle is true from all points of view. The universal is a concept, not an image. Corresponding to the object thought noematically is the thinking, reflecting subject, intellection as opposed to perception. More specifically, a certain kind of reflection is present, understanding as the grasp of an intelligibility. Understanding here is distinct from judgment, which in grasping the virtually unconditioned verifies the intelligibility as true or false.

Still a third kind of objectivity is the thematic. Here again the most obvious example is perception, in which I actively attend to or thematize what I am perceiving. When I look at the table to determine its color, I am actively attending to that and am only implicitly, vaguely aware of other things in the room forming part of the background. If a piece of music catches my attention, then the table slides into the background and the music now becomes the theme. Thematization is present on all levels of conscious experience. Other examples are the working out of a mathematical proof, in which I actively attend to the argument and its conclusion; and daydreaming, in which I imagine myself in Bermuda enjoying a winter vacation.

For such thematizing to be objectifying in the proper sense, there will also be a distancing, a "standing back from." Such distanciation moves between two extremes: one of them, that of the pure observer; the other, that of a total belonging with little or no distance. When there is a thematizing with little or no distance—for example, in ecstatic sexual encounter, mystical experience, or aesthetic experience—there is thematic attention but not objectification.

One can, however, overstate the above point, for objectification is certainly compatible with and present in less intense forms of belonging. In having a loving conversation with my friend or lover about our relationship or discussing with excitement Picasso's *Guernica* at which I am currently looking, there is certainly both involvement and objectification. The dichotomy between objectification and belonging seems to be a romantic myth that cannot be sustained by the phenomenological facts.

A fourth kind of objectivity is factual, the objectivity arrived at through the "yes" or "no" of judgment. When I affirm that the bread is on the table or that f = ma or that Columbus discovered America in 1492, I am affirming facts. This kind of objectivity goes beyond what is merely conceptually true to what in fact is so. A mathematical definition of a triangle is conceptually true, but that there are some triangular things is a fact. Factual truth also gets us beyond what is merely hypothetical or possible. When I entertain the theory of relativity as an hypothesis, I am considering the merely possible. When I verify such a hypothesis, I know a fact.[24] Corresponding noetically to such a fact is judgment, the act of affirming or denying an hypothesis.

A fifth kind of objectivity is alienation. When, without prior provocation, I call a person a name, slap or shoot her, I am objectifying her in a degrading sense. I am ignoring her character as a free, self-conscious intelligent subject and treating her like a thing. Here I attempt to harm, dominate, control, or manipulate the other. In a broader sense alienation is any kind of inappropriate objectification that estranges me from myself, other people, or being. For example, if I think of being simply as the sum total of mathematical objects or as totally comprehensible, then I am overlooking all aspects of being that cannot be mathematicized or comprehended.

Normative objectivity is still a sixth kind of objectivity—the fidelity to the dictates of inquiring intelligence and reasonableness. When I tell a person to "be objective," I am asking him to give the voice of reason priority over other voices, to be attentive to evidence, and to ignore irrational bias. I am asking him to be faithful to the standards of evidence as they pertain to a particular field of inquiry. The explicitly and methodically rational disciplines such as science, logic, and philosophy are the best examples of such normative objectivity, but this fidelity to standards is present in other areas as well. If a film critic insisted on applying the standards of stage drama to film, she would not be objective in the normative sense. In criticizing a film stressing the visual possibilities of the medium for having little or no dialogue, she would be imposing on one sphere standards appropriate for another, the stage. In reading such a critic, we would find her observations arbitrary and unfounded.

The noematic component here is the standards governing a particular realm of inquiry; the noetic is the striving to conform to and realize such norms. For example, in empirical science there is the canon of parsimony, which insists that hypotheses should be verified in sensible data and should not say more than can be justified by the data. There is, as well, the canon of complete explanation, which insists that all data be explained. Newton's theory of mechanics is less adequate than Einstein's special theory of relativity because the latter can account for the constant velocity of light and the former cannot. Finally, there is the canon of statistical residues. Some data give rise to classical laws such as f = ma or Einstein's theory of special relativity. Other data cannot be explained by these laws and give rise to laws of a different kind, statistical laws. If f = ma is an example of the former, 1 : 2, the probability that a tossed coin will come up heads, is an example of the latter.[25]

The seventh kind of objectivity is experiential—the given data crucial for reaching truth in any inquiry.[26] These data are basically of two kinds, data of sense and data of consciousness. Data of sense are the realm of perceived objects, the first kind of objectivity mentioned above. Data of consciousness are the human subject's experience of himself in relation to the world. Data of sense, to be understood not as isolated atoms but as gestalts, are crucial for verifying the propositions of the physical and social sciences. Data of consciousness are essential for verifying propositions in philosophy. For example, in trying to distinguish eight different kinds of objectivity, the philosopher must reflect on her own experience of these kinds of objectivity.

An eighth kind of objectivity is expression. As I have already shown in Chapter 2, thought must externalize itself and complete itself in expression. Such expression is objectification, a making public of what before was private, inner, vague, implicit, inchoate. Objectification as it occurs in language, interaction among people, and art is the fruit of subjectivity and is necessary for subjectivity to realize itself.

Interrelationships

The relationships between and among the kinds of objectivity are of two kinds, negative and positive. Negative relationships are present simply because there are eight distinct types of objectivity, none of which is simply identified with the others. However, this non-identity has a strong and a weak sense. The strong sense is that A is not and can never be B. For example, perceptual objectivity is not universal objectivity; nor is factual objectivity experiential objectivity. The weak sense of non-identity is inexhaustibility. For instance, perceptual objectivity is a type of thematic objectivity, but cannot be simply identified with such objectivity because universal and factual objectivity are also thematic. All perception is thematization, but not all thematization is perception. There are important implications, to be explored in the next section, flowing from these negative relationships.

Positive relationships are of three kinds, class inclusion, eidetic unity, and foundation. One example of class inclusion has already been mentioned: perception, as well as universal, factual, degrading, and experiential objectification, is a type of thematization. Indeed, thematization seems to be the most universal kind of objectification, present on all levels of conscious experience. All consciousness is consciousness of an object or theme explicitly present to consciousness. Whether I am looking at a table, imagining a pleasant trip to Canada, thinking about a mathematical proof, or choosing a life's vocation, I am considering a thematic object.

Eidetic unity between and among types justifies us in calling them "objectivities." What are the common threads that run through all the types of objectivity? One such thread is the structure of thematization, in which a theme is present to consciousness but not reducible to it, and there is a distancing. Thematization is not merely a kind of objectivity existing alongside other kinds, but a structure permeating all other kinds. One aspect of this structure is consciousness-independence or consciousness-transcendence. Thus the meaning of a perceptual thing or a mathematical proposition such as $2 + 2 = 4$ is present to consciousness but at the same time transcends consciousness because of the experienced difference between the multiplicity of conscious acts and the one public meaning. The act of perceiving is experienced as private, proceeding from me as the perceiving agent, in contrast to the many acts of one knower and many individual knowers.[27]

Independence is also present in the different kinds of objectivity insofar as they are different and specific. Any objectivity is essentially related to a subjectivity engaged in transcending itself. Indeed, there are two relationships to subjectivity here, two types of transcendence: negative and positive. The negative is the factual as opposed to merely wishful thinking, the universal as opposed to the merely individual, the normative as opposed to merely subjective, irrational bias. The positive relationship is present insofar as the act of judging is related to the noematic fact, the act of conceiving to the content thought, the act of fidelity to the norms of a particular discipline or level of consciousness.

Objectivity as foundation is present when A cannot be itself without B; B is the foundation of A. For example, perception can exist without the universalization of science, but science presupposes perception. As I have already indicated, science has to verify its hypotheses through perception. Again, insofar as perceptual, universal, and factual objectivity operate according to their own proper norms, they are founded on normative objectivity, a fidelity to the rules for correct perceiving, and so on. In a third example of foundation, factual objectivity presupposes experiential objectivity insofar as the claims of science, psychoanalysis, and philosophy are founded on the evidence that is given.

Consequences

Two consequences, to be explored in further chapters, of my account of objectification is that objectification of myself and other persons at times can be legitimate and enlightening. Denial of this claim by phenomenologists and existentialists rests upon confusing kinds of objectification. A third consequence of my analysis is that a conceptual knowledge of being or the life-world can reveal and enlighten. Conceptual, representational thinking is not, as Heidegger claims, necessarily a thinking that distorts and covers up being.[28] Only if one identifies the thematization proper to philosophy with that of perceptual, scientific, alienating, or experiential objectification can such a claim be true.

Philosophy as practiced in this book is phenomenology, the universal, reflective, conceptual thematization of human subjectivity in relation to being. Being is the life-world as ultimate context, as unity of subject and object. Thinking is conceptual because it is universal and expressive, a working-out into language of notions initially vague and incomplete. What the thinker experiences is a movement from an initially indeterminate, vague, incomplete notion to one that is determinate, explicit, and complete. Thinking has a preconceptual moment, but I experience this as incomplete until I express it and conceptualize it. Just as the painter does not fully know what she wants to say until she has added the final brush stroke, so the philosopher reflecting on subjectivity or being does not know what he wants to say until he has said it.

Such a claim has to be true because any attempt to deny it refutes itself. Any attempt to deny the conceptual and universal ends up implicitly asserting them. Thus Heidegger's attempt to arrive at a post-conceptual, post-metaphysical, post-representational thinking actually uses such concepts as "presence," the "fourfold," "involvement," and "releasement."[29]

Is "being" an object? Clearly, Heidegger has a point in denying that being is an object in the sense of perceived thing, scientifically known thing, or dominated, reified person or thing.[30] Experience of being is not of an object, but of an implicit context or ground within which objects appear. Reflection on such experience, however, thematizes being as "horizon" or "that which regions."[31] In this sense being is an object. In describing being this way Heidegger is articulating a definite, universal, thematized notion of being. Otherwise his very illuminating discussion would mean nothing to us.

In making such a claim for conceptual knowledge, I am not, however, arguing for a total comprehension of being. Such a claim would be alienating in the broader sense of that word—an inappropriate objectification. Because of our finitude and our immersion in a necessarily implicit context of language and being, Heidegger is surely correct in denying the possibility of such comprehension. The language that I use in discussing anything is always composed of sedimented meanings that I cannot totally thematize at the time I use them. For example, if I am discussing music with a person, there is always a taken-for-granted set of meanings and words that we use but do not explicitly reflect upon or justify. The world is always present to me as more than I can thematize or conceptualize at any one time. There is always an implicit background from which the explicit meaning emerges, always unanswered questions enveloping those that I do answer.[32] If I have answered the question about the eight kinds of objectivity, their interrelationships, and their consequences, there are always further questions. Does my analysis reopen the possibility of metaphysics? What are the implications for ethics, political philosophy, aesthetics?

I am arguing for a middle ground between saying that objective, conceptual thought can tell us nothing about being and saying that it can tell us everything. Although there is no space to develop the point adequately in this chapter, I would suggest that Heidegger's practice, in contrast to his explicit conception of what he is doing, is on such middle ground. To think being in a non-alienated fashion is to think it conceptually as mystery, as gift, as beyond total comprehension.[33] Philosophical knowledge is not total enlightenment about ourselves in the world, but light emerging from darkness, unconcealment arising from concealment. The task of philosophy is conceptually to articulate, as much as possible, this necessary concealment, not to remain silent about it or to overlook it.

CONCLUSION

Objectivity turns out to be many-splendored. Because of this fact, objectivity can have a role to play that is authentic and liberating. One question that might arise is whether my description of the eight kinds of objectivity is exhaustive. A claim of exhaustibility goes beyond the evidence presented in the chapter and is not essential to its argument. This claim goes beyond the evidence because I have given no argument against the possibility that there may be other kinds. Exhaustibility is not essential to the argument because I have shown that there are *at least* these eight kinds, and that they have important implications for certain issues in phenomenology and existentialism. A possible ninth or tenth kind of objectivity would not affect the argument here.

I have argued for a restoration of objectivity to its proper place in relation to subjectivity. Only with such a restoration can existentialism and phenomenology avoid replacing a one-sided objectivism with an equally one-sided subjectivism. The conceptual knowledge that is restored is chastened and humble, aware of its own limits but also capable of illuminating our quest for truth.

NOTES

1. For a discussion of concern, see Heidegger, *Being and Time*, pp. 95–122.

2. On science as essentially, internally related to interest, see Jürgen Habermas, *Knowledge and Human Interests*, trans. Jeremy Shapiro (Boston: Beacon, 1971), pp. 301–17.

3. See Karl Otto Apel, *Towards a Transformation of Philosophy*, trans. Glynn Adey and David Frisby (London: Routledge & Kegan Paul, 1980), pp. 225–85, for a fuller discussion of this argument. In Chapter 5, I shall develop further the role these four validity claims play in an account of practical, moral intersubjectivity.

4. Søren Kierkegaard, *Concluding Unscientific Postscript*, trans. David Swenson (Princeton: Princeton University Press, 1941), pp. 33–34, 37, 74–75, 107, 131–35, 200, 267–70, 273–75, 279, 288, 296.

5. Ibid., pp. 54–55, 85–86, 181–82; the quotation is found on p. 182. "Passion" here is not to be confused with passion in the ordinary sense, such as fear or hate. "Passion" refers to freedom, to that capacity of the self to give or commit itself totally.

6. Ibid., pp. 178–80.

7. Søren Kierkegaard, *Fear and Trembling*, in *Fear and Trembling and The Sickness Unto Death*, trans. Walter Lowrie (Garden City, N.Y.: Doubleday Anchor, 1954), pp. 121–24.

8. Kierkegaard, *Postscript*, p. 381.

9. Søren Kierkegaard, *The Journals of Søren Kierkegaard*, ed. and trans. Alexander Dru (London: Oxford University Press, 1938), p. 291.

10. Kierkegaard, *Postscript*, p. 31.

11. Friedrich Nietzsche, *Thus Spake Zarathustra*, in *The Portable Nietzsche*, ed. and trans. Walter Kaufmann (New York: Vintage, 1967),

pp. 124–25, 171, 308–309, 399; *Twilight of the Idols*, in ibid., pp. 481–83; and Friedrich Nietzsche, *On the Genealogy of Morals*, trans. Walter Kaufmann (New York: Vintage, 1967), pp. 147–48, 150–53.

12. Nietzsche, *Thus Spake Zarathustra*, pp. 137–39, 305; and *Beyond Good and Evil*, trans. Marianne Cowan (Chicago: Gateway, 1955), pp. 202–206.

13. Nietzsche, *Genealogy of Morals*, pp. 118–19, 136–39, 150–51; *Twilight of the Idols*, p. 489; *Thus Spake Zarathustra*, pp. 171, 402; and *The Antichrist*, in *The Portable Nietzsche*, ed. Kaufmann, p. 638. Karl Jaspers, *Nietzsche*, trans. Charles F. Walraff and Frederick J. Schmit (Tucson: University of Arizona Press, 1965), pp. 185–86, 287–88.

14. Kierkegaard, *Postscript*, pp. 377–78. In making such a criticism of Kierkegaard, I realize that I am not just taking his arguments as expressions of a pseudonymous character with little or no relation to his real convictions. On the legitimacy of such an interpretation of Kierkegaard, see Mark C. Taylor, *Kierkegaard's Pseudonymous Authorship* (Princeton: Princeton University Press, 1975), pp. 18–26.

15. Kierkegaard, *Postscript*, pp. 117, 318.

16. Søren Kierkegaard, *Either–Or*, trans. Walter Lowrie, 2 vols. (Garden City, N.Y.: Doubleday Anchor, 1959), II 47, 69, 89, 95, 168–70, 193, 200–10, 212, 215; *Fear and Trembling*, p. 103; and *Sickness Unto death*, p. 163.

17. Jaspers, *Nietzsche*, pp. 309, 317–18. Nietzsche, *Genealogy of Morals*, pp. 77–79, 135–36.

18. Nietzsche, *Beyond Good and Evil*, pp. 1, 19–22, 43, 159–60, 201. Jaspers, *Nietzsche*, pp. 182–228.

19. Husserl, Merleau-Ponty, and Ricoeur have aimed at scientific, universal, conceptual, eidetic truth in phenomenology. See Husserl, *Cartesian Meditations*, pp. 7–17, 69–72; Merleau-Ponty, *Phenomenology of Perception*, pp. vii, xiv–xvii; Paul Ricoeur, *Freedom and Nature: The Voluntary and the Involuntary*, trans. Erazim V. Kohak (Evanston, Ill.: Northwestern University Press, 1966), pp. 13–17.

20. Jean-Paul Sartre, *Being and Nothingness*, trans. Hazel E. Barnes (New York: Citadel, 1964), pp. 235–50.

21. Nietzsche, *Genealogy of Morals*, pp. 148–56.

22. Heidegger, *Question Concerning Technology*, pp. 107–109.

23. Karl Marx, *Economic and Philosophic Manuscripts of 1844*, ed. Dirk J. Struick, trans. Martin Milligan (New York: International, 1964), pp. 170–93.

24. Lonergan, *Insight*, pp. 377–80. My "factual objectivity" is "absolute objectivity" for Lonergan.

25. Ibid., pp. 380–81, for a definition of normative objectivity; pp. 70–102, for a discussion of the canons of empirical method.

26. Ibid., pp. 381–83.

27. Husserl, *Formal and Transcendental Logic*, pp. 162–66.

28. For Heidegger's argument that thinking is not conceptual, see *What Is Called Thinking?* trans. Fred D. Wieck and J. Glenn Gray (New York: Harper & Row, 1968), pp. 211–13. For his argument that genuine thinking of being is not objectifying in any sense, see *The Piety of Thinking*, trans. James G. Hart and John C. Maraldo (Bloomington: Indiana University Press, 1976), pp. 22–31. For a description of representational thinking, see his *Question Concerning Technology*, pp. 127, 130–31; *On the Way to Language*, trans. Peter Hertz (New York: Harper & Row, 1971), p. 74; and *Discourse on Thinking*, trans. John Anderson and E. Hans Freund (New York: Harper & Row, 1966), pp. 67, 69.

29. Heidegger, *What Is Called Thinking?* pp. 235–39; *Poetry, Language, Thought*, trans. Albert Hofstadter (New York: Harper & Row, 1971), pp. 149–51; and *Discourse on Thinking*, pp. 67, 74.

30. Heidegger, *Discourse on Thinking*, p. 67.

31. Ibid., pp. 67–73.

32. Such sedimentation is an important dimension of what Heidegger is getting at in his rejection of philosophies of expression. For example, see his *On the Way to Language*, pp. 57–108, and Gadamer's discussion in *Truth and Method*, pp. 345–66. In developing this notion of sedimentation in my chapter on consciousness and expression and in further developing the notion of tradition as intersubjective and historical in Chapter 6, I have tried to meet Heidegger's objections to expression and to incorporate his insights concerning the self's dependence on language and tradition into my own account. Once again I criticize and attempt to overcome the isolated Cartesian ego.

33. Heidegger, *Discourse on Thinking*, pp. 55–56, 85, 90; and *What Is Called Thinking?* pp. 30–31, 140–41, 146–47.

4

The Free Self

Up to this point in our phenomenological recovery of the self, we have been focusing on the cognitive dimensions of the self: perception, expression, reflection, and objectivity. As crucial as these dimensions are, however, they do not exhaust selfhood, for there is also the existential dimension of freedom. Not only do I know perceptually and reflectively, but I can also choose, love, commit myself to a cause or person, celibacy or marriage, capitalism or socialism, atheism or theism.

The level of freedom complements, lifts up, and completes the levels of cognition. Freedom complements cognition insofar as the existential and personal appropriately balances the cognitive and conceptual, lifts up the cognitive insofar as cognition enters into any choice, and completes the cognitive insofar as choice actualizes abstract possibility. The full constitution of the free, authentic self, then, in this chapter will have two stages: first, the fact and meaning of freedom; second, self-affirmation. Appropriately also, the chapter has two main parts.

The Irony and Ambiguity of Freedom

The argument of this part has two steps: one, dialectical; the other, descriptive. The first is that neither strict determinism nor strict indeterminism is tenable because each is self-refuting. Determinism and indeterminism, contrary to their original intentions, imply indetermination and determination. The conclusion of the first section is that determination and indetermination, albeit redefined, *must* go together in the sense of implying each other.

That they must go together, however, leaves open the question of *how* they go together. The second section answers this question by describing the actual experience and essential structure of freedom. The two parts of the argument are both necessary, and each complements the other. Without the prior dialectic, there would be the possibility that freedom as we experience it is an illusion. The dialectical moment removes this possibility once for all. Description must also complement dialectic if the affirmation of mutual implication is not to remain empty and abstract. The total argument is phenomenological, but perhaps more in an Hegelian than in an Husserlian sense. Both the dialectical and descriptive moments are essential to an adequate phenomenology of freedom.

As a result, freedom is both ironical and legitimately ambiguous. It is ironical in that attempts to defend as true either strict determinism or strict indeterminism refute themselves and become untrue. Also, the content of each of these extremes implies its opposite; determinism implies indetermination and indeterminism implies determination. This irony manifests itself most fully in the first section.

Freedom is also paradoxical and ambiguous because it is a thoroughgoing unity of indetermination and determination not accurately described by the clear and distinct idea of either determinism or indeterminism. This reciprocity itself has at least four different meanings. Determination and indetermination imply one another. The first section demonstrates the necessity, the second the content, of this ambiguity. The meanings of "determination" and "indetermination" grow out of the dialectic in the first section, and will be fully defined in the second section.

The Dialectic of Determinism and Indeterminism

Determinism · The thesis of strict determinism is that there are no free acts, no acts in which a person could have acted otherwise. Both the necessary and the sufficient conditions for an apparently free act lie in conditions and causes prior to the act. If the antecedents are given, then the consequence necessarily follows. Freedom is an illusion that cannot withstand rational, critical examination.

Yet the problem with determinism as a philosophical position is that it has to justify itself as true. Consequently a contradiction emerges between the content of determinism and the act of affirming it as true. If determinism *is*, then truth and freedom of any kind are impossible. If determinism is *true*, then determinism is false because of the logic of any truth claim.

Such self-refutation, depending on the kind of determinism defended, has three forms. The first involves a contradiction between the conscious form that a truth claim must necessarily take and posited unconscious forces. For example, physiological determinism argues that a person's actions and thoughts have their necessary and sufficient conditions in previous states of the brain. If this claim is true, then it is true of the determinist's claim itself. She holds a certain position not because of reasons or standards of evidence, but because of previous physical states of the brain. If so, then appeal to good reasons or standards of evidence is illusory or irrelevant; what really causes her to hold a position is previous physical states as understood through the laws of physiology. If the physiological determinist is correct, then she cannot defend the truth of a position consistently by appeal to good reasons. If she can defend her position, then she is not physiologically determined.[1]

Another example of this kind of self-refutation is the psychological determinist's saying that human acts are really determined by the unconscious. Yet since the psychological determinist appeals to conscious evidence and reasons to justify his position, he contradicts himself. Consciousness can only announce itself as a dupe before a consciousness that is undeceived and rational.

Ayer objects to this analysis by arguing that a computer can arrive at true results and yet is also clearly determined.[2] My response to this objection is that the results can be true only for a mind, which can evaluate and test them. Short of the presence of a mind, there is no truth, only facts that have resulted from physically determined objects. Such a claim is easily intelligible if one reflects on what occurs when a question arises about the "competence" of a computer and the validity of its results. If it is working well, then that competence will be known by recourse to rational inquiry, checking the machine's results against those of competent mathematicians. If it is not working well, then that fact too will be known through rational inquiry.

A second kind of self-refutation occurs when there is a contradiction between an explicit class-inclusion of all acts and an implicit class-exclusion, leaving out the determinist's act of asserting something as true. For example, if a sociological determinist wishes to argue that all theories are class influenced and consequently false, then either her own theory is included in the class or it is not. If it is, then it is a false theory. If it is not, then not all theories are class based and the initial claim turns out to be false.

A third kind of self-refutation depends on the conscious logic of the truth claim itself. On the side of the object known or proposition asserted, there is the necessary "questionableness" of what is asserted. To say that something is true is to have a good reason for what I assert. But a good reason is known only in the context of its possibly being a bad reason or a less good reason. If a reason is not possibly "bad," then it cannot be possibly "good" either. In the language game of making truth claims, "good" and "bad," "true" and "false" have meaning only in terms of each other. Because of this logic, holding something to be true implies freedom, in the sense of openness to at least two possibilities.

On the side of the subject considering the proposition, there is a necessary open-mindedness involved in saying that determinism is true. He must have the ability and willingness to look at both sides of the question, to consider alternative evidence, to raise further questions. Such open-mindedness must be present at least as a possibility in saying that anything is true.

Without such questionableness in the object and open-mindedness in the subject, any truth claim becomes indistinguishable from a rigidly held dogma. If Skinner wishes to argue for environmental determinism,[3] then either he has considered both sides of the question or he has not. If he has considered both sides of the question, then he is not determined to hold the position he does and is, therefore, free. Unless the possibility of determinism's being false is a real possibility for Skinner, he cannot argue that his determinism is true. If such falsity is a real possibility, he is free.

On the other hand, if Skinner has not considered both sides of the question, then we cannot and should not take him seriously, any more than we would take seriously the claim of a prisoner brainwashed by the Soviets about the relative merits of capitalism and socialism. It may be that the prisoner is correct, but we could discover that only by a process of critical inquiry that differs from brainwashing.

Thus even a determinist such as Blanshard, arguing that we are determined to believe something by reasons for the belief,[4] convicts himself through self-refutation. Because a reason that literally coerces us to believe in such a way as to exclude its possible falsity is not and cannot be a good reason, Blanshard cannot defend his position as true. If, on the other hand, he does have good reasons for his belief, then he is free. The explicit deterministic content contradicts the implicit, free act of defending it as true.

Determinism is thus ironical in two senses. It is formally self-refuting in the three above senses; the truth of determinism changes into its opposite, untruth. In a second way, determinism is ironical in that defending it as true implies indeterminism or freedom, the ability to consider alternatives. This second meaning of irony is present in the third kind of self-refutation. Such self-refutation applies to all deterministic claims because each gives reasons for itself, reasons that imply freedom.

Indeterminism · Perhaps, since strict determinism does not work, a strict indeterminism is the answer. Since essence does not determine existence, perhaps existence or freedom is the source of essence. I am the freedom to create my own essence. It is not written in the heavens that I am to be reasonable or unreasonable, homosexual or heterosexual, Catholic or Protestant, peaceful or warlike. Because it is not so written, none of these is objectively preferable to another. One person's virtues are another's vices; one person's sacrifices, another's follies. The consequence of Sartre's indeterminism, as of all indeterminism, is an absurd, arbitrary world where nothing is objectively better than anything else.[5]

There are only two alternatives: "Either man is wholly determined (which is inadmissible, especially because a determined consciousness—i.e., a consciousness externally motivated—becomes itself pure exteriority and ceases to be consciousness) or else man is wholly free."[6] An appropriate philosophical method, phenomenology, is necessary to describe consciousness as it actually experiences itself. Phenomenology takes consciousness on its own terms and does not assume that it is a thing or basically similar to things.

What careful phenomenological description reveals is that consciousness is negativity, the internal negation of the external thing. To be aware of a chair is to be aware of my non-identity with the chair. The chair does not exhaust my possibilities of perception because there are other things I could perceive. Because consciousness is this negativity, total identity with the chair would imply unconsciousness, an impossibility.[7]

Consciousness is a lived paradox: it is what it is not and is not what it is. It is aware of possibilities that are not yet realized and in the light of which it distances itself from what it is in the present. The external thing is simply what it is. It is purely positive, not able to question itself or negate itself the way consciousness can. A chair cannot suddenly decide not to be a chair, but I can choose to leave my business for the teaching profession, to desert my wife for another woman, to reject my middle class status for political radicalism.[8]

Consciousness is pure spontaneity from which all positive determination or definition is absent and which is not influenced by anything other than itself. Consciousness is totally free, therefore, not in the sense that it encounters no limits or obstacles, but in the sense that the meaning these have for consciousness comes from consciousness itself. A person climbing a mountain who becomes fatigued is not forced to stop climbing. If my fundamental project, that basic commitment underlying and giving meaning to everything else, is a life of ease, I may cease climbing. But if my fundamental project is a life delighting in hardships and obstacles that test my courage and ability, I may complete the climb at great cost to myself.[9] Freedom is not influenced by motives or reasons; these are simply expressions of the fundamental project. There is no reciprocity between motivation and freedom because motivation is not really other than freedom.

Nonetheless such an affirmation of absolute freedom has its problems. The first is that if existence precedes essence, the world is arbitrary and absurd. If absurdity is total, however, Sartre cannot defend the truth of his position. For he presumably uses phenomenological method to describe freedom because it is better than other methods, and he argues that his account of freedom is superior to other accounts. In a totally absurd world "better" and "superior" and "truer" make no sense. Sartre's recourse to a method and to standards of truth and falsity that are not absurd contradicts his affirmation of absurdity.

A similar tension arises in Sartre's discussion of good and bad faith. Good faith is living according to the nothingness that I am and accepting responsibility for the choices that I make. Bad faith is the attempt to live like a thing, to avoid the anxiety of freedom, and to shift responsibility from myself to some external agent. The former is definitely preferable to the latter because it is more reasonable and more honest. Yet why, we may ask, are reason and honesty more valuable than their opposites in a totally absurd world?[10]

Another tension exists between Sartre's existentialism and his phenomenology. If existence precedes essence, then there should be no universal, necessary essences prior to freedom. Yet the assumption of phenomenological method is that there are such essences, and Sartre spends some six hundred pages of *Being and Nothingness* describing such structures. For example, consciousness is an internal negation of the external thing, is totally lucid, is temporal, is non-thematically aware of itself, projects value and possibility, is present to the world through embodiment, and desires to be God. Such structures, which limit and define freedom, have not been chosen and are prior to existence. In a sense broader than Sartre intended, I am "condemned to be free."[11]

Freedom, therefore, is not totally empty of content, is not the mere absence of determination. Neither is it totally spontaneous. Even some of the experiences mentioned by Sartre imply receptivity in freedom, experiences such as fatigue, the resistance of external obstacles, the shame before another person catching me in a degrading act. For whether I wish to or not, I experience fatigue in climbing a mountain. Whether I wish to or not, my attention is drawn momentarily to the loud report of an automobile outside my window. Such experiences are not just bare factual events, but inherently meaningful. I do not experience mere noise, but the loud report of an automobile. Certainly I experience this noise in the context of certain projects such as reading a book or writing a letter. These projects determine the value that such an experience may have at the time, irritating, stimulating, or disturbing, but such values presuppose a meaning that I perceive in a receptive manner.

The positing of total spontaneity also is inconsistent with the experienced difference between arbitrary and non-arbitrary interpretations of phenomena, a difference tacitly presupposed by Sartre when he admits that we intuit external things and qualities in things. If I cannot make this orange peel cease being green, then perceiving consciousness to some extent is determined or informed by what is not itself. Such intuition is impossible without a receptivity to meanings in the thing, which are not imposed but discovered.[12]

Sartre's strict indeterminism is ironically self-refuting; in attempting to maintain his position, Sartre has recourse to determination.

His freedom turns out to be a freedom that should be reasonable and honest, possesses certain essential structures, has positive content, and is receptive. Since both strict determinism and strict indeterminism are self-contradictory, determination and indetermination imply one another.

The Description of Determination and Indetermination

We have established the necessary, mutual implication of determination and indetermination. The task now is to indicate the content of this relationship, to show how they go together. In this section, which is heavily indebted to Paul Ricoeur, determination and indetermination signify four kinds of reciprocity: motive and "leap," reflection and choice, essence and existence, and necessity and consent.

We can view decision either as a static whole, in which I prescind from its involvement with the body and personal history, or as a dynamic whole, in which such involvement is crucial. Considered as a static whole, decision is the project, the chosen action to be performed because of certain motives. Motive and "leap" are essentially related moments or aspects of a decision considered in this manner. This project is the whole, and motive and "leap" are parts.

Motives are not causes that compel me to act in a certain way; rather, they incline without compelling. A cause is distinct in its being from that which it causes, whereas a motive fully becomes a motive only in the "leap" of a decision, in the final *fiat* of choice whereby I opt for one course of action rather than another. The leap involved in making a decision is never indifferent to motives or arbitrary; rather, the decision itself is the result of a search for the right motives. "I decide because . . ." is the basic model for a decision. To determine is not to compel, but to legitimize or justify.

It is essential that I know a motive, whereas I could be ignorant of causes influencing me. If I announce that I am going to the grocery store and I am asked why, the answer "I do not know" makes no sense. On the other hand, if I am feeling irritable, the cause of that feeling could be unknown to me at the time. It could be a lack of sleep, inadequate diet, or too much sun the day before.

To decide to do something is not to predict that I will do it; this mistake confuses causal explanation with motivated decision. For example, on the eve of an exam, I say "I will fail tomorrow," which could mean one of two things. If it is a prediction, it means that in spite of all my efforts to pass the exam, I will fail, due to circumstances beyond my control. If it is a decision, the statement means that I intend to fail. In this case, I experience the future action as dependent on me, as within my power to execute. The certitude of the prediction is more or less probable and uncertain, whereas the certitude of the decision is total because trying to fail is both a necessary and a sufficient condition for failure.[13]

Because all decisions have a history, a decision is not only project but process. It can last a few seconds, as when I decide to have a cup of coffee, or several years, as when I decide to marry. When I need to make a decision, I initially appear as a question to myself because I experience a conflict between many possible motives and projects. If I am trying to decide where to take a vacation, for instance, many considerations appear. How much will it cost? How far away is the place? Once I arrive at my destination, are there activities that I will enjoy? Of the two or three possible vacation spots, which would be the most enjoyable and most restful?

The process of making a decision is a unity in multiplicity; the unity is supplied by the question "Where should I take my vacation?" and the multiplicity is the various temporal phases through which I pass in making up my mind. At each stage of the way there is a dynamic unity of past, present, and future as three essentially related aspects of the process. Each present slides back into the past and is retained in consciousness as past; the above question, once asked, becomes a question that *was* asked but nonetheless continues to influence my deliberations. Each consideration, each alternative accepted or rejected, each motive clarified or qualified I automatically retain as a part of the ongoing process of making up my mind. What I intend is also a unity, a resolution of many possible projects and motives into one project and constellation of motives. The one question, asked in the present because of motives deriving from the past, is an anticipation of a future unity.

Motives initially appear involuntarily, and the basic involuntary is the lived body, or body subject. Not all motives are bodily, but awareness of higher values is founded on these motives. I can respond to bodily hunger by eating a hamburger, or I can endure such hunger for the sake of justice or love of God. I can give in to my fear of the enemy in battle, or I can overcome such fear through patriotism. All motives are either bodily or elaborated and constructed in relation to bodily motives.

As I have already shown, I experience my body as subject, not object. It is my incarnate self present to the world, not as something I have but as something I am. At the beginning of the process of making a decision, therefore, I experience myself as an embodied self, hesitant, open to many possible courses of action, confused, unclear. The process of making a decision is the movement from confusion to clarity, multiplicity to unity. What makes such progress possible is the power of attention whereby I sort out motives. Fatigue, financial considerations, desires to see friends, interest in stimulating cultural activities—all are competing in the decision about a vacation. Which can I safely ignore or relegate to secondary status? How much weight should I give to financial considerations as opposed to need for a rest? Attention enables me to answer these questions.[14]

The attention involved in choice is analogous to perception. When I am looking at a table in this room, I am aware also of my ability to shift my attention, to look at something else, a book, a picture on the wall, another person in the room. When my attention shifts from the table to a book, the table slides into the background, a background of which I am prethematically or implicitly aware.

There is similar freedom of attention operative in choice. I experience my power of controlling the internal debate, of making one motive the theme of my reflections and relegating the others to the background. Because of my desire to see a friend, I may focus on that motive rather than on my fatigue. Because of my desire to witness good theater, I may concentrate on that and minimize financial considerations. Such shifts of attention are themselves not arbitrary, but motivated. If my goal is to have a relaxing vacation, I see that New York in August would not be as relaxing as Canada. Consequently, I shift my attention to Canada.

The considerations of possible motives and projects can be endless. Because the projected action is always uncertain, risky, and imperfect, no possible vacation can be the perfect vacation, and there is no guarantee that it will turn out well. Also the possible motives and projects cannot all be exhaustively tested and probed. Because of the lived body there will always be a darkness and obscurity that are not totally clarified. If I am to make a decision, therefore, something has to bring reflection to an end. It is an act of freedom itself, choosing one project and set of motives to the exclusion of others, that cuts the reflection short.[15]

The act of choice that terminates reflection is both continuous with what preceded it and discontinuous. Choice is continuous in that it is the last judgment in a series of judgments. This judgment is an act of freedom, a fixing of attention on one motive or hierarchy of motives to the exclusion of others. The rationalistic reading of choice, which excludes or minimizes discontinuity, is, therefore, a mistake. At the beginning of a choice, being reasonable is itself a possible motive; I am not compelled to be reasonable. Because attention is free, it can always listen to the irrational and reject reason. Even in a choice that approximates the classical ideal of rational clarity and continuity, the final judgment is always undergirded by an act of freedom.[16]

There is also a novelty or discontinuity in a decision. I move from consideration of a multiplicity of possible projects to one actual project: going to Canada for a vacation. I experience the decision as a "leap," as not compelled by the reasons I have for it. This aspect of decision, emphasized by Sartre, can tempt me to view decision as totally arbitrary. All reasons would be rationalizations or pretexts created by freedom itself.

Such a reading of choice is false for two reasons. First of all, affirmations of a totally spontaneous freedom end up making freedom itself a motive, as we saw in the case of Sartre. Freedom as described by his phenomenological method becomes a reason for choosing in good faith rather than bad faith. Hidden behind the apparently arbitrary act is a reason: namely, to prove oneself as free. Such, for example, is Raskolnikov's murder of the old woman in *Crime and Punishment*.

Second, in any act for which I give pretexts, I am aware of a deeper, truer motivation. I may rationalize my trip to Canada by telling myself I should visit this friend, but my real reason is that I need a rest, some sunbathing or fishing, and a cooler climate.

At each stage of deciding, determination and indetermination are present and require each other. At the beginning certain possible motives and projects appear involuntarily, but because they have not been sorted out and clarified, there is an indetermination of hesitation. I know what I could do or might do, but not what I wish to do or will do. In the course of resolving my doubts, there is the indetermination of attention seeking to be "determined" by the "best" motives.

Finally, in the actual *fiat*, the final act of choice itself, there is the determination of the self by the self in the creative irruption of a project, the fixing of a free act of attention on this project rather than that, on this motive rather than that. Such determination implies the indetermination of attentive freedom because only freedom can stop the internal debate and constitute a motive in the full sense. For a motive to be efficacious implies not only its content, but its actuality, the fact of its being chosen. There is determination of content and indetermination of form because even though I have committed myself to one project, I have the implicit awareness that I could always reopen the debate, that I am not coerced to choose this content. It is always possible for me to consider other motives and projects.[17]

Summarizing my reflections on decision, I conclude that we can view decision as either a static or a temporal whole. Viewed statically, the "leap" or decision is determined by motive, and the motive becomes a motive in the full sense only by being chosen. Viewed as a temporal whole, decision is, first of all, a movement from the indeterminacy of multiplicity to the determination of unity. Second, there is the indetermination of hesitation related to the determination of possible motives. Third, there is the indetermination of attention searching for the best motive and project. Fourth, there is the *fiat* of self-determination, whereby a possible project and motive become actual. Indetermination here is the indetermination of possibility. Fifth, there are a determination of content and an indetermination of form. Content becomes determinate in the full sense only through the indetermination of form, the awareness that I can change my mind.

Such is the first main kind of reciprocity, that between motive and "leap." A second is that between reason and choice. All motives are not rational; there are motives deriving from my body and my passions. Whereas all choices are motivated, all choices are not necessarily guided by reason. Reason is that capacity to distance myself from my life, bring it into question, conceive of possibilities, and criticize them as authentic or inauthentic. It is possible for a person to elect as a matter of policy to live an irrational life. Therefore, the determination of choice by reflection is an "ought"; when there is conflict between the rational and the irrational, one should listen to reflection and prefer it to other sources of motives.

Such an "ought" becomes apparent when the irrationalist tries to defend her position. When Sartre argues for his concept of freedom and for the superiority of good faith over bad faith, he is implicitly presuming the superiority of reason to other sources of motives. If one is to live an authentic life, one has to know the authentic possibilities and be able to distinguish them from inauthentic possibilities. Reflection makes this possible. Freedom without reason becomes dark and destructive. A woman contemplating a serious decision such as marriage must ask herself questions about the genuineness of her love, compatibility with her prospective spouse, and so forth. Not to do so is to invite personal disaster.

Not only is reason necessary for freedom, but freedom is necessary for reason. Even when I am considering theoretical reasons, as we saw when discussing Blanshard's determinism, I must have the requisite distance from two contradictory hypotheses in order to ascertain the evidence for each. If questioning is essential to theoretical reasoning, then such questioning is impossible without freedom. Freedom is also necessary for practical reason to move from possibility to actuality. Without the actual *fiat* by which a possible motive becomes an actual motive, reflection remains a plaything of possibility, a pitiful Hamlet caught up and stifled in a world of speculation, struggling in vain to escape.

A third kind of relationship between determination and indetermination is essence and existence. Freedom is not an airy nothing, but a structured indetermination; freedom has an essence that it does not choose. The essence of a decision is "I decide because. . . ." Freedom is essentially temporal, a dynamic unity of past, present, and future. It is founded on reason and on the body, both as the basic source of motives and as that through which its projects are realized. Making a decision and carrying it out are essentially related to one another as "empty" to "full."[18] Going to Canada is the realization of the decision to go to Canada, and the lived body is the necessary condition of such fullness.

A determinist still might object that I have not looked at the whole picture. Surely a person's bodily constitution, innate talents, and emotional disposition are not results of choice. If a person has a weak heart, there are certain things that he simply cannot do. If a pianist has her hands cut off in an accident, she is determined by circumstances not to be a pianist.

Because of this kind of determination, the determination of necessity, it is necessary to distinguish between decision and consent or revolt. Decision projects a future action dependent on me. Consent accepts or revolt rejects necessity: what existed prior to my freedom occurred independently and cannot be changed by it.[19]

Nonetheless even here there is not an either–or dichotomy between the voluntary and the involuntary, but a reciprocity, in two senses. Necessity is first of all the servant of freedom, the essential basis for its presence to and expression in the world. My temperament is not something I choose; it is the way I can carry out and realize my projects in the world. Braque and Picasso could work from the same still-life model, but their pictures are different because their temperaments are different.

I also do not choose the automatic, necessary functioning of my body, but this enables me, as I have already shown, to realize projects that would otherwise remain abstract possibilities. Also because I do not have to think about my heart rate, circulatory system, or digestion, my mind is freed to think about possible projects such as vacations, political action, or marriage. Necessity is the condition of freedom, and freedom realizes itself only through necessity.

Second, the necessity of the body poses a question to freedom, the question of acceptance or revolt. Do I accept my incarnate situation, with the kind of body, temperament, and unconscious I have, with all my limitations and deficiencies, or do I revolt? Ricoeur suggests that only a religious and metaphysical answer to this question is fully satisfactory, but I think that a limited answer is also possible within the scope of phenomenology.[20]

Since necessity is rooted in the body, revolt would mean revolt against the body. But such a revolt would mean a freedom continually at odds with itself, with the conditions for its possibility. This is the freedom Sartre defends: limited by necessity, yet striving to be unlimited; dependent, yet striving for total independence; receptive, yet yearning for complete spontaneity. A freedom at odds with itself in this way must affirm that both it and the world are absurd, but it cannot do so in a consistent way. If freedom is a good, then the conditions of its possibility are also good and should be affirmed. With

such an affirmation freedom becomes one with itself and fully concrete because in a sense it has taken necessity into itself. Necessity
ceases to be an alien, brute fact because it has been understood, affirmed, and accepted.

Conclusion

The argument of this first part of Chapter 4 is a disjunctive syllogism.
Strict determinism or strict indeterminism or a unity of determination
and indetermination is true. Since both determinism and indeterminism are self-refuting, we must affirm a unity of determination and
indetermination. The first section of this discussion of freedom demonstrates the necessity, and the second section the content, of this
unity.

The experienced reality of freedom is an ambiguous unity of opposites, a unity that itself has several meanings. Both determinism and
indeterminism distort this reality by absolutizing one opposite and
excluding the other. Only a notion sufficiently nuanced to do justice
to freedom in all its paradoxical complexity is an adequate account
of freedom. Such is the notion I have advanced and defended in this
part: the reciprocal, mutual implication of determination and indetermination, the involuntary and the voluntary.

THE SELF

We have now come to a very important part of our investigations,
that concerning the self. Because all phenomenology rests upon an
examination of conscious experience, it becomes important to inquire into the "who" and "what" of the experience. If self and world
are related to one another as the two ultimate sources of meaning,
then it becomes important at this point to define this self more
precisely.

Although the self has been with us implicitly from the beginning
of our study, I have deliberately avoided considering it explicitly
until now. Rather than performing a Cartesian reduction and initially
affirming a self with no content, I have followed Husserl's lead in the
Crisis and postponed the investigation of the self to a later part of our
investigations.[21]

First of all, because of the historical, linguistic character of the self, we know that it is essentially intersubjective. As I will explore more fully in the next chapter, all subjectivity is intersubjectivity. Because the self doing phenomenology is itself a product of history, such philosophizing itself is intersubjective and social. Because all thinking, even thinking philosophically to myself in my study, is essentially expressive and linguistic, as I argued in Chapter 2, thinking is essentially intersubjective.

Second, the self at its most basic level is a questioning self. To be in the world is to be a question for myself in both a practical and a theoretical sense. Practically I am aware of many possibilities, among which I must choose. Theoretically I must question and reflect on my being in the world in order to answer the practical question. Whether I choose the scientistic or humanistic alternative depends on who and what I am, and I can discover that only by the most profound theory. Practice leads to theory and theory realizes itself in practice.

Third, the self is a questioning self because its opening onto the world is initially perceptual, and perception is essentially ambiguous. The perceived thing is questionable because it is present only from a point of view, is indeterminate, arises from a context, and is subject to misinterpretation.

Fourth, because consciousness is founded on perception, and perception is essentially embodied, consciousness is essentially embodied at the perceptual level. The *cogito* is an incarnate *cogito* present to the world as an embodied subject.

Fifth, the self is not only a perceiving self but a reflecting self, moving from experience to understanding to judgment. Perception and reflection function together in a full act of knowing, and it is a mistake to reduce one to the other. Rather than mere duality or mere unity, there is a unity in duality.[22]

Sixth, such unity in duality is present both on the level of cognition and on the level of affectivity and freedom. To make a decision is to move from a level of immediate, spontaneous, confused apprehension of objects as good or bad, pleasant or unpleasant, attractive or repulsive to a mediated choice of the object, to go to Canada for vacation, to become a doctor, or to marry this person.

Freedom is present not only in practical decision-making, but also in cognition itself in the selective attention to certain contents, in the raising of questions, and in the decision to pursue questions through to the final judgment about truth or falsity. Most often in cognition such freedom is only implicit, not explicit. Only when I move to the level of explicit, practical choice does freedom become an explicit, practical question for itself.

Seventh, I cannot account for such unity in multiplicity in any merely Humean manner as a mere collection of impressions or acts. For presupposed in the notion of any collection is their unity as a known collection, and for there to be a collection there has to be one knower. The premiss is analytic: a necessary condition for unity in the known object is unity in the knowing subject. But this unity in the subject cannot be an object or an impression without the vicissitudes of an infinite regress; if that unity is an object or part of an object, then we would have to posit a second unified knowing in order to understand the first. If the second is an object, then we would need a third and so on. Consequently we must posit a non-objectified knower as the condition of the possibility for one known.[23]

Eighth, not only must I affirm a unified knower, but I can experience and describe such knowing phenomenologically. Such a unity is both horizontal and vertical, present on one level of conscious experience and between and among many levels. When I perceive a table, move around it, touch it, and explore it, I am aware of the same table from many different points of view and of the difference between the table as perceived and my acts of perceiving it.[24] However, there is a unity not only in the object, but also in the subject, not only in the contents perceived but also in the acts of perceiving. For the acts succeed one another temporally; in the present I spontaneously anticipate seeing another side, the present act recedes into the past, and I move forward to another vantage point. There is, therefore, a dynamic unity of past, present, and future, of retentions, present perceptions, and protentions. Past, present, and future are internally, dynamically related aspects, and none is present without the other.[25] Any attempt to break down internal time consciousness into a series of externally related "nows" fails because each "now," whether it be a minute, a half-minute, or a second, is laden with past and future. Once again, at the price of avoiding an infinite regress, we must posit internal time consciousness as an internally related unity of past, present, and future.

Such a unity is also vertical in that it is a relation between and among different levels. Because an imagined object, such as a centaur, presupposes prior perceptions as the source for the materials of such an imaginative construction, the act of imagining is founded on perception. For such a founding to occur, there has to be a conscious unifying of perceiving and imagining. Such a unifying cannot be an object because the acts which it initially unifies are not objects and, therefore, the act of unification cannot be. Also if the unifying consciousness were an object, we would again have the problem of an infinite regress. If that consciousness were a thematic object, we would need a second in order to unify the first as an object and so on.

Ninth, such a unity can be static or dynamic. In listening to a person, I spontaneously understand his meanings with no obvious gap between perception and reflection. Or I can move from perception to intellection to judgment dynamically—I am hit on the head by an apple, formulate hypotheses about the law of falling bodies, and verify those laws. Here the unity of consciousness is experienced as a dynamic unity. Dissatisfied with the mere flow of perceptions, I raise questions for intelligence: "What is the law that explains falling bodies?" Dissatisfied with mere bright ideas, I raise the further question for reflection, "Is the hypothesis true?" Consciousness is the desire-to-know in operation, aware of itself as agent in moving from experience through understanding to judgment. No one act is sufficient for the emergence of the known, but rather a unity of experiencing, understanding, and judging. Crucial to the process is my consciousness as a dynamic unity: retaining of the known, awareness of present, cognitive contents, dissatisfaction with these as incomplete, and asking the further relevant questions.

At this joint we are ready to make the argument more precise: if I experience, understand, judge, and choose, then I am a unified, conscious incarnate subject. I have already defined experiencing, understanding, judging, and choosing in the course of this study. A unified, incarnate subject is one consciously aware of herself as an embodied, horizontally and vertically unified agent in the world. The syllogism is a conditional syllogism grounding a virtually unconditioned judgment. The conditioned, "I am a unified, incarnate subject," presents no problems since it is merely the expression of what is to be affirmed. The link between conditioned and conditions is materially analytic: if there is knowing and choosing, then these, as I have already shown, are unified and conscious. The problematic area is the fulfillment of the conditions, which fulfillment occurs in conscious experience and in my reflection upon it.[26]

Knowing cannot be knowing unless it is conscious of itself over time as unifying dynamically linked levels of experience, understanding, and judgment. If there were not such unity, there would be no knowing and no known. Choosing cannot be the choosing of a project unless there is a movement from an initially indeterminate, complex of motives to the *fiat* of choice. Implied in choosing and knowing are the practical and the theoretical questions "What should I do?" and "What do I truly know?" But essential to every question is the taking up of a past motivation and knowledge into a present orientation that anticipates a future answer. Questioning is essentially temporal and, therefore, implies a unified consciousness.

If I truly perceive, imagine, remember, reflect, understand, choose, and love, then I am an incarnate, unified subject. But does the antecedent prevail? Here the answer lies in my own inability to avoid experience, understanding, judging, and deciding. Suppose I answer "no." Either the answer is arbitrary or it is not. If it is arbitrary, what is arbitrarily asserted can be rationally questioned or denied. If the "no" answer is rational, then that denial presupposes the very experience, understanding, judgment, and decision that I am denying. For I perceived the person asking the question or listening to my answer, remembered the various words contained in the question, understood the meanings of those words, judged on the basis of evidence in my experience, and chose to pursue the question and abide by the results. As I argued in the section on freedom, even the asking of the question presupposes a freedom open to possibility. Every asking of a question implies a choice to pursue or not to pursue the question. Freedom is essentially related to rationality.

Here the issue is one of contradiction between explicit claim and implicit performance. I can claim that I know nothing for certain, but would not wish to deny the groundedness in evidence and experience, intelligibility, rationality, and responsibility of that claim. I can despair of many things but would never wish to deny that I have perceived, imagined, remembered, coherently understood, judged, or chosen. But if I should wish to make such a claim, the very conditions of the denial would contradict the explicit statement.

This dialectic takes place within the arena of consciousness, but I can easily misinterpret consciousness. Consciousness is not an object, an impression, a concept, or a collection of impressions. Operating on such assumptions Hume looks within himself and finds no self, and Ryle argues for an infinite regress.[27] Consciousness is not object but subject, not explicit but implicit, not an idea but the prethematic awareness that accompanies all ideas. Consciousness is not something I take a good look at but rather the immanent awareness of the self as agent and source of its own activities that accompanies all looking, imagining, remembering, reflecting, and choosing. As Sartre says, all thetic consciousness presupposes a non-thetic consciousness.[28]

With self-affirmation, we are now at a point to reflect more profoundly on transcendental, phenomenological method. Transcendental method in the full sense is an explicit experience, understanding, judging, and choosing of myself as an experiencing, understanding, judging, deciding subject in the world, relating through those activities to various noematic objects. On a pre-philosophical level we are all of us, of course, perceiving, imagining, remembering, questioning, hypothesizing, conceiving, criticizing, choosing, committing ourselves, loving.[29] Most of the time, however, we do not explicitly recognize that fact. We have a rough, vague awareness of ourselves as persons but little or no explicitly grounded knowledge of ourselves.

Because such knowledge is worth having for its own sake and because industrial society, as we saw in Chapter 1, can easily seduce us into forgetfulness of ourselves, philosophical reflection is useful and essential. Philosophical recovery of the self in its *a priori* structure of experience, understanding, judging, and choosing is necessary in order to recover the self from the alienating social structures of modern, industrial mass society. Practical self-recovery fully engaged in and followed up on in all its implications requires theoretical self-knowledge as I have developed it in these first four chapters. As the last five chapters will show, there is also a necessary return to such practical self-recovery from theory. Such practical self-recovery becomes necessary, for theory itself, indeed, becomes a part of theory. This book, therefore, inscribes a circle in which there is a movement from practice to theory and back to practice, or a movement of ascent from practice to theory and of descent from theory to practice, movement out of the cave of late industrial society into the sunlight of self-knowledge and then back into the cave for an enlightened praxis flowing from that self-knowledge.

The discussion of freedom in this chapter is crucial in that such a discussion represents the theoretical recovery of the final level of the self and at the same time represents the first stage of a practical return to the world. For insofar as the choice of myself as perceiving, reflecting, and choosing subject is essential to transcendental method, transcendental method is a kind of praxis, the most fundamental kind of self-recovery that grounds or founds all other forms of praxis. Other, further stages of practical self-recovery discussed in this book will be the practical engagement with other selves discussed in the next chapter, the hermeneutical retrieval of the past, and the hermeneutically suspicious reflections on unconscious psychological and sociological structures.

As a theoretical praxis or practical theory of self-recovery, therefore, transcendental method gives rise to four transcendental precepts. Corresponding to the necessity to adequately, phenomenologically describe experience in all its richness, there is the precept "Be attentive." Corresponding to the necessity to be logically consistent and coherent and to see for myself apart from the pressures of the "they," Husserl's distinctness, there is the precept "Be intelligent." Corresponding to the necessity to judge responsibly on the basis of the evidence, Husserl's clarity, there is the precept "Be reasonable." Corresponding to the necessity of choosing a method that adequately reflects who and what the self is in its full range and being faithful to that method, there is the precept "Be responsible."[30]

I am now prepared to give precise phenomenological content to the notions of "authenticity" and "inauthenticity."[31] Authenticity, whether on a lived or a theoretical level, is the self's fidelity to itself, fidelity to the four transcendental precepts. Inauthenticity is the self's infidelity to itself. Alienation, then, in its most fundamental sense is inauthenticity, infidelity of the self to its own internal structure of selfhood in such a way that there is loss of self. This most fundamental sense of alienation grounds social alienation, but also, as I shall show in Chapter 8, is encouraged by such alienation. If all the preceding is true, then it follows that self-knowledge and self-recovery are the first stage in overcoming social alienation.

Differences in accounts of the self ground the most fundamental differences in philosophy. If my conception of the self tends to be sensate, reducing all other levels of the self to a model of sensuous perceiving and enjoying, then my philosophy, if it is to be consistent with such a conception, will take such forms as empiricism, positivism, behaviorism, and scientism. If my conception of the self is idealistic in a bad sense, reducing the self to a model of conceptual, intellectual knowing, then my philosophy will be, correspondingly, a form of idealism or conceptualism or logicism.

But if my account of the self is critically comprehensive and nuanced, then it will include the sensuous and the intellectual, the cognitive and the existential, in a dynamic, intelligible unity. What I have done throughout this book is to show that this account of the self is not just an arbitrary preference but, in keeping with the method of dialectical phenomenology, dialectically and descriptively superior to other accounts. My account is dialectically superior to other accounts insofar as these positions negate themselves and lead into my position. For example, behaviorism's defense of determinism negates itself and passes over into indeterminism, and Husserl's attempt to be totally free from prejudice reveals itself to be a prejudice against prejudice. An empiricist account of perception negates itself insofar as "this red" and "this patch" turn out to be not immediate but mediated, not mere particulars but particulars saturated with universals. An idealistic Kantian attempt to ignore the structured gestalt of perception and to derive all meaning from abstract reflection makes that reflection itself arbitrary.[32]

My position has proved itself descriptively more adequate insofar as my account of the self is more comprehensive and nuanced. Empiricism can account up to a point for sensible experience, but cannot account for the distinctiveness of reflection and choice. Idealism can account for the level of abstract reflection, but cannot account for the distinctiveness of the perceptual level and the relation of abstract reflection to perception. If empiricism tends to reduce experience to sensuous experience of sensuous objects, then empiricism cannot account for there being data of consciousness as well as data of sense, a domain of interiority that is the proper purview of philosophy as well as a domain of external objects that is the purview of positive science. What empiricism forgets is that phenomenology is the true positivism.[33]

If my account of the self is correct, then I am also in a position to talk about authenticity as a law governing the relationship between limitation and transcendence.[34] Because I am an embodied self, born in a particular place and time, with particular talents and prejudices, I am limited. Because I am an intellectual, free self, I am oriented toward the ideal, toward possibility, toward the perfect, toward the infinite. Because I am both reflective and embodied, however, I fail in authenticity when I focus simply on one of these poles and exclude the opposite. For example, I fail in authenticity when I remain simply what I am and ask no further questions, engage in no further projects, and generate no further hopes. Such an existence would be that of a vegetable, not a human being.

On the other hand, a more subtle mistake is to live simply in the realm of the ideal or the possible. If I do, then a quixotic overreaching of myself becomes possible or a neurotic perfectionism rooted in a strict superego or a comical forgetfulness of myself next to the castle of my own system. Authenticity is, then, the entering into the tension between limitation and transcendence in such a way that I accept facts and limits without giving into defeatism and despair and embrace ideals and hopes without giving into false utopianism or a repressive idealism.

What the foregoing implies is that the self is a limited self in a limited personal and social situation and that authentic practical and theoretical reflection starts from that situation and returns to it.[35] As my reflection on freedom has shown, there is a personal and social necessity that I cannot transform but simply must accept and that limits what I can do in any situation. This rootedness in situation made it necessary to begin with reflection on my particular historical situation in Chapter 1 and to return to that situation in the last four chapters.

Objections

First of all, insofar as such an account is a thematization of the self, it is an objectification of the self.[36] But there are those within the phenomenological tradition who would wish to deny that such objectification is possible and desirable. Is it not contradictory to objectify the self experienced as subject, and is not such objectification alienating, a distortion of my experience?

Much ink has been spilled over this issue in phenomenology and existentialism because insufficient attention has been paid to the kinds of objectivity, their distinctions, and their interrelationships. I cannot objectify the subject, so the argument goes, because in trying to do so I turn myself into an object. I lose subjectivity in the process of conceptualizing it, and I thus become alienated from myself.[37]

In two respects there is some truth to the argument. First of all, any reflection on human experience is necessarily on past experience. For example, to reflect on the experience of perceiving is to reflect on this experience as having lapsed. I cannot reflect on the experience of reflection as present. If I try to do so, then that experience slips into the past and becomes the object or theme of a second reflection taking place in the present. Second, in no reflection does the original experience in its immediacy survive on the level of reflection. What does emerge is the universal and thematic meaning of that experience. Just as the original experience of green does not survive in the scientific account of green in terms of wave length, so the original experience of perception does not survive in the reflective account of perception.

Do these concessions to the arguments against objectifying the subject imply that there is no valid sense in which it can be objectified? As the reader must suspect, the answer has to be a resounding "no." To say that the subject cannot in any way be objectified because of the reasons mentioned above is to confuse experiential with thematic objectivity. To say that objectification of the subject cannot occur because such objectification turns the subject into a thing is mistakenly to identify thematic with perceptual or scientific objectivity. What is thematized in a philosophical account of subjectivity is its meaning as no-thing, as conscious, free, and intentional.

Such accounts are not just pale reflections of the original, rich experience. This empiricist claim does not recognize that reflective thematization and insight *enrich* our experience—we know more about ourselves afterward than we did before. What is merely confused and vague on an immediate, experiential level becomes clear and explicit on a reflective level. For example, on a pre-reflective level our awareness of the kinds of objectivity, their rules, and interrelationships is at best implicit and unclear. When we philosophically distinguish and define the eight kinds of objectivity, not only our reflection but our common sense and scientific practice are illuminated and clarified.

What gives the argument against objectifying the subject plausibility is the lumping together of various kinds of objectivity, perceptual, scientific, thematic, and experiential. Once we distinguish these senses, the paradox disappears. Not only *can* I objectify myself, but at times, if I am to know myself, I *should* objectify myself.

Second, Sartre objects to a personal consciousness; to him consciousness as nihilating and empty of content is "nothing," impersonal, and non-egological.[38] (a) However, we have already rejected in the section on freedom Sartre's dichotomy between a positive thing with content and a negative freedom with no content. (b) If the body individuates and consciousness is essentially embodied, then it is essentially personal. (c) To be in the world is to be confronted with the distinction between self and other. But to be aware of myself in contrast to other things and selves is to be a determinate, situated self.

(d) To move onto the level of decision and freedom is to be confronted with a choice between authentic and inauthentic living, good and bad faith.[39] Do I simply remain part of the inauthentic crowd and choose according to its dictates, or do I choose for myself responsibly, according to my own lights and my own experience? Authentic living presupposes authentic choosing, and authentic choosing presupposes an authentically choosing self.

(e) The product of authentic choosing is an authentic self. There is a distinction between self as constituting and self as constituted. But the point is that unless the constituting self is authentic there is no authentic, constituted self; authenticity cannot flow from inauthenticity. Sixth, the constituted self as habitual and sedimented becomes internally related as past to the constituting self. To choose is to choose in relation to a past, present, and future in such a way that the self in the full sense is a circuit of selfness, a dialectic between constituting and constituted self. In constituting an habitual self the constituting self is constituting itself. Insofar as the constituted self is related to an aspect of the constituting self, this self is personal.

Still a third objection comes from the side of structuralism, which in its emphasis on the unconscious, impersonal, self-enclosed structures of language minimizes or excludes human subjectivity and consciousness entirely. Assuming that language is to be conceived as an object scientifically, the structuralist excludes all that is merely contingent and evanescent in the actual conscious usage of speech acts. Here is perhaps the strongest challenge in the postwar era to a philosophy of subjectivity.[40]

Nonetheless such a philosophy has resources of its own within which to construct a reply. If, as I have already argued, all scientific inquiry takes place within the life-world, then any scientific investigation into language, be it structural or otherwise, has already abstracted from that world in a partial manner. The initial phenomenon to be investigated, actual language use, founds the subsequent scientific account. Moreover, the structuralist account of language remains partial and one-sided and has to be complemented by an account of the way people use speech in actual situations. As Ricoeur puts it, de Saussure's contrast between *La Langue* and *La Parole*, with the latter subordinated to the former, has to give way to a contrast between semiology and semantics, a science of the word and a science of the sentence. With respect to the life-world, a science of the word is merely potential and becomes actual only in conscious use.[41]

The crucial notion is discourse conceived as a dialectic between concrete event and abstract meaning. The concrete event is one individual speaker talking to another and referring to things in her talk; abstract meaning is the sense of the sentence "The cat is on the mat" or "Mary is in the kitchen" or "John Searle is teaching at Berkeley." Structuralism is partial in that it gets at only the formal aspects of this abstract meaning—for example, the relations of sounds or letters to one another or formal relationships of masculine to feminine or noun to verb. Left out is the relation of language to a world.[42]

Yet the structuralist, in justifying his approach, has to use language in this way, to relate to other persons in the life-world, and to appeal to evidence that is conscious. Either his choice to regard language as a scientific object is reasonable or it is not. If it is not, what is arbitrarily asserted can be rationally questioned or denied. If it is, then there is a tacit appeal intersubjectively available to other speech users. The structuralist, in order to justify his approach, has to presume a conscous life-world context that his own approach explicitly denies.

Also structuralist form presupposes the content of the life-world. Lévi-Strauss analyzes the Oedipus myth by organizing the sentences into four columns. In the first column are all sentences speaking of an overesteemed kinship relation, for example, "Oedipus weds Jocasta." In the second are those speaking of an underesteemed kinship relation, for example, "Oedipus kills his father." In the third are those concerned with monsters and their destruction and in the fourth proper names whose meaning suggests a difficulty in walking upright: "lame," "clumsy," "swollen foot."

When we compare the columns, there is a correlation between one and two, in which kinship relations are in turn overesteemed and underesteemed; and between three and four, in which there is affirmation and negation of autochthony. It follows that column four is to column three as column two is to column one. Overrating of blood relations is to the underrating of blood relations as the attempt to escape autochthony is to the impossibility of succeeding in it. The myth appears as a logical instrument to draw together contradictions in order to overcome them.

The prescientific life-world founds such a formal analysis in three senses. First of all, the bundles of relationships are articulated as sentences in our life-world. Lévi-Strauss articulates such sentences to other subjects in the life-world and refers to a meaningful real referent in the life-world, the Oedipus myth as remembered and known historically. Second, the formal opposition is rooted in an opposition of content, without which the former would be meaningless. Without the existential conflicts, there would be no logical conflicts to overcome. Third, as I shall develop more fully in Chapter 6, such a formal explanatory analysis has meaning only in a process of moving from an initial understanding through explanation back to a more mediated understanding, from a surface to a depth semantics.[43]

It thus is apparent that structuralism is a chosen approach, adopted freely and consciously, but it is not inevitable or necessary. There are many other equally valid or more valid ways to approach language. Structuralism is simply one project among many in the life-world. In relationship to such a context, structuralism is founded in two ways: it depends on a prescientific context that is prior to it, and it is part of a life-world conceived as a totality of projects.[44] Therefore, structuralism, if it is to be fully scientific, must transcend itself and admit its roots in the life-world as consciously experienced by human subjects. The formal structures of structuralism are grounded in the material structures of the life-world. Insofar as it tries to remain a total account, structuralism is ultimately unscientific and fails to recognize the triumph of ambiguity. Any attempt fully to understand human beings or language in a way that is positively scientific, totally clear, and exact must fall to the ground.

A final objection is that proposed by Jacques Derrida to any philosophy of consciousness, that is, that such a philosophy gives into a metaphysics of presence that fully critical thinking should renounce and overcome. Rather, what emerges in any attempt to affirm the presence of consciousness is that it is saturated with *différance*. Language differs, in the sense that any particular meaning implies reference to another meaning; and language defers, in the sense that no meaning is simply present but is saturated with traces of absent, past meaning.[45]

First of all, Derrida sees himself as continuing Heidegger's project of overcoming metaphysics. Heidegger fails, Derrida argues, because he falls into affirming being as presence. Now, insofar as the project of overcoming metaphysics rests upon a confusion about the meaning and kinds of objectivity, Derrida's project itself is suspect. To objectify is not necessarily to alienate or falsify; nor is it necessarily to affirm a presence that is total with no negativity. All objectification, I have argued, is surrounded by a zone of the unsaid, the presumed, and the tacit. Any attempt to say anything always presupposes a linguistic context that is taken for granted and implied. All positivity, all presence, is saturated through and through with negativity of various kinds.

Derrida explicitly and validly criticizes Husserl for emphasizing presence in a way that denies or minimizes the relationship of consciousness to time, to language, to the body, and to the world.[46] However in my own account of the self I have stressed all these relationships as essential to the self. Consciousness is essentially expressive in such a way that it finds itself and fulfills itself only through such expression. Pre-linguistic insight finds itself and fulfills itself through such experience. Language is not external clothing draped over a thought already complete in itself but is necessary to realize thought itself.

I deny, along with Derrida, a total presence untouched by any negativity or difference. I affirm, however, the reality of a presence internally related to *différance*, a presence that Derrida must also necessarily invoke. For in arguing about the reality of *différance* he must appeal to evidence that is present in some way, a text, gaps and contradictions in a text, or his own experience of negativity. Otherwise his assertions are merely arbitrary, and what is arbitrarily asserted can be rationally questioned or denied. *Différance* must, therefore, be present if it is to make a difference and not leave us indifferent to the argument.

Presence also is absent in that negativity of one kind or another permeates it. Any attempt to think a pure presence negates itself and passes over into difference. An attempt to think without presuppositions about consciousness as merely externally related to language reveals language at the core of that very thinking.

Pure *différance* as thought, therefore, differs from itself and passes over into presence; pure presence negates itself and passes over into difference. What emerges is the dialectical unity of absence and presence and various ways in which absence and presence play off against one another. The unseen side of a perceived table is different from the hidden thought of a person with whom I am talking; the presence and absence of a remembered person is different from her actual perceived presence. *Différance*, because it has different kinds, differentiates itself and differs from itself. Nonetheless, whether in my experience or in reflection upon it, certain kinds of differences become present and relevant in a way that others do not. When thinking about Pierre, I find that his own absence is present to me explicitly in a way that that of a chair is not. When I am looking at Matisse's *Red Studio*, the absence and presence of that is present and relevant to me in a way that a mathematical equation is not; both these examples reveal an important difference between a presence–absence explicitly attended to and one that is not.

Derrida would reply to such criticism that it is impossible to avoid using traditional metaphysical arguments and concepts such as "evidence" or "presence" because he himself, as well as we, has been formed by that tradition. Nonetheless such factual impossibility does not imply that we should retain metaphysics.[47]

This reply, however, puts him in a difficult situation. First of all, self-refutation is a strong form of argument. Second, referring to necessary dependence on a dead tradition does not get Derrida off the hook. For I am arguing here that rational necessity for evidence and for presence present in any tradition, Western or Eastern, compels us to reject Derrida. The main issue is not whether one is rooted in a particular tradition or not, but rather how seriously one takes the dictates of one's own inquiring intelligence and reasonableness.

Third, in arguing that we transcend the Western tradition, Derrida is cutting the ground out from under his own feet. For if I have to use arguments and concepts from a bankrupt tradition in order to transcend that tradition, then the very bankruptcy of that tradition, if we are to agree with Derrida that the tradition is bankrupt, should incline us to reject his argument. On the other hand, logically, if we except from the charge of bankruptcy those terms and concepts that are essential for Derrida's argument, then the tradition ceases as a whole to be bankrupt. It becomes, as I think it is, more dialectical, more ambiguous, a mixture of truth and error, light and darkness.

Derrida's argument for transcending rationality is unlike others that can be made. I can argue and would argue that there are demands other than philosophy that are more intuitive, mystical, and irrational and that involve a certain transcending of philosophy. If I cease writing my book and go listen to some music, visit friends, engage in political praxis, or pray, I am leaving behind the strictly conceptual and philosophical. Indeed, on good phenomenological grounds I can argue the necessity and possibility of moving into those other areas, at least to some extent, in order to live a full human life.

But let us suppose now that after convincing you through a phenomenology of aesthetic experience or sexual encounter or mysticism to take up these worthwhile domains of human activity, I were to say to you, "By the way, philosophical arguments, even the ones I just presented to you, are bankrupt and have no value because they are saturated with false forms of presence and identity." You, after having been convinced by my arguments, would now be compelled to withdraw your assent. You might still engage in those other activities, and I hope you would, but your choices would be arbitrary. There would be as much reason for abstaining as for engaging in mysticism, sexual love, or aesthetic experience.

Derrida's arguments, I would suggest, leave us in a similar position. If we wish to follow him into a post-metaphysical realm of *différance*, we might do so, but there is no more reason for doing that than doing the opposite. Yet, Derrida's practice, as opposed to what he says he is doing, suggests otherwise. According to him, there are compelling reasons for rejecting metaphysics and moving into a post-metaphysical realm.

The role of philosophy, I would argue, is to reflect on the play of absence and presence and the different forms that takes.[48] The notion of play, so important to both Heidegger and Derrida, reappears here.[49] But this is a play within philosophy itself, not in some kind of thinking beyond philosophy. Philosophy, and more specifically phenomenology, playfully moves between the poles of ambiguity and objectivity. Objectivity with no ambiguity implies a total presence that is false. Situating oneself firmly within the play of ambiguity and objectivity allows one to give up the seriousness of total mastery and still stay within the confines of philosophy itself. Philosophy can be playful without ceasing to be philosophy; it can say something conceptual, universal, and true without invoking a false presence.

NOTES

1. James N. Jordan, "Determinism's Dilemma," *Review of Metaphysics*, 23 (1969), 48–66. William Hosker, "The Transcendental Refutation of Determinism," *Southern Journal of Philosophy*, 11 (1973), 175–83.

2. A. J. Ayer, *The Concept of a Person, and Other Essays* (New York: St. Martin's, 1963), pp. 266–67.

3. Skinner, *Beyond Freedom and Dignity*, pp. 77, 92, 99, 191–92, 195.

4. Brand Blanshard, "The Case for Determinism," in *Determinism and Freedom*, ed. Sidney Hook (New York: New York University Press, 1965), pp. 3–15.

5. Sartre, *Being and Nothingness*, pp. 38, 414–28, 455; and *Existentialism and Human Emotions*, trans. Bernard Frechtmann and Hazel E. Barnes (New York: Philosophical Library, 1957), pp. 15–16. It is questionable whether the later Sartre accepts completely this notion of freedom; nonetheless I am using his existentialist defense of a total freedom here because it is the strictest, most rigorously argued version of indeterminism I could find.

6. Sartre, *Being and Nothingness*, p. 418.

7. Ibid., pp. lii–liii, 98, 151, 156; and "Consciousness of Self and Knowledge of Self," in *Readings in Existential Phenomenology*, edd. Nathaniel Lawrence and Daniel O'Connor (Englewood Cliffs, N.J.: Prentice-Hall, 1967), pp. 126–33.

8. Sartre, *Being and Nothingness*, pp. lxii–lxvii; and "Consciousness of Self and Knowledge of Self," pp. 126–33.

9. Sartre, *Being and Nothingness*, pp. lviii, 419, 430–31, 458, 464, 471, 472, 473, 499, 507.

10. Ibid., pp. 38–45, 543–46; and *Existentialiam and Human Emotions*, pp. 44–47.

11. Sartre, *Being and Nothingness*, pp. lviii, 93, 96, 99, 102, 152, 296–97, 461; and *Existentialism and Human Emotions*, pp. 63–67.

12. Sartre, *Being and Nothingness*, pp. 152–57, 162–65.

13. Ricoeur, *Freedom and Nature*, pp. 7, 41–43, 67–68. Stuart Hampshire, *Thought and Action* (New York: Viking, 1960), pp. 92–135.

14. Ricoeur, *Freedom and Nature*, pp. 149–63.

15. Ibid., pp. 163–81.

16. Ibid., pp. 158–59, 163–71.

17. Ibid., pp. 182–89.

18. See Husserl, *Logical Investigations*, II 694–701, for this important distinction.

19. Ricoeur, *Freedom and Nature*, pp. 343–54.

20. Ibid., pp. 444–81.

21. Husserl, *Crisis*, p. 154.

22. See Chapter 2, pp. 61–72.

23. See Hume, *Treatise on Human Nature*, pp. 251–63, for one version of such psychological atomism; see Charles Hartshorne, *Creative Synthesis and Philosophical Method* (LaSalle, Ill.: Open Court, 1970), pp. 173–204, for another.

24. See Chapter 2, pp. 47–48.

25. See Chapter 1, pp. 36–37.

26. I owe much in the method and content of this argument to Lonergan, *Insight*, pp. 319–47.

27. Gilbert Ryle, *The Concept of Mind* (New York: Barnes & Noble, 1949). pp. 162–63.

28. Sartre, *Being and Nothingness*, pp. 1–lvi.

29. Imagining and remembering, because they have as objects the sensuous particular, would be internal forms of sensible experience. For an excellent discussion of imagining, see Edward Casey, *Imagining: A Phenomenological Study* (Bloomington: Indiana University Press, 1976). For the limited, non-Husserlian sense of "transcendental" in this context, see above, Chapter 1, p. 39.

30. See Bernard Lonergan, *Method in Theology* (New York: Herder & Herder, 1972), pp. 13–25, for a discussion of the transcendental precepts. For his own definition of distinctness and clarity, see Husserl, *Formal and Transcendental Logic*, pp. 56–62.

31. Heidegger, of course—in *Being and Time*, pp. 169–224, 312–423—has made these terms famous in the tradition of phenomenology. Although my use of them has the theme of self-recovery in common with Heidegger, my use is also different because of my differing phenomenology of the self. In the next chapter, I use the terms in a more orthodox Heideggerian way.

32. See Chapter 1, p. 6; Chapter 2, pp. 51–53 and 67–70; Chapter 4, p. 95.

33. Husserl, *Ideas*, p. 86.

34. Lonergan, *Insight*, pp. 472–79. What I describe as "authenticity" Lonergan describes as "genuineness." See Kierkegaard, *Sickness Unto Death*, pp. 162–207, for an existentialist discussion of authenticity carried on through relating opposites such as necessity and possibility, finitude and infinitude.

35. See Marcel, *Creative Fidelity*, pp. 82–103, for a phenomenology of being-in-situation.

36. See Chapter 3 for an account of thematization and objectification.

37. Karl Jaspers, *Philosophy*, trans. E. B. Ashton, 3 vols. (Chicago: The University of Chicago Press, 1969), I 56–58, 65–68.

38. Jean-Paul Sartre, *The Transcendence of the Ego*, trans. Forrest Williams and Robert Kirkpatrick (New York: Noonday, 1957), pp. 31–42.

39. Heidegger, *Being and Time*, pp. 203–24. Sartre, *Being and Nothingness*, pp. 21–45, 543–46.

40. Ferdinand de Saussure, *Course in General Linguistics*, ed. Charles Bally and Albert Sechehaye, trans. Wade Baskin (New York: McGraw-Hill, 1976), pp. 7–17. Paul Ricoeur, *Interpretation Theory: Discourse and the Surplus of Meaning* (Fort Worth: Texas Christian University Press, 1976), pp. 2–8.

41. Ricoeur, *Interpretation Theory*, pp. 2–8.

42. Ibid., pp. 8–12.

43. Ibid., pp. 80–87. Claude Lévi-Strauss, *Structural Anthropology*, trans. Claire Jacobson and Brooke Grundfest (Garden City, N.Y.: Doubleday Anchor, 1967), pp. 206–21. For the development of the relation between explanation and understanding, see Chapter 6, pp. 174–77.

44. See Chapter 2, pp. 69–70.

45. Jacques Derrida, *Writing and Difference*, trans. Alan Bass (Chicago: The University of Chicago Press, 1978), pp. 79–168; and *Speech and Phenomena*, trans. David Allison (Evanston, Ill.: Northwestern University Press, 1972).

46. Derrida, *Speech and Phenomena*.

47. Jacques Derrida, *Positions*, trans. Alan Bass (Chicago: The University of Chicago Press, 1981), pp. 1–12.

48. Robert Sokolowski, *Presence and Absence* (Bloomington: Indiana University Press, 1978), pp. 144–71.

49. Heidegger, *On the Way to Language*, pp. 29–106; and *Poetry, Language, Thought*, pp. 179–82. Jacques Derrida, *Dissemination*, trans. Barbara Johnson (Chicago: The University of Chicago Press, 1981), pp. 64, 93, 142, 154–55, 163–64, 169–70, 216–21.

5

Knowing the Other and Being with the Other

To DISCUSS OTHER PERSONS is not to introduce a totally new topic. The other has been with us implicitly from the beginning in the discussions of history, language, perception, reflection, and freedom. Because a book such as this has to be written from a moving viewpoint, however, I have had to postpone explicit and methodical consideration of the other until now.

In a post-Cartesian philosophical context, there are basically two questions about the other. The first is epistemic and concerns our knowledge of the other. How do I know that the other exists? What is the meaning of the other? How does she manifest herself to me? Here our post-Cartesian developments in language, embodiment, intentionality, and perception will be of great value. Husserl raises the question in a Cartesian context but remains too Cartesian to give it a satisfactory answer.[1]

The second question, the problem of freedom and the other, and its solution are both post-Cartesian. Assuming that the other exists, can I relate to him in a way that is mutually fulfilling and that enhances both our freedoms? If one grants that there is some conflict between and among persons, is such conflict necessary? Are human beings in their life with one another condemned to a war of all against all, as Sartre seems to suggest in his existential–phenomenological period?[2]

KNOWLEDGE OF THE OTHER

Dialectical Considerations

The question about the epistemic status of the other receives its first decisive formulation in Husserl's *Cartesian Meditations*. Husserl poses the question from within an egological context. If the ego constitutes its world intentionally in the sense of discovering or creating all the meaning in its world, is it not paradoxical to discuss the constitution of other egos? How can I constitute as object someone who is essentially subject, who is constituting a world? Sartre also, responding to and taking over this formulation of the problem, decides that I cannot know the other self. Husserl gives an affirmative and Sartre a negative answer to the question "Can I know the other?"[3]

We resolve this paradox of objectifying another subject if we recall our discussion of the different kinds of objectivity and reflection. There we briefly discussed the difference between objectification as thematization and objectification as degradation. Because one type of objectification is logically distinct from the other, there is no contradiction involved in saying that I perceive or philosophically thematize others as subjects. What emerges in such acts is the sense and reality of the other subjects. What emerges in such acts is the sense and reality of the other person, who is not the same as a perceived thing, a scientifically verified series of events, or a slave.[4]

Objectification of the other person can occur without degradation or alienation because thematization and degradation are two distinct senses of objectification. If I say to another person "You are very wise," such a statement certainly is a thematizing, but I do not intend to degrade the other person; nor does the person experience it as such. Rather what can and does happen is that such a statement builds up the relationship and contributes to the other person's sense of worth and dignity. The other feels exalted, liberated, and enlightened by my expressed esteem.

There are, of course, forms of behavior that do objectify in a degrading sense. If with insufficient provocation, I call another person an idiot or scoundrel or charlatan, then clearly I am using language to humiliate that person. What I am denying here is that such degradation is an inevitable result of my thematizing the other person and our relationship. Sartre gets mileage out of his argument for such a claim by uncritically lumping together the three distinct senses of perceptual, thematic, and alienated objectivity.[5] However, not all looks are alienating; some merely thematize, whereas others degrade and humiliate. Looking at the other with reverence and esteem is essentially, logically different from harshly judging, shaming, or staring down the other.

There are times when the other experiences objectification of her body as liberating. For example, when she has a broken leg, she wishes the doctor to objectify her, to use scientific knowledge to help her get well. The doctor's objectification of her body is liberating because the doctor is helping her to do what she wishes to do, get back on her feet. This kind of objectification is different from that experienced by a man who is insulted because of his appearance. The first is positive and enhancing; the second, degrading and disconcerting.

A second difficulty is that knowing the other seems to involve an inference from within myself to someone existing outside myself. However, I have already established that consciousness is intentionally present to what is not itself and, therefore, in principle is open to otherness in general. The issue about other persons, therefore, is a question about a specific kind of otherness, not otherness in general. Confusing these two questions makes the problem insuperable; distinguishing them and answering them in the order of their logical priority makes the problem surprisingly easy to resolve.

One final problem that suggests itself, one often confused with the immediately preceding one, is the accessibility of the other, even if one grants the claim of intentionality. If the other is noumenally hidden behind her body and only contingently related to it, then the other would seem to be forever inaccessible. The relation of the other to her body would be analogous to the noumenon–phenomenon relation discussed by Kant.

However, if the basic argument of this book is correct, the former claim is as much a mistake as the latter. For I have been arguing that to be a person is to be essentially embodied, expressive, and in the world. There is no consciousness without expression, and there is no expression without embodiment. Perception grounds even the highest and most exalted activities of consciousness, and perception is impossible without embodiment. If a human person is essentially embodied and expressive, then other human persons are as well. They would be essentially related to their own embodied behavior and, therefore, accessible to me in a behavioral manner.

Husserl is ambiguous on this issue. On the one hand, he makes the distinction between transcendental and embodied ego and implies that the latter has only a contingent relationship to the former. On the other hand, he argues that the embodied behavior of the other is essential to knowing the other. If the other's real constituting ego is only contingently related to his own embodied behavior, it is difficult to see how Husserl can say that we can know the other. I choose to resolve this dilemma by giving up the distinction between transcendental and embodied ego. Human consciousness is essentially in and present to the world, and the lived body is the condition of the possibility of such presence.[6]

The Meaning and Reality of the Other

The Other as Individual and Immediate · If I can know other perceiving, understanding, judging, and choosing subjects through their own embodied behavior, then I can know other persons. Here once again there is a conditioned, a condition, and the link between the two. The conditioned is the virtually unconditioned judgment "I can know other persons." The conditioned is simply the conclusion, and the link between the conditioned and the condition is a materially analytic claim, defining what other persons are. To know others is initially perceiving them in all three senses of that word, experience, understanding, and judgment. Again the other person will not be a noumenal spirit in some noetic heaven, but one essentially related to her body and manifesting herself through her own embodied behavior, in a body perceived as distinct from mine.

The fulfillment of the conditions is given in phenomenological reflection upon conscious experience. Here, as in the discussion of perceptual objectivity, it is not a matter of inference from private states of consciousness but of explicating evidence that is already there implicitly. Such an explicitation has four steps: the evidence for otherness in general, the evidence for specific kinds of otherness, the evidence for the otherness of human persons, and a richer, stronger sense of objectivity.

The evidence for otherness in general has already been articulated. In our discussion of perception, we discovered five notes of perceptual objectivity: (a) the unity of the thing in contrast to many perceptual acts; (b) the presence of the thing as detachable, "there," and thematic, in contrast to my own lived body as inseparable from me, "here," implicit; (c) the presence of the thing as perspectival and subject to only presumptive synthesis, in contrast to the massive, mute, non-perspectival presence of my perceiving body; (d) the independent content of the thing in contrast to acts proceeding from me as perceiver; (*e*) the thing as gestalt emerging from a background, in contrast with the lived gestalt of my body, the subjective background from which my act of perception proceeds.

We are in a world, moreover, in which different kinds of otherness manifest themselves. Rocks, trees, and dogs are all objects of my consciousness and, therefore, independent of me, but rocks, trees, and dogs are specifically, qualitatively different from one another— they have a different kind of presence. I can grow a tree but not a rock; I can train Fido to hunt ducks, but I cannot so train a tree. My interaction with rocks, trees, and dogs rests on manifested, verifiable properties and activities in these objects, such as the hardness of the rock, the growing of the plant, and the running of the dog. Plants and dogs reveal themselves to me as different forms of life, self-moving, growing, self-maintaining organisms. Dogs, moreover, can move and sense, whereas plants cannot. Here then are forms of behavior manifesting themselves in bodies that are experienced as other, as having the five aspects of objectivity described above.

It is in the context of multiple kinds of otherness that I experience other persons. For what becomes clear is that there is another kind of embodied life with a different kind of presence. It not only grows, senses, and moves, but talks, gestures, and paints pictures. I can talk at Fido, but I can talk with this other kind of life, which can also talk back and sometimes disagree with me. I can put my plants anywhere I want in my apartment with no protest from them, but these other beings can resist me, disobey, refuse to go or be where I wish. I can train and indoctrinate Fido, but these other strange beings can resist being trained and indoctrinated and express their indignation in being so treated.

There is, therefore, a sense in which I feel and sense a community with these other beings; they reveal themselves as "like me." We should not, however, take this "like me" quality in an explicit, inferential sense. Rather, my lived body implicitly resonates with the lived body of the other in a way that I do not with trees or dogs. With other persons I spontaneously anticipate a certain kind of response that answers to and corresponds with my experienced behavior: anger when I am angry, love when I am loving, joy when I am joyful. When I ask a question, I expect to get an answer and am disappointed when I do not. When I make a proposal, I expect agreement or disagreement. Such responses I do not demand or expect from my plant or dog. They can respond to me only in a limited, relatively exterior way. The full riches of my interiority are closed to them; with the human other, however, there is no limit to my self-revelation.

Therefore, in his behavior the other manifests himself to me as an expressive consciousness in his language, gestures, and actions. As I perceive the gestalt of a table in a room immediately, so I can read anger in the face of the other as he perceives the wreck I have made of his car. As I can enlighten and criticize the other through what I say, do, or create, so he can enlighten and criticize me. In contrast to my relationship to things, plants, and animals, the other can relate to me in a fully *reciprocal* way. As I can lie, resist, or withhold myself from the other, so he can do the same to me. Indeed the ability of the other deliberately to deceive me or hide something from me, rather than being evidence against his existence, is evidence for his existence. Through such behavior the *interiority* of the other manifests itself and reveals him as specifically different from a rock, plant, or dog. I can deceive myself and have mistaken perceptions about all these objects and about the other person as well. But only he can deceive me about himself, i.e., lie to me, hide himself from me. I can dominate my dog, order it around, and treat it in an unfair way, but among all the objects of my experience only the other can alienate me, dominate me, "look" at me in Sartre's sense. I will consider in the next section whether the alienating look is necessarily paradigmatic for human interaction, but in any event the possibility and actuality of the "look" is certainly one important bit of evidence for the meaning and reality of the other.

As I know all objects of my perceiving consciousness, I know the other only in a presumptive way. I can look at a department store mannequin and think it is a person; I can look into the distance and mistake one person for another. Just as mistaken perceptions about particular objects presuppose the validity of perception in general, so mistaken perceptions of the other presuppose the sense and existence of the other. I can know only in the light of a subsequently true perception that the other has deceived me, and I can know only in the light of past behavior indicating such interiority that the other is capable of deceiving me.

With the presence of the other we have objectivity in the full sense of the word. Objectivity means not simply what I perceive, understand, or judge for myself but what is intersubjectively true. The perceived thing is present to me as something that not only I but the other perceives, and her perceptions can correct, complement, or deepen mine. An objective claim in science, mathematics, or philosophy is one that is universally true for all persons. Such claims, as we saw in the discussion of perception and reflection, presume intersubjectivity in the prescientific life-world. This kind of objectivity is presumed in the constitution of the more complex domains of society, culture, and the state.

Such is the evidence for the claim that we know other persons. Such an argument is not an argument from analogy and therefore does not succumb to the objections against that. One of the objections questions the legitimacy of inferring from one self-enclosed person to another; but my argument is not an inference, and consciousness is intentionally present to the world. Another objection is that one necessarily assumes the existence of the other while trying to prove one's own existence. But the only kind of otherness I assume is otherness in general, established in the chapter on perception. I use a definition of human person, established in the chapter on the self, but this definition does not assume ahead of time that other human persons exist; it does, however, clarify the issue by helping us to see that the other we are seeking is not a Cartesian ego only contingently related to his body and the world.

My approach, however, does remain first person and egological in a qualified, important sense. The evidence for the meaning and reality of the other is established by reflection on my own conscious experience. In this sense I constitute the other pre-reflexively and reflexively. To say otherwise is to fail in the task of philosophical self-responsibility and regard for evidence characteristic of phenomenology. This methodological priority of my self to the self of the other does not imply an ontological or genetic priority. Others certainly have existed before me, influenced me, and contributed to my socialization. I can make such claims, however, only by having recourse to my conscious experience and discovering myself as already having parents, language, and national identity. I discover that I have already been constituted by the other or, to put it more paradoxically, I constitute my having been constituted by the other. Such a paradox can be regarded as vicious only by someone who lumps together different kinds of priority that should be kept distinct, a failure responsible for much of the confusion on this issue.

But such a priority has to be very seriously qualified. Insofar as I have the responsibility to verify what I myself have conceived eidetically in responding to nature and other human beings, phenomenology is egological. However, the thesis of intersubjectivity has implications even for phenomenology itself. I perform imaginative, eidetic variation not in an isolated fashion but in relation to what persons in my own culture and in other cultures can experience, imagine, and conceive. Apodicticity in a qualified sense is possible, but part of what forces me to speak of a weak rather than a strong apodicticity is that any eidetic claim remains presumptive in relation to a community of past, present, and future investigators. Any eidetic claim has to be open to testing not only by the possible counter-example that I come up with, but by those that occur to others as well.

Therefore, the unity that phenomenology intends is a unity of ideal agreement among investigators. To the extent that unresolved disagreements remain, to the extent that I have not considered counter-claims or qualifying claims from other thinkers, my relative apodicticity is a deficient, relative apodicticity. To the extent that I do resolve disagreements and consider counter-claims or qualifying claims, I approach an adequate, relative apodicticity.

Even the personal verification in phenomenology is intersubjective and dialogal, either directly through some kind of discussion or indirectly through my own inner taking account of the possible claims and objections of the other. The internal dependence of phenomenology on the past, historical other that Husserl discovered in the *Crisis* has to be broadened to include the essential relation to the present and future other. Phenomenology not only in what it affirms about intersubjectivity but in its actual practice and method is essentially dialogal and intersubjective.

One main reason for such a claim is that perceptual experience founds phenomenology as a form of abstract reflection. Because perceptual experience in its full sense is intersubjective, the objectivity and the unity that it strives for are intersubjective. To see this point we can imagine a person who witnesses a murder in a hotel room across the street and experiences in a personal way all the five aspects of perceptual objectivity. When that person reports the murder, however, she receives no intersubjective confirmation. When the police come to the scene of the crime, there is no body, no sign of blood, no weapon, no indication of violence, no other witnesses.

Determining whether the witness was hallucinating or not depends upon further inquiry and intersubjective confirmation. Short of such confirmation internally qualifying the five notes of perceptual objectivity as fully and certainly one, objective, and so on, she experiences a contradiction between a personal sense of what is true and the community's lack of belief. Like all contradictions, this one demands rational resolution. Because perception presupposes a community of perceivers, therefore, phenomenological inquiry presupposes a community of inquirers.

The weaker sense of perceptual objectivity, stage one in my constitution of the other person, is logically and phenomenologically prior to the fuller sense built up genetically from the weaker sense. The fuller sense of objectivity, however, is normatively and teleologically prior, in the sense that intersubjective agreement is the norm of truth on all levels and the goal toward which individual thinkers strive. Such a norm and such a goal have been present implicitly in all the eidetic claims made in this book. At all points dialectically and descriptively I have tried to take account of and learn from positions differing from my own. At all points my descriptions have benefited from and learned from the prior descriptions of others. Both the dialectical and the descriptive aspects of dialectical phenomenology have intersubjective implications. At this point in my argument I am reflecting explicitly on such implicit intersubjective practice, and in this manner my explicit phenomenology comes to correspond more closely with such practice. There is a circle here, but one that is fruitful, not vicious.

The Social Life-World · As I have developed it so far, my account of intersubjectivity is incomplete, for it has dealt mostly with the face-to-face encounter with the other. This is indeed the most fundamental kind of intersubjectivity, that which founds the others. My task in this section is to show how other more mediated forms of intersubjectivity emerge.

The immediate contact with the other, in which he or she is present spatially in the living present to me, can have two forms, reciprocal and non-reciprocal. The non-reciprocal mode occurs when I am observing someone who is not aware of me or paying attention to me.

If the other is chopping wood, for example, I can know the objective meaning of the act "chopping wood," but the subjective meaning, the motive, may not be clear to me. Is the person chopping wood to get exercise or to work off steam after a quarrel with a spouse or to make money?[7]

There are three different, indirect ways to try to figure out the motive. I can search out my own memory for similar actions of my own, I can resort to my own knowledge of the customary behavior of the person chopping wood, or I can try to infer the motive by asking whether the motive would be furthered by the act in question. Here, as in all other knowledge of motivation, there are two kinds of motivation, "because" motives deriving from the person's past and "in order to" motives present in a project directed toward the future. A person can chop wood because of anger in order to work off steam or because of overweight in order to work off five pounds.

Time consciousness, as we saw in Chapter 1, is a dynamic unity of past, present, and future internally related to one another. When I am reciprocally involved with the other person, that person's subjective meaning is more accessible to me through gesture and direct revelation. If I am in doubt about the person's motives, I can question that person. But because of the possibility of willful deception, I never have total certitude about motives. The immediacy and directness are always mediated, never totally immediate.

In trying to understand and communicate with another person, relevance structures, meanings essential for understanding a particular theme in a situation, are necessary. There are three kinds of relevance structures, imposed thematic, motivational, and interpersonal. The first causes forced attentiveness, as when my attention is drawn away from my work by a car noisily whizzing by my apartment. The second I take up consciously and choose, as when I deliberately look at Cezanne's *Mt. St. Victoire* in terms of its color organization or the movement of planes back into space. The third occurs when a theme is present to my attention and I bring in elements from my habitual stock of knowledge to interpret it. Such interpretation can be either routine, when I enter my study and discover the book I thought I had lost, or problematic, when there is a gap between my habitual stock of knowledge and the theme. For example, the woman who I thought was going to accept my invitation for a date refuses me, and I have to reinterpret our relationship. All three kinds of relevance structures reciprocally interact when I encounter and try to understand other persons.[8]

I know the meaning of the behavior of others through various kinds of self-expression or self-objectification. Here there are three kinds, in ascending degrees of mediation. The first occurs when I observe someone doing something, swimming or playing tennis or driving a car; and I learn something from that observation, such as why the person is swimming or how to play tennis or how not to drive a car. The second form of objectification occurs when the other person explicitly indicates knowledge of a situation, by sticking a hand in a pot of boiling water and coming away with a pained facial expression or communicating something to me through waving a hand or saying something.

If objectification is embodiment of subjective processes in everyday occurrences and objects, then both these first two occur in an immediate face-to-face situation. In such situations persons express themselves in action in such a way that someone else can learn something from that activity. When I leave a mark such as a notch on a tree or a wooden sign, create a work of art such as a painting or a piece of sculpture, make a tool such as a knife or a hammer, or write something such as a poem or a novel, then other possibilities emerge. My objectifications can become detached from me, and others can learn from them in different places and times. Such knowledge acquired through detachable objectifications is essential for knowing others, predecessors or contemporaries, outside the face-to-face situation. Such detachable objectifications are also necessary conditions for the hermeneutical function of distanciation that will be discussed in Chapter 6.[9]

In the face-to-face situation, I am in immediate contact with the other as a particular human being with easily knowable objective and subjective meanings. Two other, indirect, social relationships are those with contemporaries and predecessors. Contemporaries are those present to me temporally but not spatially in a face-to-face manner. I know them anonymously, universally, and objectively, in contrast to the personal, individual, and subjective emphases of the face-to-face situation. I can infer some subjective meaning in such idealizations as the "postman," "the consumer," "labor," or "capital" because I can move from the kind of behavior typical of such persons to typical, generally expected behavior. Social sciences such as economics, sociology, or political science operate on the basis of such enriching abstractions, founded on the more primordial face-to-face encounter.

This relationship of foundation is indicated by the three ways we come to know contemporaries. The first occurs when I derive my knowledge from a previous face-to-face encounter with someone now outside the range of direct observation, for example, a previous acquaintance at the university where I teach. A second occurs through description by someone in a face-to-face situation, in the light of which I form a concept or picture of someone who is absent; my brother describes his friend to me.

A third way of knowing contemporaries is through cultural objects such as artifacts, institutions, and conventional, habitual ways of doing things. But even this form of knowledge presupposes direct experience of others. Contemplating an artwork presupposes that I know what it means to paint or draw or sculpt, either through watching others do it or by being taught by others. If I did not have the benefit of such experiences, I would not know what to make of an art object and might even treat it as just another material object. As we have already seen in our discussion of expression, more elevated, abstract forms of reflection and activity are founded on, though not reducible to, the public world of the immediate face-to-face situation.[10]

In knowing predecessors, I emphasize the past modality of time consciousness. A predecessor is a person in the past not one of whose experiences overlaps with mine. I cannot influence predecessors; they influence me. I can come to know predecessors through being told about them by another person, through monuments and records, and finally through the sharing of a common language. English is not a language that I construct for myself *ex nihilo*. Rather, as I have already shown in the discussion of expression, I am born into and learn from a culture and a community that predecessors have already constituted. My life-world is filled with historical objects like the Washington Monument, historical documents like the Constitution, traditions such as the American political tradition, languages such as English. As internalized by me and made a part of me, these realities exemplify the essential historicity of my consciousness. My consciousness as internal time-consciousness not only extends back into a personal and social past, but is formed by that past. The past is a kind of womb that forms me linguistically, culturally, and politically and that I never completely leave. Just as the doctrine of intentionality forbids me to separate inner from outer, so the doctrine of my historicity, because there is no pure present separable from the past, forbids me to separate my present self from my past self.[11]

Because intentionality not only extends outward into a world but backward into a past that continually comes forward to meet me and forward toward a future that I rush to meet, because intentionality is essentially linguistic and expressive, because I can know others and they me, because I am essentially social and not simply individual, I am essentially historical. Because I am in my own being historical, objective history in the sense of documents or monuments or history as a science has meaning for me. History in these latter two senses, we could say, is founded on history in the former sense. Were I not fundamentally historical, objective historical documents would be alien, tales told by an idiot full of sound and fury signifying nothing. I am interested in the past because I have a past, whether shameful or edifying, impoverished or rich, unhappy or happy.[12]

For these reasons, my life-world is shot through with history. History is both outside me, in the form of documents, monuments, and institutions, and inside me, in the form of a social temporality, sedimented meanings, and learned language. I am part of a social life-world both product and producer of institutions and traditions. To the very core of my being I am Irish, Catholic, and American, with certain ways of thinking, certain mannerisms, certain forms of expressions that betray those origins and influences. At the same time, as an active participant in the world I can contribute to and form the traditions and institutions that formed me. Though Irish, I can ignore or criticize old-fashioned attitudes and opinions of my Irish parents and grandparents. Though Catholic, I can criticize the Church's teachings on birth control or celibacy or the ordination of women to the priesthood. Though American, I can criticize our involvement in a foreign war.

Traditions and institutions, then, are depositories of socially sedimented meanings simultaneously outside me and inside me, forming me and being formed by me. If the common language that is a part of my social life-world is the most basic and the most common tradition, there are others, founded on that, that are more specific. Corresponding to the activity of labor and production, there is the economic institution of capitalism. Corresponding to the domain of symbolic interaction, there is the political institution of legal, constitutional, representative democracy. Corresponding to various activities on the level of abstract reflection, science, philosophy, and formal logic, there are the historical traditions out of which individual scientists, philosophers, and logicians emerge. Institutions and traditions educate me. Because capitalism has educated me, personal independence, money, private property, and pleasurable consumption are important to me. Because the institution of constitutional democracy has educated me, a President cannot get away with Watergate, conduct an unconstitutional war, or wiretap citizens illegally. Because certain sub-traditions within the history of philosophy, phenomenology, existentialism, Hegel, Kant, and critical social theory have educated me, I have a sensitivity to the value of the human subject, the importance of freedom, and the problem of alienation in twentieth-century industrial society.

But traditions and institutions can not only enlighten but distort, can not only inform but leave out, can not only educate but alienate. Capitalism can make us so individualistic that we ignore the fundamental, social character of human beings, so materialistic that we forget the self in industrial mass society. Individual philosophical traditions can emphasize some ideas and omit others that are important. Analytic philosophy leaves out too much of human subjectivity; existentialism and phenomenology, too much of the socially practical and political; Marxism and critical theory, too much of the ontological and religious. For these reasons, and because there are gaps and uncertainties in our inherited stock of knowledge, the social life-world is profoundly ambiguous. Any knowledge of others that I have in the life-world is essentially partial and one-sided. I can know X only if I leave out Y, can enjoy a symphony only if I forsake a baseball game, can commit myself to one woman permanently only if I renounce all other women. For these reasons there is a fundamental opacity to the social life-world that can motivate a Descartes to move to radical doubt and that serves as a necessary condition for my own more limited, circumspect suspicion discussed in Chapter 6.

Because of the ambiguity of the life-world, I can misinterpret the historicity of myself and others. My historicity can be either authentic or inauthentic. Inauthentic historicity is a splitting-off of the modes of temporality from one another in such a way that I try to flee into the past or live in a pure present or dwell in a pure future of mere possibility. If authenticity is conformity to the four transcendental precepts, discovered in Chapter 4, and fidelity to those precepts leads to a unified, coherent understanding, judgment, and choice of the self and the self's temporality, then inauthentic historicity will be a splitting-off of the self from itself.[13]

Even though its emphasis at one time or other may be more on one aspect than on the other, authentic historicity, in contrast to inauthentic historicity, brings past, present, and future together internally in an explicit manner. For example, when I do history, my focus is on the past, but authentic temporality prevents me from sinking into mere antiquarianism. In contrast to the forgetting characteristic of inauthentic temporality, authentic temporality reverently confronts and remembers its past. In contrast to a curious, idle, consuming approach to the present, a questioning wonder permeates authentic temporality. In contrast to an inauthentic future full of momentary novelties that I drift toward, do not choose, and experience as imposed by the "they," as authentically temporal I choose my future actively, individually, and responsibly. Whereas inauthentic temporality experiences the historical, social world inauthentically as the alienating presence of the "they," authentic temporality can experience the social life-world as enhancing, not necessarily negating, its own individuality and freedom.

Authentic temporality is, then, a temporality in which the explicit conception of the self matches or fits what it is essentially. Inauthentic historicity is at odds with itself because it is fleeing from itself. Trying to flee the past into a pure present or a pure future, I nonetheless remain subject to the past through the language I use, the inherited values and prejudices I employ in making choices, and the limitations of character that I have built up through the years. Trying to flee the future and merely drift, I nonetheless choose to drift; not choosing is itself a choice. If I try to flee the present into a safe past or a romantic future, nonetheless this attempt to flee is itself something that takes place in the present. Even when I try to flee from myself, I remain caught up in myself, ambiguous in a bad sense, vacillating, inconsistent—in a word, inauthentic. As we saw in Chapter 1 and shall explore further in Chapters 8 and 9, contemporary industrial society is a continual, structural invitation to such loss of self.

Authentic historicity grounds historiology in its three aspects: the antiquarian, the monumental, and the critical. I interpret a document not to flee my present or my future into some kind of antiquarianism, but to discover lived, monumental meanings that have a bearing on my present and disclose future possibilities. In the light of such an uncovering of possibility disclosed by a reverent openness to the past, I can become critical of a lived, inauthentic present lost in the "they."[14]

With the recovery of an authentic temporality involving an interpretative openness to my past, an attention to the lived present, and the choice of a critical future, I now have the basis for talking about phenomenology as hermeneutical, descriptive, and critical. As we saw in Chapter 1, a mere descriptive openness to the present is not sufficient for phenomenology because both phenomenology itself and the life-world are historical. As we shall see in the last four chapters, description and interpretation are insufficient without critique and suspicion. Both in its disclosure of the world and in its own account of itself, phenomenology has to contain a critical future.

Up to this point we have been considering merely the genesis of knowledge from more immediate to less immediate forms. We need still to consider the genesis of the content of knowledge. What are the various types of content known through these forms of knowledge? We can distinguish among the face-to-face, the group, the crowd, and very mediated realities such as "class" or "state" or "race."

In the face-to-face relationship I am dealing with others as individuals in a context more or less immediately accessible; a conversation between friends or lovers or siblings might be examples of such a relationship. In a group, the others are still present to me as a whole, but I have shifted the accent from their individuality to more general notions or concerns; a professor lecturing to a class on a topic in philosophy, a politician giving a speech to some of his constituents about the dangers of nuclear war, and a musician playing Bach for an audience are typical examples.

In a crowd, the concerns remain general, communication among all the members remains possible, and the members are all physically present in the same place and time. What distinguishes a crowd from a group is the difficulty or impossibility of perceiving everyone at the same time from my own vantage point. A large peace demonstration in Washington, D.C. in which the members are strung out for several miles is an example.

The most complex social realities, however, are those that are the most mediated and most universal, such as "the United States," "the black race," or "the capitalist class." These transcend any particular, local time or place. These realities are founded on the experiences of face-to-face encounters, groups, and crowds, on shared objective characteristics such as nationality, race, or similar relationships to the means of production; representation, shared institutions such as the Constitution, the NAACP, or the United Auto Workers; and finally structures and systematic effects of which we are, for the most part, not ordinarily, directly conscious but which can be theoretically elaborated and explained.

Let me expand further on a couple of these points. First of all, by representation I mean a systematic, conscious relationship between the larger social reality and small couples, communities, groups, and crowds. In the Constitutional Convention of the United States, for example, the states sent representatives to determine the type of government under which we would live as a nation. In large industrial societies representation of some kind is essential to the constituting and maintaining of these societies.

There are, however, in large industrial societies structures that transcend the immediate consciousness of any of the participants. I refer to these structures in Chapter 8 as the "social unconscious," of which we can become aware through a conscious attempt at interpretation, explanation, and critique. Similar to the process of psychoanalysis, in which a person becomes aware of unconscious motivations and forces, in social interpretation and critique we become aware of the hidden structures of race, sex, class, and government power. Day in and day out institutionalized practices lead systematically to effects that transcend the intentions of the participants. Contrary to the intentions of the participants, for example, low interest rates and a high degree of speculation in stock lead to an economic crash.

Such hidden structures and effects rest upon a very complex network of immediate experience, habitual, customary practices, and institutions. Whenever groups of people live in a certain place for any length of time, they experience one another in certain ways, develop certain habitual ways of dealing with one another, allow these to be sedimented in custom, and explicitly formalize, legalize, and regularize them in law, economics, and government, and finally experience the effects of the hidden structures of race or class or sex or government. Experience leads to regular practices to custom to institution to unconscious structures. Such structures are founded on conscious experience, practice, custom, and institutions but transcend them as well.

Blacks and whites living in the South, for example, encountered one another as different, developed habitual ways of dealing with one another, regularized them in customs of exclusion—"blacks don't eat here"—and finally institutionalized some of these customs in various practices and laws of exclusion, such as forbidding blacks to vote. These regular practices, customs, and laws of exclusion gave rise to racist structures and structural effects such as the economic impoverishment and political powerlessness of blacks in relation to whites.

Not only do practices, regularities, customs, and institutions found structures and structural effects, but structures mediate experience. Being raised in a working-class black family is to have my experience limited, determined, and influenced from the very beginning in a way different from growing up in an upper-class white family. The values taught, the self-esteem communicated, the social mobility experienced, the culture absorbed, and the hopefulness about life prospects enjoyed are all highly dependent upon such structures and structural effects. The mediation, therefore, is mutual: practices, regularities, customs, and institutions found structures; structures mediate practices, regularities, customs, and institutions.

A reality such as "class consciousness," therefore, has many different levels and aspects: the immediate experience of my family as working class, middle class, or wealthy; the experience of the work place in which I am subordinate or dominant, regimented or free, mindless or creative; institutions such as labor unions or corporations or states, the awareness of being part of a national movement such as a strike or revolution in which there is some communication between parts of the movement and some representation; and, finally, the explanatory, critical account of the hidden structures of class domination that relates these to the various levels and kinds of conscious class struggle.

It is usually the last that Marxists refer to when they are speaking of class consciousness in a full, ideal sense. We should note, however, that this clear, explicit, comprehensive sense builds on and co-exists with others that are less clear and more ambiguous and, therefore, more easily misinterpreted. A United States worker in the 1980s can become fed up with his low pay, bad working conditions, and poor neighborhood, but can easily blame the wrong agency: "big government," "Eastern intellectuals," or "Ivy League academics." For this reason, the experience of class domination and class struggle needs to be understood, interpreted, and communicated theoretically. Experience leads to understanding and judgment; understanding and judgment rest on and presuppose experience.

The understanding and judgment achieved theoretically need to be communicated, not imposed. As I shall show in the next section, such communication should take the form of appeal, not coercion. Just as I have to understand and verify the validity of any psychoanalytic interpretation of my experience by my analyst, so the group involved in class struggle has to understand and verify any theoretical account proposed inside or outside the group. There are a built-in democratic ethos and a rejection of elitism in dialectical phenomenology. Elitism is anti-philosophical.

A PHENOMENOLOGY OF COERCION AND APPEAL

Even though we can know the other, there is still some doubt about the possibility of fruitful, practical interaction with the other. One thread uniting many thinkers is the denial of any possible reciprocity among men and women. To the claim that I can teach another Socratically in such a way that the student becomes freer, one writer objects that such teaching is just a form of weak control, of positive reinforcement. To the notion that I can genuinely love another person in such a way that the person's very being is enhanced, another answers that such love is just a form of domination, of seducing away the other's very being and turning it into an object. Another asserts that technocracy is the only rational form of government and that any plea for freedom, democracy, or participation is anachronistic. Still another insists that truth is essentially a function of power and that power is essentially conflictual, coercive, dominating.[15]

For politics the debate has important implications. If genuine dialogue among free men and women is impossible, then political domination and manipulation are not only inevitable but justified, and we must jettison the classical notion of democracy. Thinkers such as Marcuse, Arendt, and Habermas have criticized twentieth-century capitalist states for being technocratic and for turning real democracy into merely formal democracy, a mere appearance of popular decision-making.[16] The norm for such criticism is an ideal of rational, free discussion among equals taking place in such a way that the freedom of each is enhanced—in a word, appeal.

For the above reasons, therefore, a phenomenological inquiry into the experience of coercion and appeal is essential. A totally unprejudiced description is, of course, impossible; but as much as possible I shall describe different experiences of coercion and appeal without assuming ahead of time that one is reducible to the other. Within phenomenology, Sartre's is the strongest, best-argued disagreement with my position. I shall briefly consider his position before moving into my own positive account.[17]

Freedom and the Other: The Look

Sartre's paradigm for relations with the other is the "look." When I am in the hallway and am looking through a keyhole at something, I hear footsteps on the stairs and am caught in the act, transfixed before the gaze of the other. I feel my freedom drain out of me as I become an object before her gaze—I am ashamed.[18]

To deal with this situation, I can do one of two things. I can stare back and try to reduce her to an object; I can say "Who are you to condemn me, for I have caught you doing the same or worse," or I can grovel in my shame. The situation becomes a contest between freedoms, each trying to subdue the other.

Sartre's claim here is that I do not become aware of the other as subject by knowing her, because such knowledge objectifies the other and, therefore, does not really present her as subject. Any look is an objectifying and degrading look that robs the other of her freedom. I can be aware of the other only by being "looked at," by being the object of her knowledge. Only this experience gives me an indubitable certainty of the other.

Real human mutuality between persons is, therefore, impossible because that would involve mutual looking and thus a contest of freedoms in which one ends up being dominant. Human intersubjectivity is essentially conflictual because freedom presupposes an absolute independence, negativity, and lack of receptivity. Since any mutuality presumes mutual influence and dependence, any attempt at mutuality would be the negation of freedom. I can be either free or dependent on another, but not both. I can be either in charge of my destiny or open to another's influence, but not both.

In a chapter in *Being and Nothingness* entitled "Concrete Relations with Others," Sartre uses this general paradigm to explore specific kinds of intersubjectivity: sadism, masochism, and so on. In each instance there is a capitulation to the other or domination of the other. If I am the stronger, I become sadistic; if weaker, then I go the masochistic route. Even apparently mutual and loving relationships turn out to be hidden forms of domination in which one person is controlling or using the other.[19]

What are we to make of Sartre's intriguing account of intersubjectivity? First, as we have already seen, there is an inadequate account of objectivity and objectification in which perceptual, thematic, and alienated objectivity are uncritically lumped together. If such a procedure is incorrect, then to objectify is not necessarily to alienate. There are many kinds of looks—loving, encouraging, respectful, friendly—that have a different logic from Sartre's accusing look, as well as a different result.

Second, Sartre describes freedom as totally independent, negative, and unreceptive to motives or values.[20] If this account were true, genuine dependence of any kind on another would detract from freedom, and true mutuality would be impossible. But, as I have shown, this notion of freedom is one-sided and to that extent false.[21] Rather true freedom is a unity of determination and indetermination, motive and "leap," receptivity and activity. "I choose because . . ." is the model of such a freedom, which is open and receptive to the world, the body, and motives. Consequently, with this more comprehensive notion of freedom, mutuality between persons emerges as a possibility.

One example of such a receptive freedom is philosophical discussion itself. When Sartre tries to persuade us of the truth of his position, such receptivity on the part of the hearer or reader is necessary. Otherwise the discussion is an exercise in either futility or domination. Yet such a receptivity, tacitly presumed by Sartre in his attempt to convince us, he explicitly denies. "Either man is wholly determined (which is inadmissible, especially because a determined consciousness—i.e., a consciousness externally motivated—becomes itself pure exteriority and ceases to be consciousness) or else man is wholly free."[22]

One consequence of positing a total freedom is that all reasons become rationalizations for my fundamental project. Yet such a consequence contradicts Sartre's attempt to convince us of the truth of his position, an attempt tacitly presupposing a distinction between reasons and rationalizations. Such a distinction presupposes a motivated, receptive freedom.

Third, Sartre's attempt to convince us of the truth of his account presumes the possibility of genuine dialogue, of what I call "appeal." For he is attempting to convince us of the truth of his position by appealing to criteria that are not arbitrary. Yet, according to his account of intersubjectivity, any attempt at persuasion is an attempt at domination, no more objectively binding than any other such attempt. The explicit claim, therefore, conflicts with the implicit performance, tacitly presupposing a communication free from domination.

Fourth, in tension with Sartre's own account is the admission that we perceive the other and, therefore, know him. Perception would seem to be at least a necessary condition for such knowledge even in Sartre's own account. "But all of a sudden I hear footsteps in the hall. Someone is looking at me."[23]

Fifth, our awareness of the other does not seem apodictic, as Sartre claims. Even he admits that we can think we hear footsteps and be mistaken. Nonetheless, he attempts to meet this difficulty by saying that the other "is present everywhere, below me, above me, in the neighboring rooms."[24] But this vague, general sense is corrigible because it rests on present and past perceptions and memories that are corrigible: memories of being caught in the act in the past, past perceptions of muted conversations in rooms, radios blaring, record players sounding.

Sixth, it seems that Sartre overgeneralizes from one kind of intersubjective encounter, that of the accusing look, to all encounters. Yet phenomenological description, such as that of appeal in the next section, disputes Sartre's generalization. His descriptions are valid for certain types of negative encounters, but they fall desperately short as the general story.

Seventh, we have to make this kind of phenomenological point against Sartre, but it is not enough. For he goes from a description of the immediate experience to a further kind of necessary claim: even if certain experiences with others seem to be mutually liberating, they really are not because they cannot be. And they cannot be finally because of an "either–or" logic, which Hegel describes as the logic of understanding, that is in tension with and dictates to the phenomenological results. Because Sartre affirms a necessary disjunction between activity and passivity, positivity and negativity, determination and indetermination, dependence and independence, people *cannot* participate in mutually liberating relationships even when they seem to be doing so.[25]

What seems to motivate such a logic is a will to absolute freedom in Sartre. To confront Sartre at his deepest is to confront him here. We do so by arguing that such an "either–or" approach to conscious experience is both self-refuting and phenomenologically false. The approach is self-refuting because, as I have already shown, any truth claim implies a commitment to reason and to criteria of truth and, therefore, a union of determination and indetermination, passivity and activity, motive and "leap." The very attempt to defend indeterminism rests on a tacit appeal to a "both–and" conception of logic. Sartre's conception is phenomenologically false because human consciousness emerges in phenomenological description as a unity of opposites: subjectivity and objectivity, perception and intellection, body and mind, positivity and negativity, determination and indetermination, motive and "leap." Perception, for example, is both active and passive and takes place through a lived body experienced as subject. Aesthetic experience involves an active attention to the object, an attention that is at the same time deeply receptive. Freedom is both negative and positive, implying not only the ability to distance myself from my environment but the adherence to values. Even an apparently totally negative social revolution justifies itself by an appeal to positive values such as freedom or justice.[26]

To think phenomenologically in a way that is faithful to experience is to understand experience and thought as a "bacchanalian revel," a play of opposites that is fruitful and mediated.[27] Husserl and Hegel come together here: Sartrean *Verstand* must give way to Hegelian *Vernunft*. The irony is that, with the possible exception of Ricoeur, Sartre uses the Hegelian language of dialectic more than anyone else in phenomenology. Yet there is no one in that tradition who is farther away from the genuine spirit and intention of Hegel.

To the extent, therefore, that Sartre rests his claims on phenomenological description, they can be disputed. To the extent that he appeals to an "either–or" logic, possibly motivated by a desire that freedom be absolute and God-like, his claims are arbitrary, and what is arbitrarily asserted can be rationally questioned or denied. The interest and power of *Being and Nothingness* to a large extent derive from this tension between his phenomenology and his existentialism, between a description attempting to be faithful to the limits and dialectical complexity of human experience and an existential will toward an absolute autonomy.[28]

A Positive Account

We have seen from the preceding section that Sartre's account of intersubjectivity is contrary to experience and self-refuting. Not only are there many other kinds of intersubjective encounter that do not fit his model, but Sartre's own attempt to persuade his readers of the truth of his viewpoint presumes the necessity of appeal or dialogue. If Sartre's argument is simply one more attempt to dominate us, then we cannot and should not take it seriously as an argument. But if his truth is what should appeal to us, then there is a contradiction between what he explicitly says and what he implicitly does.

Appeal emerges, then, as a dialectical necessity from the preceding argument. However, we still have to determine the content of appeal. What is it in itself and how is it distinct from coercion? What are the different kinds of coercion and appeal? With the purpose of answering these questions, I will reflect first on the general nature of dialogue as this is expressed in language, and then move to consider specific instances of appeal and coercion.

Let us return briefly to the dialogal situation where Sartre is trying to convince someone of the truth of his position. In the linguistic interaction between two persons, certain presuppositions emerge that allow us to make the distinction between coercion and appeal. What anyone tacitly presumes when she is trying to convince another of the truth of an argument are four validity claims: comprehensibility, truth, sincerity, and appropriateness. To say anything presumes that it is intelligible and that I am telling the truth; otherwise the conversation could not go on. Even lying presupposes the general intention of truth, for someone else will believe a lie only if he thinks it to be the truth. Consequently, sincerity is also implied; if all speakers were universally insincere and recognized to be such, no argument could go on. And because even such recognition in language is a true, sincere recognition, universal insincerity is impossible.[29]

Appropriateness, the final validity claim, involves reciprocity between speakers as the rule and any departure from that rule as the exception. If Sartre asks me just to take his word for the truth of indeterminism, then I sense the arbitrariness of this request and ask why I should take his word on the matter. I resist an inappropriate assuming of authority in this situation or any lack of reciprocity in the assumption of roles. If Sartre has the right to ask questions, state opinions, and express feelings, then so do I.

We normally take for granted such validity claims in dialogue. What we also tacitly assume is that we can bring them into question and give reasons for any claims that are made. We tacitly assume an ideal speech-situation of total reciprocity and complete freedom in questioning, asserting, and role playing. This is not to say that such a speech-situation is ever totally realized; in any dialogal situation, there will be unexamined presuppositions and prejudices.

The distinction between coercion and appeal, therefore, depends on the recognition or lack of recognition of validity claims. Because consciousness is essentially expressive and linguistic, consciousness of intersubjectivity based on appeal is the consciousness that validity claims are being mutually observed and realized. Coercion, on the other hand, rests on a violation of one or more of the validity claims.

One of the most striking examples of appeal is the Socratic situation, in which the teacher through a process of questioning and answering helps someone to understand something—for instance, that God is intelligent, that the categorical imperative is true, or that capitalism is irrational. What characterizes such a learning situation is that, first, there is an appeal on the part of the teacher to the reason of the other person, an invitation to participate in the search for truth. Second, there is the mutual openness on the part of each toward the other. At any point in the process, the student can raise questions about presuppositions or ask that a different hypothesis be considered. This freedom is essential if the Socratic method is to be authentic and to avoid becoming propaganda for the teacher's truth rather than *the* truth. Any arbitrary assumption of authority by the teacher, a violation of the fourth validity claim, would reveal itself as dogmatic.

Third, the activity of the student is called forth; the teacher functions as the midwife for this activity. The point of Socratic method is to help the student see for herself, not take the teacher's word for it. Fourth, there is an experienced fulfillment on the part of the student in reaching the truth. That which she did not know she knows; the questions that she was asking now have answers. Finally, the teacher's intention is altruistic: the student's growth in autonomy. The point of Socratic method is to help the student become her own woman as a thinker and person; the student realizes in herself the four validity claims. She sees and judges for herself that an argument is comprehensible, true, sincere, and appropriate.

Socratic method, then, approximates the ideal speech-situation. There is unlimited freedom to raise questions, express disagreement, and assume different roles. The participants in the dialogue can question and explore any claim that seems unclear, false, insincere, or inappropriate. If the teacher has authority here it is not one that he arbitrarily assumes, but one that the student freely, rationally grants. But his is an authority that can itself be questioned any time he becomes dogmatic or makes untrue claims. His authority is that of a guide who aims to make himself dispensable; at any time the student can question whether he is a good guide or not.

Now let us take another example, that of a discussion between equals about one of these same questions. Here there is the same recourse to reason, the same tacit willingness to question anything and everything, the same emphasis on activity rather than passivity, the same sense of fulfillment in reaching the truth, the same altruism. What is not present here is the relation of authority. The dialogue here takes the form of mutual questioning and answering, with each being free to raise any hypothesis he wishes. If one arguing that capitalism is irrational is using dubious presuppositions, her partner can bring these into the discussion. If one person is being unconsciously dogmatic about a certain point, that dogmatism can be made thematic.

Now it is true that this is an ideal case, that any real dialogue will fall short of this ideal to a greater or lesser extent. Nevertheless we all have experienced discussions which approximate the ideal in their concern for truth and the better argument alone prevailing. We have also experienced discussions in which the opposite is true, where there is some constraint introduced into the argument. People are trying to score debating points, assert their authority in covert ways, or refuse to question beyond a certain point. We are aware of these situations as coercive, however, because of their contrast with the ideal speech-situation, where appeal not coercion is dominant.

Now let us consider kidnapping, an obvious example of coercion. A criminal or group of criminals kidnap the child of wealthy parents to get money from them. The use of force is an attempt to bypass the reason and freedom of the parents: because the kidnapper realizes that a donation of $1,000,000 to his own bank account is not something the parents would spontaneously give through rational persuasion, he is violating the fourth validity claim of appropriateness. Therefore, and this is another contrast, the kidnappers introduce constraint and forcibly limit options. They have no confidence in the merits of the case or that the better argument will prevail; they depart from the second validity claim of truth. The kidnappers rely on force, not truth. Because the parents love their child and want her back, they refrain from bargaining with the kidnappers or questioning their demands. In contrast to the emphasis on the personal activity of the agent in the first two cases, here the will of the kidnapper is dominant, rendering the parents and child more or less objects in the hands of the kidnapper. The equality and reciprocity of the ideal speech-situation is violated.

In contrast to the non-alienated character of the first cases in which both persons are trying to see for themselves and want the truth for each other, there is an element of alienation. Here the kidnappers try to force the parents to "do what they really do not wish to do." Freedom is not totally absent in the parents, of course, because they can still choose to comply or not comply with the kidnapper's demands. But there are constraints introduced making it unlikely that the parents will refuse to comply. The parents are pressured to consider only the options suggested by the kidnappers. In the examples of appeal, on the other hand, there is no gap between action and desire and no forcible limiting of options. Both persons are discussing a certain topic because they wish to do so, not because they are forced to do so. Here the actors "choose to do what they really wish to do."

Finally the goal of the kidnapping subordinates the good of parents and child to the goal of the kidnappers. In this instance of coercion, people become mere means to an end. In the two examples of appeal, on the other hand, the good of the other is an essential concern. That the student reach the truth on his own and grow through such activity is the goal of the teacher. That the opinions and questions of the other be taken seriously is an overriding concern of the discussion between equals.

Is such selfishness present in all instances of coercion? Although it does seem to be present in many instances, at times the good of the other can be intended and achieved. A parent disciplining a child, a policeman pulling a potential suicide away from a bridge, and a court order forbidding people to swim in polluted water are all examples of coercion that intends the good of the other and does not merely use the person. Whether or not such coercion is moral is beyond the scope of this chapter, but at least coercion is not obviously immoral in all instances.

There are other, more subtle examples of coercion that must be considered. For instance, a daughter informs her mother that she wishes to be a scientist rather than the lawyer her mother always wanted her to be. The mother subtly lets her daughter know that if she chooses the microscope over the courtroom, she will forfeit her mother's love and respect. Here the coercion is psychological rather than physical, but no less real. Here there is a similar attempt to bypass the person's freedom and reason by introduction of alien considerations, a similar limiting of options, and similar domination, alienation, and exploitation. The mother here subordinates the good of the daughter as the woman conceives it to her own desire that the daughter follow in her footsteps. Total disregard for the autonomy of the daughter masquerades as genuine love. The mother covertly violates all four validity claims; lack of love, untruth, insincerity, and inappropriateness clothe themselves in their opposites.

Up to this point we have been confining ourselves to personal forms of appeal and coercion exercised among two or three persons. However, in addition to the legal coercion already mentioned, there are even more subtle forms. Various types of political propaganda and advertising present themselves as in earnest about the people they are addressing, but such appearances are highly questionable in many instances. If I am looking for an automobile, I may become convinced through patient reflecting and consulting *Consumer Reports* that a fairly inexpensive Toyota is the best car for me. However, I am constantly assaulted by advertisements informing me that my masculinity will be enhanced if I buy a bigger, more expensive, flashier car such as a TransAm.

If certain social critics such as Ewen are correct,[30] advertising violates all four validity claims. It violates the claim to comprehensibility because it manipulates and obfuscates such terms as "freedom," "happiness," and "power." The MasterCharge advertisement of a few years ago identified "true clout" with having a MasterCharge card. Such "power" and "freedom" really imply and conceal their opposites, the impotence of men and women to change their lives in a substantive way and their enslavement to consumption.

There is untruth because such "clout" turns out not to be the real item; the real power that comes from effective individual and collective decision-in-action advertising tacitly shunts to the side and ignores. There is insincerity because the advertisement presents itself as looking out for my good but is really interested primarily in profit, in getting me to charge as much as possible and to pay the twenty-two percent interest on what I charge. There is inappropriateness because the advertisement tacitly assumes that its version of the good life is the true one and discourages questioning of that claim by its appeals to emotion. By tacitly shoving reason to the side, the advertiser hopes to avoid the criticism that would bring such emotional appeals into question.

What is interesting about such blandishments is that they are not negative but positive. They are not trying to coerce me through threats but through psychological seduction, promising me that I will be a better man, more sexually fulfilled, and more socially acceptable if I buy a certain kind of product. Like the earlier forms of coercion, this kind tries to bypass reason and freedom through addressing feeling, imagination, and the unconscious, forcibly limiting options, rendering me passive by manipulating me, and alienating me. Such coercion introduces a division between what I should do and what I feel like doing. Unlike the earlier forms, however, this comes bearing gifts, presenting itself as the answer to my problems, consolation for

my grief, rest for my weary bones. This type of coercion, positive reinforcement in Skinner's sense, is difficult to see through because it
does not present itself as coercion.

Finally, like negative coercion, this type is not necessarily selfish
in the sense that the good of the person addressed is always consciously subordinated to the good of the ruler or businessman. In
positive coercion exercised in political affairs, presidents and kings
can be well-intentioned when they use propaganda "for the national
interest." However, we also often are aware that such pleas of disinterestedness are specious. When McDonald's tells me that "You,
you're the one" or MasterCharge urges me to "get real clout," a little
reflection indicates that the bottom line is profit.

Not all advertisements are positive in the sense described above.
There are many that are negative as well, threatening the person with
a loss of job, sex appeal, or status if she does not buy the requisite
product. Nor are social and political coercion the only kinds of positive coercion. Only brief reflection on some of the previous examples
is necessary to see how widespread positive coercion is. Both the
teacher suggesting that his students will be sophisticated and up-to-
date if they agree with him, and the parent showing her daughter
what a respected member of the community a lawyer is, are exercis-
ing positive coercion. Indeed, in many stances negative and positive
coercion alike are present in varying degrees of emphasis and explic-
itness, and each can be dominant at different times in the same
situation. A student resisting the pressure of his teacher or a daughter
the arguments of her mother may experience a gradual shift from
promise and love to threat and intimidation as the dominant form
of interaction.

It is obvious here, then, that the distinction between coercion and
appeal is operative and valid as we pass from individuals to groups
to crowds to large institutions and social structures. Hitler giving a
racist speech to a large crowd is operating differently from a Martin
Luther King giving a reasoned speech against racism to a large crowd
in Washington, D.C. In the former are all the aspects of coercion already mentioned: constraint, violation of the validity claims, inequality, lack of openness to the further question, evasion or negation
of rationality and freedom. In the latter are all the aspects of appeal already mentioned: freedom, fulfillment of the validity claims,
equality, openness to the further question, emphasis on rationality

and freedom. King's speeches were filled with passion and rhetoric, but these supplement rationality and freedom in his presentation.

Conclusion

Appeal is a rational, free addressing of another as a rational, free, active center, initiating a relationship in which both are not alienated but fulfilled and one with themselves and each other. Such fulfillment expresses itself as a realization of the four validity claims. Coercion, on the other hand, is irrational and unfree in its address, rendering the other passive and alienated even when his own good is intended. By "irrational" and "unfree" here I mean "irrational" and "unfree" in form, not content. A parent disciplining a child can have good reasons for doing that, but her coercion does not address directly the free, rational center of the child. Coercion can be divided into negative and positive, selfish and altruistic. In positive coercion there is an appearance of rationality, always contradicted by the facts; and altruism, often contradicted by the facts.

One consequence of this analysis is that there is an essential difference between control and influence. Control has a different logic, the logic of coercion, whereas influence is possible through appeal. Because Sartre ignores this distinction, he ends up with no possibility of genuine mutuality in social life.

A second consequence is that this reflection on coercion and appeal has implications for the discussion between modernism and postmodernism. Foucault's reduction of truth to power and his rejection of ideology critique have many of the same difficulties as Sartre's analysis. In my opinion, Foucault misses the essential distinction between coercion and appeal, in which the only force is that of the better argument. Also, his rejection of the possibility of ideology critique, because it presumes an interest-free knowledge, misses the essential connection between truth and the interest structure of appeal governed by the four validity claims and an orientation toward the better argument. His account likewise misses the distinction between an illegitimate imposition of interest from without a particular realm of inquiry or action—rejecting a job applicant because she is a black or a woman—and a legitimate, essential connection between knowledge and interest. As a result, Foucault is unable to give any normative account for a distinction between liberation and domination for his own leftist project.[31]

It is important to distinguish at least the following five essential kinds of power: appeal, influence, manipulation, coercive non-violence present in such actions as a sit-in, and straightforward violence. In contrast to a phenomenological account of the differences among these kinds of power, Foucault's account is "de-differentiated."[32] In typically post-modern fashion, there is an obliteration of difference contrasting ironically with the post-modernist's proclamation of *différance*. If Husserl legitimately complained about Descartes and Kant philosophizing from on high without a prior descriptive account of experience, we can legitimately criticize thinkers such as Foucault for too often engaging in anti-philosophical philosophizing from on high that refuses to conduct a prior descriptive inquiry into experience. Dialectical phenomenology emerges as the true friend of difference.[33]

Foucault also has performative difficulties similar to Sartre's. Either "all truth is a function of competing power claims" is universal or it is not. If it is universal, then it has an objectivity that contradicts the content of the proposition. The performance of asserting a universally true proposition contradicts the relativistic content implying that nothing is universally true. On the other hand, if the claim is not universally true, if it is simply the assertion of my will to power, then I do not have to take it any more seriously than I would any other act of mere self-assertion. In a way similar to Sartre's attempt to convince us in a non-coercive way that human relations are essentially coercive, Foucault's attempt to convince us of the universal truth of his claim contradicts the relativistic content of that claim. Both Sartre and Foucault fail because they are unable to recognize the distinctive non-violent, non-coercive character of appeal.

A third consequence is that genuine democracy and participation are possible; human interaction escapes the alternatives of abject submission and arrogant domination. Human beings can interact with one another politically, set goals and question arbitrary assumption of authority by an "expert" claiming better insight. Indeed, one criterion that emerges for the social, economic, and political health of a society is the degree of its freedom from domination and openness to a dialogue governed by the four validity claims. I shall use this critique in Chapter 8 to criticize the technocratic irrationality of late capitalism. Appeal functioning as an aspect of symbolic inter-action is essential to such ideology critique.

NOTES

1. Husserl, *Cartesian Meditations*, pp. 89–157.
2. Sartre, *Being and Nothingness*, pp. 197–278, 337–406.
3. Husserl, *Cartesian Meditations*, pp. 89–90. Sartre, *Being and Nothingness*, pp. 197–228.
4. See above, Chapter 3.
5. Sartre, *Being and Nothingness*, pp. 235–50.
6. See Husserl, *Cartesian Meditations*, pp. 18–26, 92–105. See my "An Inconsistency in Husserl's *Cartesian Meditations*," *New Scholasticism*, 53 (1979), 460–74, for a fuller development of this point.
7. Alfred Schutz, *The Phenomenology of the Social World*, trans. George Walsh and Frederick Lehnert (Evanston, Ill.: Northwestern University Press, 1967), pp. 31–38, 172–75.
8. Alfred Schutz, *The Structures of the Life-World*, trans. Richard Zaner and H. Tristam Englehardt, Jr. (Evanston, Ill.: Northwestern University Press, 1973), pp. 182–223.
9. Ibid., pp. 261–86.
10. Schutz, *Phenomenology of the Social World*, pp. 176–207.
11. Ibid., pp. 207–14. Heidegger, *Being and Time*, pp. 444–49.
12. Heidegger, *Being and Time*, pp. 424–55.
13. Ibid., pp. 383–403. See above, Chapter 4, p. 112.
14. Heidegger, *Being and Time*, pp. 448–49.
15. Skinner, *Beyond Freedom and Dignity*, pp. 84–87. Sartre, *Being and Nothingness*, pp. 337–406. Niklas Luhmann and Jürgen Habermas, *Theorie der Gesellschaft oder Sozialtechnologie—Was leistet die Systemforschung?* (Frankfurt: Suhrkamp, 1971), pp. 7–100, 291–405. Michel Foucault, *Power/Knowledge*, ed. Colin Gordon, trans. Colin Gordon, Leo Marshall, John Mepham, Kate Soper (New York: Pantheon, 1980), pp. 78–165; and *Language, Memory, Counter-Practice*, ed. Donald Bouchard, trans. Donald Bouchard and Sherry Simon (Ithaca, N.Y.: Cornell University Press, 1977), pp. 162–63.
16. Marcuse, *One-Dimensional Man*. Arendt, *Human Condition*. Habermas, *Towards a Rational Society*, pp. 81–122.
17. It is true that later Sartre goes beyond or attempts to go beyond the position articulated in *Being and Nothingness*. On the possibility of reciprocity, see his *Critique of Dialectical Reason*, pp. 109–21. Because

the argument in *Being and Nothingness* remains the strongest argument within the phenomenological tradition against my position, I am considering that argument here.

18. Sartre, *Being and Nothingness*, pp. 228–78.

19. Ibid., pp. 337–406.

20. Ibid., pp. lviii, 419–20, 430–31, 458, 464–65, 471–73, 499, 507.

21. See Chapter 4, pp. 96–99.

22. Sartre, *Being and Nothingness*, p. 418.

23. Ibid., p. 36.

24. Ibid., p. 253.

25. Georg Wilhelm Friedrich Hegel, *The Logic of Hegel*, trans. William Wallace, 2nd ed. (London: Oxford University Press, 1892), pp. 143–55.

26. Mikel Dufrenne, *The Phenomenology of Aesthetic Experience*, trans. Edward Casey, Albert Anderson, Willis Domingo, and Leon Jacobson (Evanston, Ill.: Northwestern University Press, 1973), pp. 370–434. Paul Ricoeur, *History and Truth*, trans. Charles Kelbley (Evanston, Ill.: Northwestern University Press, 1950), pp. 305–28.

27. Georg Wilhelm Friedrich Hegel, *The Phenomenology of Spirit*, trans. A. V. Miller (Oxford: Clarendon, 1977), pp. 27–28.

28. This treatment of Sartre may seem oversimplified in its neglect of certain passages such as the famous footnote at the end of the section on hatred in the chapter "Concrete Relationships with Others" (*Being and Nothingness*, p. 388), where he discusses the possibility of an ethics of deliverance coming out of radical conversion. If commentators such as Thomas Busch ("Coming to Terms with Jean-Paul Sartre," *Philosophy Today*, 24 [1980], 195–96) are correct in arguing that Sartre's description of relations with others is a description of inauthentic, bad faith leaving open the possibility of reciprocal relationships in good faith, then Sartre is indeed manifesting some awareness of the problems I am concerned with in this chapter. However, to make such a claim seems to be in tension with his account of freedom, affirming a disjunction between passivity and activity, determination and indetermination. Given this account, good faith or authenticity could only be moving away from any kind of dependence and reciprocity. Moreover, to say, as Busch does, that radical conversion involves giving up the desire to be God is in tension with Sartre's description of this desire as natural and essential. "[M]an fundamentally is the desire to be God" (Sartre, *Existentialism and Human Emotions*, p. 63).

Because of these first two points, I would admit that Sartre is more complicated than he might initially seem in my presentation, but this added complication merely intensifies the contradictoriness that I am arguing for in Sartre. The most general form that that contradiction takes is that between his phenomenology and his existentialism. The specific form that that contradiction takes here is one between a phenomenological recognition of the possibility of mutuality at odds logically and phenomenologically with his extreme existentialism, affirming a one-sided, negative, asocial or anti-social freedom. In any event the purposes of my argument demand that I give full play to the possibility of non-mutuality between persons, which purposes necessitate my stress on the existential side of his argument. If Sartre himself, even at the time of *Being and Nothingness*, begins to suspect or see, albeit inconsistently, the possibility of such mutuality, such a recognition is further textual evidence both for the contradictoriness of Sartre and the rightness of my own position on mutuality.

29. Jürgen Habermas, *Theory and Practice*, trans. John Viertel (Boston: Beacon, 1973), pp. 17–19.

30. Ewen, *Captains of Consciousness*.

31. Foucault, *Power/Knowledge*, pp. 78–165.

32. For the concept of "de-differentiation" as it occurs in postmodernism, see Jürgen Habermas, *The Philosophical Discourse of Modernity*, trans. Frederick Lawrence (Cambridge: MIT Press, 1987), pp. 112–13, 121–26, 133–37, 306, 336–52.

33. Husserl, *Formal and Transcendental Logic*, p. 278.

6

The Hermeneutical Turn: From Retrieval to Suspicion

WHAT HAS RESULTED from my analysis so far is that I see that I am in an intersubjective world through language, participation, and action. Because of my openness and receptivity to the other, I am essentially flooded with otherness. Because I am essentially intentional, I am related to what is other. I am not closed in upon myself but ecstatically outside myself in the world.

Not only am I essentially social but I am temporal, a dynamic union of past, present, and future. Such temporality is internally related to my sociality and vice versa. My relations to others have a past, present, and future, and my temporality is infused with sociality through the presence in me of sedimented language. When I think of this internal, mutual relation of sociality and temporality, I think the necessary historicity of human beings.

One example of such relatedness I considered in Chapter 1 when I argued that phenomenology itself emerges out of an historical tradition, practical and theoretical. Now I am ready to close the circle by returning to where I began and considering it more profoundly. Here I shall be reflecting in a second-level way on what I did in reflecting on such tradition; I shall consider the necessary back-and-forth movement between description and interpretation, universal and particular, abstract and concrete. In such a move to hermeneutics, the final stage in overcoming Cartesianism occurs. The last vestiges of a totally autonomous, individualistic ego disappear.

Such an overcoming itself has two stages. The first is the necessary openness to and retrieval of tradition; the second, the necessary critique of tradition. Interpretation, like all genuine dialogue, has a moment of genuine openness and trust in it and a moment of suspicion—indeed, is the movement back and forth between these two moments.

Because human knowing includes both insight and judgment, we need not only to understand tradition but to criticize it.[1] Such evaluation has to be open not only to positive but to negative judgments about the truth and value of tradition or parts of the tradition.

Openness to Tradition

We have already seen how bound up with tradition philosophy in general and phenomenology in particular are—they have a history and emerge as a result from history. To confront one's history, whether personal or collective, is to confront the particular in all its richness and fullness, the particular text, the particular symbol, the particular historical epoch. Consequently I reflected on the particular, practical historical situation in which I find myself and on the particular texts of Merleau-Ponty and Wittgenstein. To such particularity, or rather to such reflection on particularity, I now return. What makes interpretation possible?

One account of interpretation is that it is just a matter of taking a value-free good look at what is there, of letting the real Plato or the real Aristotle or the real Husserl speak for himself. And yet we have seen that not even perception is value-free, not even perception is involved in confronting a set of uninterpreted sense data. What is true of perceiving is even truer of interpreting a text or a symbol. I always approach the text with prejudices, preconceptions, values, anticipations, presuppositions. As we saw in Chapter 1 in discussing Husserl, the attempt to be free of prejudices reveals itself as an illegitimate prejudice against prejudice. No more than the perceived thing is an object existing in itself apart from conscious experience is the text a thing in itself apart from the conscious interpreter.

A second, naïve notion of interpretation is that in interpreting we are reading off the private individuality of the author, understanding the author better than she understands herself. Among the many difficulties with such a position is the difficulty of verification. There is no way of showing that the love that Shelley talks about in one of his poems or the anxiety Heidegger speaks about or the masochistic sexual relations that Sartre discusses corresponds to real events of love or anxiety or masochism in the lives of the individual authors. Surely because of the general dependence of all insight on experience there is something in the author's experience on which he is drawing, but that could include awareness of what other people have experienced and thought as well as personal experience and thought. For example, a love poem by Shelley could be based on observation of two lovers or a poem that he has read about love or experience of his own loneliness and desire for love or observation of a woman that he *could* love or *would* like to love or a love affair of his own. All these are possibilities, but none of them has to be verified in order to discover the meaning of Shelley's poem.[2]

What I reach in interpreting any text, therefore, is not the private subjectivity of the author but the world disclosed by the text itself in the text. The text is the public, noematic pole of a dialectic of event and meaning. Even on the level of immediate, face-to-face dialogue, not only the individual act of saying something but the public, universal meaning of that act—for example, "that it is raining outside," "that Socrates is a great philosopher," or "that Washington was elected President"— are present. There is also the hearer's act of appropriating that meaning, responding to it, agreeing or disagreeing with it, acting on it.

The text is objectification of discourse. Discourse is the basic, most comprehensive notion of language, encompassing speech and writing, structural form and semantic content, event and meaning. In one and the same speech act there are an objective, propositional content and a subjective, event-character. The propositional content comprises both sense and reference, which correspond linguistically and noematically to understanding and judgment respectively. When I understand what the sentence "Sartre was the conscience of a generation in France" means, I grasp its sense. When I judge that such a sentence is true, I grasp its reference. In addition to its objective, semantic content, there is the formal, semiological structure present on a phonological, lexical, and syntactical level.

Within the objective, propositional content there is also a dialectic between singular identification and universal predication. When I say that Sartre was the conscience of a generation, the subject of the sentence identifies Sartre as a singular individual and the predicate posits certain universals as instantiated in him. This semantic intertwining of singular and universal in the sentence is its basic, most important, rational structure. Present too, of course, are the semiological dimensions, but they relate to the semantic structure as form to content. The full reality of the objective dimension of the sentence is, therefore, a unity of singular and universal, form and content. Although we are usually conscious of the content, we are for the most part not conscious of the form. We have to reach such form through a movement from understanding to explanation, to be discussed later.

On the subjective, event side of discourse are the self-reference of the sentence—the implicit or explicit reference through such grammatical devices as pronouns and through such non-linguistic devices as physical expression and gesture to the speaker; the illocutionary dimension in which the same locutionary content, "that Sartre was the conscience of a generation," is asserted, questioned, or exclaimed over; and the perlocutionary reference to the hearer. As subjective, the act of speaking is noetic; as objective, it is noematic and public. Event and meaning imply one another. "If all discourse is actualized as event, all discourse is understood as meaning."[3]

Because discourse even in speech already has a public, objective character, discourse can be recorded as writing. When writing occurs, there is a distanciation of the meaning from the private subjectivity and situation of the author, a distanciation and objectification that is not negative and obfuscating, but positive and enlightening. For what writing does is to free the meaning disclosed in the initial situation from the limited confines of that situation for apprehension by a wider public. Shelley's poem, rather than being something heard by one person or group in one audience, becomes accessible to millions in different historical epochs. An objectification occurs in such expression that is not merely alienating but liberating.[4]

The author arrived at through interpreting the text is the author as author, the implied author as opposed to the real author, revealed through style, the genre of the work, and finally the work as a whole.[5] The initial distanciation of the work from the intentions of the author, the initial situation of discourse, and the initial audience is a condition for my appropriating the meaning of the text. Such distanciation is not an obstacle to interpretation but essential for it. But interpretation is not mastery. The more complex, dense, and meaningful the text is, the more efforts to control, dominate, or exhaustively interpret the text reveal themselves as fruitless and vain. There is something in the text that resists such attempts at mastery and causes them to misfire.

Efforts to describe interpretation as mastery or domination falsify the experience of interpretation. For interpretation is less one-sided mastery by a subject and more akin to a game.[6] To enter a game is to enter a situation in which the rules of the game transcend the sub- jectivity of each player. To make a right or a wrong move in chess is to verify that by recourse not to the subjectivity of each player but to what has happened on the board. In playing a game I not only play but am played upon in the sense of being in a situation that has public criteria of success or failure. In a sense the game plays me as much as I play it. I am in over my head.

The game that I play in interpreting a text is one of question and answer in which my question opens up and illumines the text and the text replies. Because I am an interpreter in a situation, I come to the text with questions that open up what has hitherto lain dormant in the text. Because of the politics of the 1960s, for example, many American interpreters of Marx are discovering the relevance and illumination that he can give in response to the question of aliena- tion.[7] At the same time because of its own structure the text more and more resists certain kinds of interpretations—for example, the notion of the two Marxes, the early humanistic and the later scientific Marx. Among many texts, the emergence of the *Grundrisse* has dealt the death blow to this view of Marx.[8]

The dialogical model that I developed in my discussion on inter- subjectivity seems appropriate again for interpreting interpretation. For the text reveals itself as a genuine other to me, as something to be taken seriously and responded to, not dominated. As in a Platonic dialogue, the idea is neither to refute the text in a one-sided way with- out letting it have its say against me nor to impose in a one-sided way my interpretation on it. Rather, not only do I bring the text into ques- tion but I allow it to bring me into question, my own presuppositions, my own critique, my own sense of what philosophy or poetry or art is. Such interpreting emerges as a back-and-forth movement, a kind of play, in which first one partner and then another has a say. To put it another way: the ideal speech-situation also operates as an ideal in interpretation. Such an ideal forbids all arbitrary imposition, all premature critique, all attempts to win the argument at any cost.[9]

Such serious, playful encounter with the text is possible because the text and I share the common bond of tradition and a language, or, more exactly, we are both in a language and tradition. Because I have learned a language and tradition that have become sedimented in me, part of my lived, habitual past ingressing into my present, I can encounter the text. Because the text is part of the same tradition and the same language, it can relate to me.

As in the relation between subject and object discussed earlier, two historical isolated monads do not encounter one another; the text as historical encounters me as historical, temporal, social, and in the world. Because I am essentially historical, therefore, I can have a past and can encounter the text as past. Because I am essentially historical, the text is other but not alien. I encounter it as part of my world, illuminating and enriching that world. It is this common embeddedness in tradition that Heidegger is getting at in his critique of philosophies of expression. There is a legitimate phenomenological sense to be given to the notion that the tradition speaks through us. Nonetheless, such a recognition entails, not relinquishing the subject, but only qualifying its claims to autonomy and independence from society and history. Such a recognition necessitates, not transcending phenomenology into thought, but transcending transcendental, Cartesian phenomenology into existential and hermeneutical phenomenology.[10]

Using such a phenomenology I can integrate a necessary emphasis on the concept, objectivity, method, and distanciation with an emphasis on thinking as thanking, as open to and beholden to being, as the shepherd of being—questioning is the piety of thinking.[11] Such stances, which Heidegger wishes to situate outside philosophy, I would put inside it. In any philosophical, phenomenological thinking worthy of the name, I am attentive to the evidence, open to the claims of the other, refusing arbitrarily to impose an interpretation on the data, and allowing being to reveal itself in my judgments.

Such chosen openness can be characterized as conformity to the four transcendental precepts "Be attentive, be intelligent, be reasonable, be responsible," corresponding to the four levels of perceptual consciousness, experiencing, understanding, judgment, and decision. The transcendental precepts translated into hermeneutics become a method of interpretation. Contrary to Gadamer and Heidegger, there is no opposition between method and truth, but thoroughgoing reciprocity.[12]

Involved, therefore, in being attentive is the canon of parsimony. Negatively the canon excludes the unverifiable. Positively the canon refers to the experience of the text, its relation to other texts, its own peculiar structure, style, and genre. Just as science excludes the unverifiable, so the interpreter excludes what is not verifiable in his interpretation and what is contradicted by evidence in the text.[13]

Conformity to the precept "Be intelligent" involves striving to reach an account that is as comprehensive as possible. Other things being equal, an interpretation is truer the more of the surface of the text it reveals and explains, and the more consistent that explanation is. Here too one must avoid imposing on the text a consistency that is not there.[14]

Obeying the precept "Be reasonable" means attaining a virtually unconditioned judgment or set of judgments about the text: a judgment is true because its conditions happen to be fulfilled. These conditions arise on the level of experience and understanding. No interpretation will be true that is not verifiable in the data of the text; nor will any interpretation be true that is not consistent and comprehensive. For example, an interpretation of Hamlet as really mad might fail on the level of experience because it ignores the comment warning his friends that he may be feigning madness, and would fail on the level of intelligence because it cannot make sense of or include this comment of Hamlet's. Crucial conditions are lacking for making the virtually unconditioned judgment "Hamlet is really mad."

Being responsible implies not only deliberate conformity to the first three precepts, but essential openness to the text as a "thou." There is a categorical imperative to interpret in such a manner that the integrity of the text, its power of revealing, and its inexhaustibility are respected. I should avoid quick, facile refutations, not letting the author have her say against me, not allowing her to bring me into question, not allowing the strongest version of her position to become manifest. I should also avoid arbitrary impositions of my categories and expectations on the author in such a way that I do not respect her place in history and her relationship to the tradition in which we both participate. Criticizing Aquinas because he does not answer the Cartesian question or Plato because he does not engage in value-free science in the *Republic* is an example of such impositions.[15]

Although the text is present to me as interpreter in my experience, the text is nonetheless other to me. No simple identity but an identity in difference is present, no mere absorption of finite horizons into an absolute horizon but a fusion of horizons.[16] We can talk, therefore, in analogy with the perceived object, about aspects of hermeneutical objectivity and about the criteria for such objectivity.

First of all, in contrast to multiple acts of interpretation of one or many interpreters, there is the one text subject to many interpretations. Consequently there is no exhaustive interpretation of the text any more than there is an exhaustive perception of the thing. There are always further questions to be asked, new aspects to be uncovered, new connections to be made. Because such is the case, any positivist claim to master the text completely is a false one. Any interpretation has to be open to being qualified or corrected by future interpretations.

This gap between the one text or symbol and the inadequate interpretations does not imply that all interpretations are equally adequate or inadequate. Just as an interpretation of the perceived thing is more adequate the more aspects I have perceived, so an interpretation of Kant's *Critique of Pure Reason* that has related it to the other two *Critiques*, to his earlier work, and to the work of his contemporaries such as Leibniz will be more adequate than one that has not. As we have seen, comprehensiveness in relation to the total surface of the texts of an author is one criterion governing the truth of an interpretation, even though such adequacy is never totally attainable.

A second contrast is that between the "thereness" of the text and my "hereness." In addition to the spatial differences between my "here" and the text's "there," however, there is the temporal difference. Its genre, style and language are different from mine because of the time in which it was written. Shakespeare's *Hamlet* could no more be mistaken for twentieth-century English than Kant's *Critique of Pure Reason* could be mistaken for twentieth-century German. Because of such temporal differences, there is an opacity in the text that I have to overcome. The objectification or distanciation of the text makes it available for interpretation, but because such objectification occurs in the author's own time and place, such objectification presents an opacity that I have to overcome in a dialectic of distanciation and appropriation through the use of language, inquiry, and research. I have to work myself into, and make myself at home in, the author's milieu and time.[17]

Just as the "body" here is not an instrument that I use but a presence that I am in relation to the perceived thing, so language is not an instrument but an interpreting that I am in relation to the world. All thinking, we have seen, is essentially expressive and linguistic. Therefore any explicit distancing of myself from a word, sentence, or text in order to objectify it presupposes language as subject. Otherwise we are in an infinite regress; if the language I am thinking with and in were an instrument or object, I would need a second language in order to use that, since a non-linguistic, a non-expressive thought would have no way of making contact with or grabbing hold of a linguistic object. If this second language were an instrument, then I would need a third, and so on.

Not only is the non-instrumentality of language necessary but I experience it. For to confront a text as object is to do so through the medium of a language that is prethematic. Such language I experience as sedimented in me and on the hither side of the subject–object distinction. Just as I confront the perceptual thing through the actions of my body, I confront the text through thinking linguistically. Just as in perceiving, I focus, not on my body but on the thing, so also in reading a text I focus on it, not on some linguistic, thoughtful presence to it. I do not experience language as an intermediary, a third object between myself and the text, any more than I experience the body as a third thing between myself and the object. The body is my conscious, incarnate presence to the perceived world, and language is my thoughtful presence to the text. Again, just as I can turn my body into an explicit object of perception only by presupposing the lived body as subject, so also I can turn individual words, sentences, or paragraphs that I am using into objects of reflection only through language as subject inseparable from my thinking. Language as object is possible only through language as subject.

Moreover, there is the experienced difference between the non-perspectival presence of language to me as subject and the perspectival presence of the text, which never totally reveals itself to me, but like the perceived thing always has hidden, implicit, unexplored aspects. For this reason, any interpretation of a text will be probable, and an interpretation of a text will be truer the more probable it is. Just as our corrected, perceptual version of the "bent stick in the water" is truer than the initial version, so an interpretation of the text that takes into account more of its aspects will be truer, all other things being equal, than one that does not. An interpretation of Husserl that takes into account his discussion of the life-world in the *Crisis* will be truer than one that does not. So also the text of *Hamlet* might make equally plausible and possible an interpretation of feigned or real madness, but exclude an interpretation that Hamlet was neither feigning nor really mad.

Such an account of parsimony does not imply that there is a difference between "seeing" and "seeing as," that I see the passages in Husserl's *Crisis* about the life-world and then interpret. Rather, such "seeing" is already an interpretation of certain letters, words, and sentences. Nonetheless the truth of this interpretation of the section as itself talking about the life-world is subject to the control of the text; such an interpretation is more likely than one interpreting Husserl as saying that Galileo and Descartes were right about secondary qualities. In an interpretation of texts, as in perception, there is no "seeing" without "seeing as," no initial contact with a pure given that is subsequently interpreted.

Because of the perspectival dimension of the text and because of its having been written over a period of time by one author, the text can have gaps, omissions, inconsistencies, contradictions. Just as there is a canon of statistical residues in the physical and social sciences, so there is a canon of residues for interpretation: be prepared for and open to such phenomena in the text. Such an orientation seems to be what Derrida is trying to get at in his concepts of *différance* and deconstruction.[18] The canon of residues will be crucial in reflecting on the psychological and social unconscious, where contradictions in individual and social behavior are present.

Finally, just as I perceive the sensible thing in a context, interpretation relates to the text in a context. In interpretation, though, in contrast to perception, time becomes as important as space in determining context. Essential to the internal gestalt of the text is its relation to contemporaries and past influences, Hegel's relation to Fichte and Kant or Kant's relation to Hume and Leibniz. The text is also related to the future insofar as it asks questions that it does not fully answer, consciously looks forward to future interpretations, and becomes available in its very distanciation to future interpreters.

THE CRITICAL TURN

At this point we have achieved something decisive and important, a turn toward the historical particular, toward tradition, toward interpretation, integrating these with the descriptive and eidetic. That I am being in the world with the eidetic structures of reflection, consciousness, freedom, and intersubjectivity is important and essential, but that I am also in a particular, historical tradition or traditions and know myself through such a tradition is essential as well. Rather than the historical particular being non-essential as Husserl initially posited, the historical becomes essential. Rather than the historical being merely particular, it becomes universal—historicity is a necessary, universal structure of human being in the world. On the other hand, as I showed in Chapter 1, phenomenology as reflection on and orientation to the universally eidetic becomes historical insofar as phenomenology itself grows out of the history of modern philosophy. The true universal is this union of universal and particular, the concrete universal,[19] and a movement back and forth between abstract universal and concrete particular as internally related.

Phenomenology as an enterprise emerged in this book with the reflection on the tradition of modern philosophy culminating in the dialectic between phenomenology and analytic philosophy. We have been reflecting on the condition of the possibility of that kind of reflection on a particular tradition.

Nonetheless another more critical reflection is not only possible but necessary. There is the possibility that the historical traditions themselves are distorted by oppressive social structures such as state socialism or capitalism. Habermas, for example, argues that a merely respectful approach to the text through a hermeneutics of retrieval implies an uncritical abandonment to tradition and is, therefore, unable to distinguish between the tradition as truth-bearing and as ideologically justifying class difference and class domination. Is not the respectful approach to the text as a "thou" excessively passive? Is not the model of dialogue inappropriate when the tradition is implicitly ideological and, therefore, violates the conditions of fruitful dialogue? What seems to be necessary is a critical suspicion in which the repression hidden in various forms of historical communication is articulated and seen through.[20]

In focusing on immediate, experiential contact with the tradition, I discover a weakness in eidetic, descriptive, hermeneutical phenomenology: namely, its inability to focus on or do justice to unconscious personal and social structures not immediately given in experience. In the stressing of individual autonomy, for example, is it not possible that I ignore the extent to which that very individual is an expression of and a product of capitalism, with its stress on individual initiative, private ownership, private profit, and competition? The structures of the capital–labor relationship as they are expressed in the law of value—that the exchange value of a product is determined by abstract labor time—are not immediately present in conscious experience but can be reached only through a process of scientific abstraction and explanation.

What can one defending a phenomenological hermeneutics say about such a criticism? First of all, even if I criticize a tradition, I can criticize it only while presupposing and using that tradition. Habermas in resorting to ideology critique is basing himself on a tradition of philosophy that goes back at least as far as Descartes and extends up through Kant, Hegel, Marx, Adorno, and Marcuse. Through such concepts inherited from that tradition as "alienation," "ideology," "autonomy," and "critique," he can then criticize that tradition. It is impossible to think critically with no inherited language or tradition whatsoever.

My earlier point, therefore, about being in a sedimented context of language over which I have to relinquish complete control applies here as well. Language "thinks me" even when I try to move to the stance of critique, and any attempt to achieve full freedom from tradition lands me in predicaments similar to those discussed in relation to Husserl; the attempt to be presuppositionless is laden with presuppositions such as the prejudice against prejudice. Any philosophy, whether phenomenology or critical theory, has to undergo an historical reduction whereby I uncover roots in history. But such uncovering reveals the impossibility of a complete uncovering that would dissolve all the ambiguity and indeterminacy.

If, for example, I try to uncover the roots of the concept "alienation" in the philosophical tradition, I embark on a task that is endless, that has no clearly defined limits—a task that can take me from early Marx to the Marx of *Capital* to the recently translated *Grundrisse* to various interpretations of it and so on. Or I can go back from Marx to Hegel's *Logic* to his *Phenomenology of Spirit* to his early writings to Kant. And then I can go forward to various interpretations of early Hegel, relationships of early to late Hegel, Kant to Hegel, Hegel to Marx, and so on. Where does one draw the line and say "This far—and no farther"? Where can one say for certain that explanation should come to an end?[21] The point is that any line drawn is arbitrary, beyond which there are always further zones of indeterminacy, questions to be asked, relationships to be explored, texts or aspects of texts to be investigated. Something can be said about all these questions, but whatever I say is only relatively, not fully, adequate to the question, texts, situation.

Moreover, it seems that the Marxist concept of ideology itself, ideology as an inverted distortion of reality arising out of class domination,[22] presupposes two more fundamental notions. First, ideology has the role of integration, which takes the form of justifying and legitimating a country's institutions through interpretation of fundamental institutions and founding acts such as, in the United States, the Declaration of Independence, the American Revolution, and the Constitution. Ideology is to the social project what motive is to the individual act of choice. Ideology both motivates and carries along, is both justification and project.

Ideology in the most fundamental sense also simplifies through slogans, symbols, and maxims. It is on this level that "isms" arise, socialism, capitalism, fascism. However, one should not be too quick to criticize. Such simplification allows ideas to be socially efficacious. Moreover, ideology is less an explicit conception of what human beings think than a context of ideas, symbols, and codes out of which they think. It is this implicit dimension of ideology that makes possible the distortion and dissimulation which Marx describes and of which he is so critical. Because ideology is contextual in this manner, total thematization of ideology is impossible. Also because ideology is part of a history and a tradition, there is a conservative tendency to assimilate new ideas and experiences to this tradition.[23]

A second notion of ideology is that of authority, linked to hierarchical aspects of social organization. All groups founding themselves as groups render themselves socially efficacious through political authority, whether that be oligarchical, monarchical, or democratic. Such authority shares in the opaque, obfuscating character of the first form of authority. "We do not desire it but desire within it." No phenomenon manifests so completely the inertia of ideology as authority. "Each power initiates and repeats anterior power: every prince wants to be Caesar, every Caesar wants to be Alexander, every Alexander wants to Hellenize an oriental despot."[24]

The proper Marxist concept of ideology, ideology as justifying and reflecting a perverted, irrational social world rooted in class domination, presumes the first two senses. Because these two senses are present, no ideology critique can be total and no ideology critique can be totally free of all ideology. Ideology critique shows the impossibility of total ideology critique. But because we not merely belong to tradition but can achieve distanciation or objectification with respect to that tradition, a limited ideology critique is possible. Because it is an ideology critique qualified by an awareness of its embeddedness in ideology in the two more primordial senses, such critique is free of arrogant, totalitarian pretensions.

Not only is tradition compatible with critique, but tradition nourishes critique and critique redeems tradition. Tradition nourishes critique insofar as it gives critique historical ground to stand on, values on which to base a criticism, criteria by which to measure validity, ideals by which to project a future. In the light of America's traditions of democracy and participation, I can criticize, for example, the contradiction between capitalist accumulation and democracy.[25]

Critique also liberates tradition redemptively by unlocking its potentials for transcendence.[26] What I did in Chapter 1, for example, and shall do again in Chapter 9 is to inquire into the history of modern philosophy in order to unlock or unleash elements in that history contributing to a fully adequate dialectical phenomenology. There are elements in phenomenology itself, such as the insights into embodiment, subjectivity, consciousness, language, freedom, and intersubjectivity, that need to be rescued from the clutches of a debilitating capitalism. Tradition is not only something to be seen through and criticized but something to be depended on and redeemed.

Second, I have developed a dialogical model for critique in which four validity claims, comprehensibility, truth, sincerity, and appropriateness, are employed. To say that anything is true implies that my statement is comprehensible and true and that I am sincere in making the claim; otherwise, the dialogue could not go on. Also, it must be appropriate for me to make the statement; participants in the dialogue must be able to test and justify any claims of authority or expertise. As initially present these validity claims are not thematic; nor is the speech situation as such even open to explicit total inspection. Habermas in this model seems to imply that the opposition between dialogue and critique is false.[27]

Third, not only in Habermas' text but in reality the opposition between a hermeneutics of respect and a hermeneutics of suspicion seems false. For such an opposition rests upon a dichotomy between activity and passivity, independence and dependence, autonomy and heteronomy that is false. From the very beginning of our discussions of perception through those on freedom and intersubjectivity we have seen phenomenologically that consciousness is a unity of opposites. On the perceptual level, for example, consciousness is open to what is not itself, yet actively interprets the perceived thing; consciousness is never totally active or strictly passive. Against the extremes of indeterminism and determinism I argued that freedom is motivated: "I choose because. . . ." Freedom is receptive as well as creative, dependent as well as independent. Finally I have argued that in a dialogical situation genuine appeal is possible, in which neither party subjugates nor dominates the other.[28]

All I have to do here is reap the benefits and implications of those analyses. Dialogue, it seems, is characterized by activity and passivity, openness to the other and critique, respect and suspicion. In a discussion with a friend about a performance of Stravinsky's *Rite of Spring*, for example, we may have a very strong disagreement. He might feel like throwing tomatoes, and I might feel like showering roses on the conductor's head. Nevertheless to carry on such a discussion, we both draw on and use a tacit, shared musical understanding and experience. When I mention Beethoven's *Fifth Symphony* as a point of contrast, I can presume he is familiar with the work and does not require elaborate explanation. When I use terms like "fugue" or "sonata" or "tonality," again I do not have to explain these. Or if I did have to explain a term to him or he to me, that explanation itself would depend on further, tacit understanding. This common understanding is the background out of which the figure of explicit discussion emerges.

Now often, of course, explicit disagreement or suspicion does not arise because people work, live, act, and think in a generally harmonious context. Habermas' point is that suspicion may arise and at times should arise. I would agree, but argue that such disagreement goes on within an intersubjectively shared context.

Finally, there is the issue of unconscious psychological and social structures not immediately accessible to direct, phenomenological description. This inaccessibility indicates the limits of such description and the necessity of moving from description to explanatory interpretation. The model of such interpretation that I would propose, drawing on Ricoeur, is understanding→explanation→understanding. Whether encountering a philosophical text, symbols from one's own unconscious, or the "text" of capitalism as a social system, one moves from an initially vague, hypothetical understanding through explanatory social structures to a more comprehensive understanding. The traditional controversy in social science between understanding and explanation is a false one. Explanation deepens understanding. Understanding envelops, grounds, and penetrates explanation as its starting point, context, and goal. As in all phenomenology, it is the experienced subject–world relationship that explanation illumines.[29]

For example, if we share Habermas' concern with understanding a text critically, then we might find it necessary to subject the text itself to ideology critique. To what extent is Descartes' retreat into the subject a manifestation of bourgeois individualism? To what extent does his mind–body dualism reflect a dualism in production between labor and capital, mindless work and mindful, central control and exploitation? As I shall show more fully in Chapters 8 and 9, the law of value as an explanatory structure can contribute to illumining the subject–object encounter between ourselves and the text or between ourselves and capitalism as a social system.

We could use a different example and move from our own experience of being in the world to reflecting on experiences such as slips of the tongue, errors, obsessive neurotic behavior, feelings of inferiority, and so on. As experienced, these do not have their adequate account in consciously described and present eidetic structures. Rather, as I shall show more fully in the next chapter, the explanatory categories of "id," "ego" and "superego" must be developed and verified. Once I have performed this task, then they can become part of my life-world as a whole illumining it and enriching it. I experience and understand my life-world illumined by these categories of the personal unconscious.

As I argued in the chapter on perception and reflection, there is similarly a process of moving from experience to initially vague preconceptual insight into that experience—the suspicion that there might be something in my unconscious sexual past that is determining me to behave in such a way—to conception or definition of categories, such as "id," "ego," and "superego"—to verification of these in psychoanalytic experience. Explanatory definition and insight are the final working out and expression of understanding, and understanding finds its own proper completion and expression in such definition and verification.

Thus there is both continuity and discontinuity between explanation in the physical–mathematical and the social sciences. There is continuity insofar as the same cognitional structure and process are present in both kinds of endeavor—experience, understanding, and judgment. In this respect, understanding a circle or a free fall is the same as understanding a text or a social system. There is difference insofar as the initial data into which I inquire are different: in one case, sensibly perceived objects; in the other, symbols, objects, and institutions produced by human beings, or groups of human beings. Because these latter kinds of data are ambiguous and many-leveled in meaning, the criteria for understanding and verification are ambiguous rather than exact, qualitative rather than quantitative. Because the field of experience into which I inquire is specifically different in both cases, some criteria appropriate to one sphere are not appropriate to another. Skinner's hypothesis about no inner life may be appropriate for physical objects, but it is definitely not appropriate for human beings. Consequently the pre-understanding that guides the social scientist is or should be different from that which guides the physical scientist. The former is guided by a pre-understanding of the world as a human world filled with interiority; the latter can dispense with considerations of such interiority as irrelevant to his inquiry.

It is not enough, therefore, for philosophy as phenomenology to reflect on our prescientific belonging to the world as distinct from our scientific explanation of it. Stopping at that point would leave us in an intolerable dualism of explanation vs. understanding, method vs. truth. What has to occur is reflection on belonging and distanciation, understanding and explanation, pre-reflective and reflective awareness. In such reflection both moments cease to be absolute as moments and become parts of a total life-world. Both prescientific understanding and science itself become partial projects within the total project of the life-world or being. Because distanciation or objectification is an essential aspect of hermeneutics, critique and explanation are possible, but they are never total because they rest upon an initial, primordial belonging to the life-world, to history, and to tradition that I can never totally thematize. Ambiguity in a good, creative sense is always with us.[30]

CONCLUSION

I have argued in this chapter for the necessity and possibility of both interpretation and critique in hermeneutical phenomenology, though I have not yet fully executed such a critique; that is the task in the next three chapters. The chapters on Freud's personal unconscious and Marx's social unconscious will have three functions: to serve as examples of suspicion in hermeneutics, to expand our analysis into wider, higher viewpoints whereby consciousness is integrated with first a personal and then a social unconscious, and finally and fully to overcome Cartesianism on the level of subjective spirit and from within phenomenology. What finally has to go is the myth of an autonomous ego fully immune from any influence of the unconscious or society. The self is finally fully placed in the world in relationship to all its myriad aspects. Isolated, individualistic autonomy is out; being in the world is in.

I also conclude that the initial distinction between interpretation and description, made in Chapter 1, has to be qualified. Description was understood as description of experience; interpretation, as understanding of particular, historical texts or symbols. Yet because all experience is mediated by tradition and language, no description is free of such experiences. Because all interpretation is interpretation of symbols arising out of personal or collective experience, no interpretation is possible apart from experience. In a certain sense, all describing is an "interpreting as," and all interpreting is a descriptive response to what is given.

Moreover, the dichotomy between interpretation and critique is false. Because all interpretation involves a "seeing through" of the way the symbol initially presents itself, all interpretation is at least inchoately critique. Because all critique is a "seeing through" that is also an interpretation of the symbol or text in question, all critique is interpretation. Finally, since eidetic description is mediated by interpretation and interpretation by critique, eidetic description is mediated by critique. Hermeneutics is the crucial middle term between eidetic description and critique.

To insist on these interrelationships, however, is not to deny a distinction among eidetic description, interpretation, and critique. In its object, the traditional symbol or text, interpretation is not the same as eidetic description, the object of which is the given human experience. Interpretation is oriented to understanding the particular symbol or text in question; eidetic description, the universal, essential structure of experience. Also, the emphasis, on the particular symbol or text in the one instance and on conscious experience in the other, is different. Interpretation is relatively mediate, whereas description is relatively immediate. Interpretation emphasizes the past within a dynamic temporal continuum, whereas description focuses on the present. Of course, past, present, and future are present as internally related aspects of time in both interpretation and description, but a different modality of time is explicit and thematic in each.

This difference in initial data, goal, emphasis, degree of immediacy, and temporal modality also applies to the difference between critique and description and critique and interpretation. Critique is oriented to and emphasizes the symbol, text, or particular personal or social system as particular and as mediated, whereas description focuses on human experience as universally structured and as relatively immediate. In contrast to interpretation that approaches the tradition sympathetically, critique approaches it suspiciously. In contrast to interpretation's emphasis on what is present to conscious experience, albeit in a more mediated manner than description, critique is oriented to those unconscious personal or social structures present in neither an immediate nor a mediate manner to conscious experience. Finally, the temporal modality is different for each.

As one moves from description through interpretation to critique, therefore, there is an increasing degree of mediation, an increasing degree of activity in relation to the given, a greater play given to praxis. As I have indicated before, praxis includes labor, artistic creativity, and symbolic interaction, as well as theory used with a critical intent. Such theory, as we saw in Chapter 4, is rooted in transcendental method as the most fundamental form of praxis. Transcendental method, then, would have three different meanings. As eidetic, it would simply include the *a priori* structures, noetic and noematic, of human beings in the world. Such abstract universals would mediate but not be reducible to the hermeneutical, in its narrow sense of retrieval, and the critical. There are two senses in which transcendental method includes the hermeneutical and the critical, the noetically formal and the union of noesis and noematic, content and form, universal and particular. As noetic and formal, transcendental method is reflection on the necessary, *a priori* connection among eidetics, interpretation, and critique. In this sense, I am practicing transcendental method in this conclusion. As a union of noesis and noema, content and form, universal and particular, transcendental method is the concrete universal. In this most controversial use of the term "transcendental method," I approach Hegel, but the reader should always remember that my concrete universal is chastened by a sense of ambiguity, of the limits of knowledge, of an open indeterminate future.[31]

What critique points toward is transformation of the given. But if transformation of the given is not to be totalitarian and violent, it has to be motivated by a descriptive and interpretative respect for the given. We thus have a circle of description, interpretation, and critique pointing toward transformation, each mediating the others, each incomplete and inadequate without the others. Description without interpretation is naïve, interpretation without critique is dogmatic, critique without description is groundless, description without critique is ideological.[32]

Just as in one sense we can speak about a movement upward from description to suspicion toward greater mediation, so in another sense we can speak about a movement downward from eidetic description through interpretation to a critique culminating in praxis. Eidetic description allows us to illumine the most general, abstract aspects of human beings in the world; interpretation is more specific and concrete; and critique is the most concrete of all because it is concerned with personal and social transformative praxis. The partisans of praxis, therefore, have a point against a philosophy that wishes to remain merely abstract and contemplative and to ignore praxis. Such a philosophy remains incomplete even as theory.

On the other hand, what devotees of praxis often miss is that eidetic description and hermeneutics have their own rights and their own criteria that cannot be reduced to political, ethical praxis. Eidetics and hermeneutics are enriching abstractions that lead up to and prepare the way for such critique and praxis. Not only is such contemplation worthwhile in itself for what I learn about myself and my world, but it is necessary for a political praxis that is informed, nondogmatic, and non-arbitrary. We have to avoid the temptation of reacting to a one-sided academic contemplation by an equally one-sided negation. Dialectical phenomenology as a differentiated unity of description, interpretation, and critique avoids such one-sidedness.[33]

NOTES

1. See Paul Ricoeur, *Freud and Philosophy*, trans. Denis Savage (New Haven: Yale University Press, 1970), pp. 80–86, for the definitions of retrieval and suspicion that I use in this book. As Ricoeur suggests, the three great masters of suspicion are Nietzsche, Marx, and Freud. Part of the originality of this work is my attempt in Chapters 8 and 9 to develop the Marxist, critical theoretical form of suspicion more than Ricoeur did in the framework of a hermeneutical phenomenology.

2. Gadamer, *Truth and Method*, pp. 153–214, 235–53.

3. Ricoeur, *Interpretation Theory*, pp. 8–44; the quotation is found on p. 12. See also J. L. Austin's *How To Do Things with Words*, edd. J. O. Urmson and Marina Sbisa, 2nd ed. (Cambridge: Harvard University Press, 1975), pp. 94–120, for the original distinction in locutionary, illocutionary, and perlocutionary acts.

4. Ricoeur, *Interpretation Theory*, pp. 8–44; and "The Hermeneutical Function of Distanciation," *Philosophy Today*, 17 (1973), 129–41.

5. Ricoeur, "Hermeneutical Function of Distanciation," 134–35. For the distinction between implied and real author, see Wayne C. Booth, *The Rhetoric of Fiction*, 2nd ed. (Chicago: The University of Chicago Press, 1983), pp. 70–86.

6. Gadamer, *Truth and Method*, pp. 91–119.

7. See, for example, Bertell Ollman, *Alienation: Marx's Conception of Man in Capitalist Society* (Cambridge: Cambridge University Press, 1971).

8. See Ollman, *Alienation*; Istvan Meszaros, *Marx's Theory of Alienation* (New York: Harper & Row, 1970); Roslyn Wallach Bologh, *Dialectical Phenomenology: Marx's Method* (London: Routledge & Kegan Paul, 1979); Karl Marx, *Grundrisse*, trans. Martin Nicolaus (New York: Vintage, 1973).

9. Gadamer, *Truth and Method*, pp. 325–41.

10. Ibid., pp. 345–66. Heidegger, *On the Way to Language*, pp. 57–108.

11. Heidegger, *Question Concerning Technology*, p. 35.

12. Gadamer, *Truth and Method*, p. xi. Heidegger, *On the Way to Language*, pp. 74–75. Lonergan, *Method in Theology*, pp. 3–25.

13. See Chapter 3, p. 84, for a discussion of parsimony in science.

14. Ibid., p. 84, for a discussion of comprehensiveness in scientific inquiry.

15. Gadamer, *Truth and Method*, pp. 325–33.

16. Ibid., pp. 273–74, 337–41, 358.

17. Ricoeur, *Interpretation Theory*, pp. 89–94.

18. See Chapter 3, p. 84, for my discussion of the canon of statistical residues, and Lonergan's *Insight*, pp. 590–94. On Derrida's notions of *différance* and deconstruction, see translator Gayatri Chakrovorty Spivaks' Preface to Derrida's *Of Grammatology* (Baltimore: The Johns Hopkins University Press, 1974), especially pp. xliii–l; see also Derrida's text, pp. 53, 68, 70, 72. Jacques Derrida, *Margins of Philosophy*, trans. Alan Bass (Chicago: The University of Chicago Press, 1982), pp. 3–27.

19. For his notion of the concrete universal, see Hegel, *Logic of Hegel*, pp. 287–97.

20. Jürgen Habermas, "A Review of Gadamer's *Truth and Method*," in *Understanding and Social Inquiry*, edd. Fred Dallmayr and Thomas McCarthy (Notre Dame: University of Notre Dame Press, 1977), pp. 335–63.

21. Wittgenstein, *Investigations*, pp. 36–37.

22. See Karl Marx and Friedrich Engels, *German Ideology, with Supplementary Texts*, ed. C. J. Arthur (New York: International, 1981), p. 47, for this description of ideology.

23. Paul Ricoeur, *Hermeneutics and the Human Sciences*, ed. and trans. John B. Thompson (Cambridge: Cambridge University Press, 1981), pp. 225–28.

24. Ibid., pp. 228–29.

25. Ibid., pp. 229–46. For explorations of the contradiction between capitalism and democracy, see Charles Lindbloom, *Politics and Markets* (New York: Basic Books, 1977), pp. 161–233. On such a contradiction in the United States, see Alan Wolfe, *The Limits of Legitimacy: Political Contradictions of Contemporary Capitalism* (New York: Free Press, 1977).

26. On the notion of a redemptive criticism in relation to tradition, see Richard Wolin's excellent book *Walter Benjamin: An Aesthetic of Redemption* (New York: Columbia University Press, 1982).

27. Habermas, *Theory and Practice*, pp. 17–19; and *Zur Logik der Socialwissenschaften* (Frankfurt: Suhrkamp, 1970), pp. 281–89.

28. Ricoeur, *Hermeneutics and the Human Sciences*, pp. 87–100.

29. Paul Ricoeur, "Explanation and Understanding," in *The Philosophy of Paul Ricoeur*, edd. Charles E. Reagan and David Stewart (Boston: Beacon, 1978), pp. 149–66. See also Lonergan, *Insight*, pp. 291–92, 332–35, 394–95, 587–88, for the necessary reciprocity between description and explanation.

30. Ricoeur, "Explanation and Understanding," pp. 156–66.

31. See Chapter 1, p. 33.

32. One could ask, however, whether the required personal and social transformation is reformist or radical. The answer, first of all, has to be that whether one is reformist or revolutionary depends on the situation. If the neurotic individual is only slightly neurotic, then reformist measures might be enough. On the other hand, if the individual is deeply psychotic, more drastic measures might be called for. Similar points could be made about the social, political sphere. Dialectical phenomenology has to be open to both possibilities and cannot exclude either, at the price of being obscurantist. I shall argue in Chapters 8 and 9 that our historical situation makes a radical suspicion of our social situation the more adequate interpretation, but even if I am wrong—and my argument is certainly disputable—one cannot deny the necessity of a moment of suspicion in philosophy and phenomenology without mutilating both.

33. David Tracy, *The Analogical Imagination* (New York: Crossroad, 1981), pp. 69–79. As should also be obvious, I am using interpretation here in the more narrow sense of retrieval of a tradition, the sense stressed in the first part of this chapter. The broader, more inclusive sense of interpretation or hermeneutics includes suspicion and retrieval as moments of itself. See Ricoeur, *Freud and Philosophy*, pp. 20–36.

7

Hermeneutics of Suspicion I: The Personal Unconscious

A HEAD OF THE BOARD opens a meeting by saying "I declare the meeting closed." After having been through a painful experience in Stockholm, a woman forgets a word associated in her mind with that experience. A man forgets where he put a gift from his wife, from whom he feels alienated, and rediscovers the item some time later, when he feels loving toward her. A woman recently married sees her husband on the opposite side of the street and, forgetting momentarily that he is her husband, refers to him as "Mr. K."[1] Another man, a scientist, who is about to marry the love of his life, forgets that it is his wedding day and goes to his laboratory instead.

Such consciously experienced phenomena have in common that they are inexplicable according to available, positively scientific methods or descriptive phenomenology. I cannot explain slips of the tongue, errors, and misplacing objects simply through inattention because they occur even with full attention or the effort to be attentive. Nor can I account for such errors by fatigue because they occur even when I am fresh. Even if such errors occur while I am fatigued, still I need to explain the reason why they take the particular form that they do take. Why do I forget this word rather than another? Why do I mislay the gift from my friend? Why do I declare the meeting closed rather than declaring it prolonged or shortened?

For these reasons I consider and affirm the hypothesis of an unconscious, a dimension of psychic life that is completely unconscious, neither conscious nor preconscious, explicit nor implicit, thematic nor prethematic. Because such an unconscious is repressed and forgotten, I have to recover it through an active remembering in psychoanalysis. It seems not only that some mental life is unconscious but also that sexual impulses, in both the narrow genital sense and the broader sense of organ pleasure, play an important part in the psychic life of human beings and contribute to the highest cultural, artistic, and social achievements. When I look at and reflect upon not only errors, slips of the tongue, and forgetting, but also dreams and neuroses, I discover the libido—the force by which the sexual instinct achieves expression—to be the most important unconscious element. Because the productive economic work of society needs to be done with efficiency and discipline, this libido is to a greater or lesser extent repressed. Discipline is the business of the important daylight hours; erotic play is reserved for evenings or weekends.[2]

The evidence that Freud uses to establish the sexual nature of the psyche is massively documented. Not only are symbols such as pens and sticks standing for the male organ and houses and chapels standing for the female organ shown repeatedly to be sexual in folklore, literature, jokes, and psychoanalytic practice, but analysis of neuroses and dreams especially also demonstrate this sexuality. In the course of psychoanalysis a woman suffering from a delusion of jealousy toward her husband, who is and has been extremely faithful to her, reveals herself as sexually desirous of a younger man. The jealousy is a means of dealing with her own guilt; if her husband is unfaithful, then she does not have to feel as guilty for having such desires. If he is playing around, then so can she.

A man dreaming about riding a bicycle in Tübingen and being bitten by a dachshund in front of two grinning ladies reveals in the course of analysis that he had fallen in love with a girl recently who owned a dachshund. She always walked the dog, and he conceived the idea of meeting her through her dog. He has eliminated her from the manifest content of the dream, and the two old ladies are probably representations of her.[3]

Phenomenology as we have defined it up to this point approaches but does not equal psychoanalysis. A first way in which phenomenology approximates psychoanalysis is that phenomenology in the reduction breaks with the natural attitude, with what obviously seems to be so, and discovers consciousness as the source of meaning. Psychoanalysis also moves from immediately present phenomena such as slips of the tongue toward a less obvious explanation.

Involved in this first kind of approach is an awareness even in phenomenology of what is not directly experienced but merely co-intended: the other side of the thing, the past, the future, the interiority of the other person. Because of this first kind of "unconsciousness," the possibility of error, of ambiguity, of self-deception is introduced.

We take a second step toward the Freudian unconscious when we discover the notion of intentionality. Such intentionality is not merely explicit awareness of an object but implicit awareness of ourselves as subjects in the world. Because I am always implicitly present to myself in this way, I can never achieve complete total self-representation; I am always going to be somewhat opaque to myself. Such presence to myself is awareness of myself as being in the world, as embodied, as ecstatically outside myself. We saw earlier how the body functions as a source of ambiguity, confused motivation, and lack of clarity, making any totally clear, apodictic presence to self impossible.[4]

We take a third step when we remember that language is a dialectic of presence and absence, absent to things by intending them with empty intentions and present to things through the very emptiness of signs. Signs themselves are present and absent because they mean something only by their contrast with other signs in a language—a vowel with other vowels, words with other words, and so on. "Black" has meaning only in its relation of difference and constrast to "blue," "red," "green," and so on. Such a dialectic of presence and absence is presumed in psychoanalysis where words in dreams refer to something repressed and forgotten, and one can mourn a lost object. Here we can see how the "ambiguity of things becomes the model of all ambiguity in general and of all the forms of intentionality."[5]

Fourth, there is an approximation of phenomenology to psychoanalysis through intersubjectivity. All our relationships to the world have an intersubjective character. As initially experienced, intersubjectivity is lived pre-reflectively, not thematized reflectively. For this reason we are not surprised when we learn that desire is intersubjective from the very beginning, desire of the boy for his mother or of the daughter for her father.[6]

As close as eidetic, descriptive phenomenology may seem to analysis, the two disciplines are very far apart on the same issues. First, phenomenology is a reflexive discipline reducing all phenomena to objects for consciousness. Psychoanalysis is a suspicion directed toward the autonomy of consciousness itself. Phenomenology's *epoche* is an act of freedom whereby suspicion is directed toward the natural attitude; psychoanalysis is a reflection aiming to show our unfreedom and bondage to the unconscious. Phenomenology is a centripetal movement from the externalized, extroverted natural attitude into the interiority of consciousness; psychoanalysis is a centrifugal movement out from consciousness, a displacing of consciousness from its privileged center in favor of the unconscious.[7]

Second, the model of intentionality gives us at best a dialectic of implicit and explicit on the level of consciousness itself. The implicit remains preconscious in the Freudian sense, but not fully unconscious. The notion of repression, which is important in interpreting dreams and neuroses, points to a region inaccessible to direct phenomenological description that cannot be described but only interpreted. The condensation of dreams, whereby one symbol can mean many objects, and displacement, whereby the wished-for or hated object is presented in distorted, symbolic guise, indicate the operation of a censor. Such a censor is engaged in repressing wishes, mostly of a sexual nature, that do not fit in easily with reality. The seething cauldron of the id's sexual desire is not directly given, but only inferred as necessary to explain the consciously experienced realities such as errors, slips of the tongue, forgetting, dreams, and neuroses.

There are many examples in Freud's writings of interpretations leading to the positing of an unconscious. Besides those mentioned in the first few paragraphs of this chapter, another is that of a woman dreaming that she and her husband are at a theater, one side of the stalls is empty, and her husband is telling her that Elise L. and her fiancé also wished to come but could get only bad seats, three for a florin and a half. When put in the context of other facts disclosed in psychoanalytic encounter, such as the recent engagement of Elise, Elise's being the same age as she, and her own booking of tickets early, these data lead to the interpretation that the dreamer feels that she married too early. "Too early" and "too late" play a prominent role in the latent content of the dream content, as does the theater, an imaginative substitute in the dream for getting married.[8]

If language is a key to understanding the language of the unconscious, there are at the same time sharp differences between phenomenology and psychoanalysis in their approaches to language. Dreams, for example, in their aspects of displacement, condensation, and contradictoriness, saying "yes" and "no" at the same time, do not follow a logic of ordinary, conscious discourse. Rather, what happens in the case of displacement, for example, is that a content is admitted into consciousness at the same time as I keep it outside consciousness. The father I would like to kill appears in my dream as another man; the mother I would like to sleep with appears in my dream in the form of a female teacher.[9]

Finally, if the intersubjective relationship is where phenomenology most approximates psychoanalysis, it is also where the two enterprises most sharply diverge. For the psychoanalytic encounter is not simply a playful exercise in interpretation akin to philosophy but a therapy that takes the form of struggle and a remembering that takes the form of overcoming resistance. Because dreams and other phenomena of the unconscious are not simply meaningful but also energic, psychoanalysis is a mixed discourse of meaning and force. Dreams not only mean something but express something of the forces of id and superego. Consequently psychoanalysis is not only an interpretation but an overcoming of resistance.

Crucial to such overcoming of resistance on the part of the patient is the phenomenon of transference, the patient's turning the psychoanalyst into a love or hate object. This part of psychoanalytic treatment functions as both a means of overcoming earlier resistance and a final resistance itself. It functions as an overcoming of resistance insofar as the conflicts from the past are experientially lived through in the psychoanalytic encounter and thus become visible. Transference functions as a resistance insofar as the relationship with the psychoanalyst becomes one final evasion or substitute gratification, which the patient must refuse by taking responsibility for her own projections and resistances.[10]

The move to a Freudian hermeneutic, therefore, is one that displaces consciousness as a center and places the accent on the unconscious. Freud's is an anti-phenomenology dealing a third blow, after those of Copernicus and Darwin, to the narcissism of human beings. At the same time as he deals narcissism a severe blow, Freud discovers the unconscious roots of such narcissism in the self's love for itself. Freud ceases to define the unconscious in relation to consciousness, but rather defines the unconscious topographically as a locality in which ideas or representations reside. Finally, the "object" means no longer the object of consciousness but the aim of an instinct.[11]

Freud, therefore, leads us to a realism of the unconscious that determines whatever we experience consciously. Freedom, seemingly so secure a possession of the immediate Cartesian, Husserlian, and Sartrean ego, seems from the Freudian perspective to be an illusion.[12] We get at such natural forces of the unconscious through a scientific approach conceived on the model of the natural sciences—science is an effort to understand phenomena, establish a connection between them, and whenever possible increase our control over them.[13]

Nonetheless such a reductionism is self-defeating and self-refuting. First of all, as we saw in Chapter 4, determinism is self-refuting. A total determinism of the unconscious would have to posit any conscious motive as illusory. However, such a determinism undermines any attempt at making claims, even that of psychoanalysis itself. For a truth claim has to appeal to evidence in order to ground itself as true; since all evidence for truth is conscious, all evidence would have to be illusory if determinism were true. Not the conscious reasons I have for making a claim are the real ones, but the subconscious reasons. If determinism were true, psychoanalysis could make no truth claims itself, since its own real reasons for making such claims would themselves be illusions, hiding the real reasons. Consciousness can announce itself as deceived only before a consciousness that is at least implicitly undeceived and rational. Also, as I have shown in the chapter on freedom, making a truth claim implies the relationship of that claim to possible falsity, and possible falsity implies freedom.

Second, the very process of psychoanalysis is a process of making the unconscious conscious. "Where id was, there ego shall be."[14] Through analysis the patient becomes aware of her own unconscious repressions and resistances and moves to a broader, deeper knowledge of herself. She reintegrates the part of herself that she has been blocking off. Consciousness in a narrow sense, conceived as opposed to the unconscious, consciously comprehends and integrates this unconscious with itself. Consciousness in the full sense is a unity of the unconscious and consciousness.

Third, the movement from genital to erotic sexuality, in which the whole of the person is related to the whole of himself and the whole of other persons integrally, is possible only to the extent that the ego freely takes over libidinal impulses, diverts them from their original aim, and directs them toward new objects. Sublimation would be impossible for a totally determined ego with no autonomy of its own. Such an eroticizing of human life through sublimation presents again a progressive, forward-moving unifying of consciousness and the unconscious.[15]

Fourth, there is a dialectic of identification such that in the son's intersubjective encounter with father and mother in the Oedipal situation, the son introduces the mother into the psyche as a love object and the father as an idealized authority figure. There is a forward movement here, a teleology of desire, which presupposes that desire is intersubjective from the beginning and not solipsistic as Freud at times indicates.[16] Because mother and father are persons to whom the son relates, essentially and not accidentally, the introduction of the mother and father into the psyche causes the emergence of the superego as a further step in the dynamics of intersubjectivity.

Fifth, we have to avoid the danger of a reductionism of all in the unconscious to the sexual. Freud wavers on this issue, arguing at times that the meaning of all neuroses is sexual and at times that the meaning of all dreams is not sexual.[17] To such reductionism or tendencies to reductionism, there are several counter-arguments. (a) If my phenomenology of the person is correct up to this point, there is non-reducibility of higher forms of reflection and freedom to the body. These levels are founded on but not reducible to the body.

(b) In many psychic phenomena, such as slips of the tongue, forgetting, dreams, and so on, the sexual dimension plays an important role, but not the only role. Slips of the tongue such as "I declare the meeting closed" can be rooted in ambition as well as sexual desire, and dreams such as giving a paper that is well received before a group of philosophers can be rooted in a legitimately ambitious freedom as well as sexuality.

(c) To complement an archaeology that would reduce all to the sexual, a hermeneutics needs to develop a teleology that does justice to the human vocation to reflection and freedom.[18] I can interpret Hamlet, for example, archaeologically by showing the Oedipal relations among mother, father, stepfather, and son; and such an interpretation is legitimate up to a certain point and does shed light on the play. However, there is much in *Hamlet* that is not reducible to such an interpretation. The play in its soliloquies, in the contrast of Hamlet with Fortinbras, and much of its action, such as Hamlet's refusing to kill Claudius at prayer or Hamlet's very decisive killing of Rosencrantz and Guildenstern, expresses the dilemma of a freedom at odds with itself, desiring too much certainty, and unwilling to take the risks that decision demands.

(*d*) There is in Freud himself a contradiction between an explicit positivism and an implicit hermeneutics present in the practice of psychoanalysis itself. Psychoanalytic experience is not a sensible object but the encounter between patient and analyst. Truth is a saying of the truth in which the person comes through reflection on herself to recognize herself in the course of the psychoanalytic process. In the next section of this chapter, I shall develop the precise meaning and status of psychoanalytic method.[19]

The result, therefore, of our critical reflection here is a transcending of the notion of a Husserlian pure consciousness with a notion of consciousness as mediated by the unconscious. Consciousness has left its own secure abode, gone outside itself, lost itself, and returned to itself. What has been restored is a relative, not an absolute, autonomy and independence. With such mediation a model of phenomenology emerges as a unity of Husserlian and Freudian perspectives.

This recovery of the self allows us justifiably to be skeptical of premature "death of self" or "death of man" talk, to the extent that is justified by psychoanalysis. Lacan, for example, shows very well that the Cartesian ego has to be given up in the light of unconscious desire. He makes very well the negative move from such an ego to unconscious desire; what he does not execute is the positive dialectical recovery of the self, as unity of conscious and unconscious, rationality and desire.[20]

FACT, METHOD, AND PROOF IN PSYCHOANALYSIS

There are five criteria of a fact in psychoanalysis. First of all, as I have already remarked, such truth is sayable through language. Second, I say such truth to another person. Through such processes as transference, I play out the essentially intersubjective nature of desire in the course of analysis itself. The analyst helps me to liberate myself critically and freely from the constrictions and illusions of the past—psychoanalysis is hermeneutical, critical social science and practice, not a positive science. Any attempt to force me into a mere adjustment to an alienating social situation violates this thrust toward liberation.[21]

Third, there is a working through of fantasies. Fantasy, rather than being irrelevant to the facts as in normal positive science, is the relevant psychical fact or an important part of it. More important than whether a fantasy such as castration is true is the role it plays in the person's behavior. The patient has to live through and see through abandoned objects, substituted objects, and mourning over a lost object. Indeed, mourning is part of the praxis or labor of psychoanalysis that situates the object on the level of the imaginary in order to understand it in relation to the person's real past and present life. Psychoanalytically relevant is what a person makes of her fantasies as she moves from the fantasy as alienating to the fantasy as symbolically founding an undivided identity.[22]

A fourth criterion for a psychoanalytic fact is narrativity. The patient must be able to reconstruct his life history as a unified, coherent story that is both accurate and comprehensive. To the extent that the story is incomplete, partial, fragmented, or inconsistent, it fails to meet this test. To the extent that there are events in the patient's life history that the story does not explain or that contradict the story, it is unsuccessful as an interpretation. Here again the verification is not any objective look at objective facts but the self-reflection and remembering of the patient.[23]

A fifth criterion is that a fact is in a context of contradiction, tension, depression, self-division. Either the fact itself is contradictory, as when I both love and hate my father, or it is part of a larger contradictory whole, as when my apparent or real fear of failure is related to and grounded in a love of failure. This fifth criterion represents the psychoanalytic translation of the canon of residues.[24]

Because of the above dimensions of a fact in psychoanalysis, any behavioristic, positivistic interpretation of psychoanalysis misses the boat; what goes on in the analytic situation is a significant counter-instance to a behavioristic, positivistic interpretation of experience and invalidates any such interpretation of psychoanalysis itself. The behaviorist or positivist can, of course, reject psychoanalysis because it does not conform to rigid, empirical criteria. Such an approach not only is question begging but rests upon an impoverished notion of experience that the whole of this book overturns. If Husserl is correct in saying that phenomenology is the true positivism,[25] then a phenomenology that is both eidetic and hermeneutical gives a more comprehensive, nuanced account of experience than either a strictly Husserlian or a strictly objective, empirical approach.

Performing the equivalent in psychoanalysis of the rules of interpretation or translation connecting observation with theory in the physical sciences is the triangular relation of a procedure of investigation, a method of treatment, and a theory. Investigatory procedure tends to give preference to relations of meaning between and among phenomena, while method of treatment tends to give preference to relations of force between systems. Theory integrates these two aspects of physical reality. Investigatory procedure treats all phenomena to be interpreted, such as dreams, jokes, neuroses, and so on, as texts to be deciphered. Treatment, however, has to deal with experiences of resistance, regression, and repression, and to overcome them. Because the analytic situation is one in which both meaning and force operate, Freud's language goes back and forth between translation metaphors and energy metaphors, and theory has to resolve the apparent inconsistency. The theory functions to explain what occurs not only in individual psychological behavior, but in psychoanalytic experience.

The notion of the superego, for example, arises to explain the phenomenon of resistance and repression as that comes out in the psychoanalytic encounter. The id arises to account for what it is that one is afraid of and is trying to repress, and the ego is the agency that mediates between the id and superego, the self and the external world. At the same time this theory of the self helps to explain the origin of meanings in dreams and neuroses. That many dreams have a sexual meaning, for example, is explained by the id, that such meaning is distorted and repressed is explained by the superego, and that such distortion is overcome in the process of interpretation is explained by the ego.[26]

What counts as a good explanation in psychoanalysis? First of all, the facts must correspond to the theory and vice versa. Freudian theory is an attempt to do justice to both the energic and the meaningful dimensions of the psychoanalytic experience. A fact that does not correspond to the theory would force an eventual qualification or rejection of the theory as a theory. It might seem, at first, for example, that the claim that all dreams are wish-fulfillments has a counter-example in nightmares, but further reflection discloses that nightmares confirm the point. (*a*) Dreams are not wholly successful in carrying out wishes because of the censorship. In that respect there is a sense of pain or deprivation, as in the case of a dreamer whose dream of drinking leaves his thirst unslaked.

(*b*) On account of the censorship the fulfillment of a wish can create anxiety in the dreamer, because she is carrying out a wish, killing her mother or marrying her father, that her superego forbids. (*c*) Because of the role of the superego there may be a desire to punish herself for certain deeds or wishes.[27]

A second main criterion of a good psychoanalytic explanation is that there must be intratextual and extratextual consistency. Not only must there be an inner consistency of the new text substituted by means of translation for the unreadable text of symptoms and dreams, but there must be consistency along analogical lines with other phenomena such as jokes, puns, tales, and so on. An account of a neurosis, for example, as rooted in rejection by the father must explain not only dreams and neurotic symptoms but also these other phenomena that have their roots in the unconscious.

A third criterion, relatively independent of the first two, is that the explanation must be economically satisfactory. The patient must be able to "work through" in terms of his own practice and emotionally accept a proposed explanation or account. Otherwise the solution remains merely intellectual, and a merely intellectual solution is no solution at all. Crucial to psychoanalytic praxis is a remembering that is both true and effective.

A fourth criterion, relatively independent of the first three, is narrativity. An explanation must satisfy the general conditions of acceptability that are present in any story, historical or fictional. The story has to be followable and in that sense self-explanatory. In a good story there should be few if any shadowy places, inconsistencies, unexplained data, experiences that the patient is unable to accept. Rather, if a particular interpretation is true, she is able to accept it as her story.[28]

THE DIALECTICAL CHARACTER OF PSYCHOANALYSIS

As should be obvious by now, there are several different ways in which psychoanalysis is dialectical. First of all, the human psyche is a playground of opposites: conscious and unconscious, id and super-ego, ego and id, repression and expression, spontaneous and controlled, irrational and rational, self and other, male and female, hidden and revealed, pleasure principle and reality principle. Initially in the process of psychoanalysis these are split off from one another.

Second, a genuine sublation in the Hegelian sense occurs that both preserves and negates. Psychoanalysis retains elements from the unconscious and consciousness, but restores them on a higher viewpoint in a new unity. Psychoanalysis rejects, however, the one-sided, repressed character of the unconscious, and posits a new higher unity of consciousness and the unconscious.

Third, there is dialectical interaction, struggle, and encounter between patient and analyst. In the process of transference and taking it back, the patient leaves himself, goes out to the analyst, and takes back into himself what he is projecting. In so doing, he takes responsibility for his own projections. If, for example, his neurosis takes the form of being a victim or anticipating rejection by perceiving others as excessively critical of him, he begins to see that he is responsible for being a victim and for being self-critical. He has to realize that, in the areas where his neurosis operates, he is his own worst enemy. The perceived hostility and criticism of the external social world, if rightly understood, are projections of his own superego.

Fourth, the phenomena investigated by psychoanalysis are dialectical in many different ways. Sublimation, for example, in which I divert a wish with an immediately sexual object to a higher aim, is characterized by retention of the initial sexual energy, rejection of the immediately sexual aim, and integration into a higher unity. Wishes can have opposite forms in consciousness from what they are unconsciously. Love of the other can take the form of hating the other; desire to fail and desire for sexual intercourse can take the form of fear of failure or anxiety in experiencing sexual desire. Contraries can express the same element, displacement can be present in which one image stands for reality other than itself, and condensation can occur in which one image or symbol stands for many objects or persons. An old man in my dream can stand not only for my father but for a friend, a teacher, and so on. Finally, in successful psycho-analysis I overcome resistance because I integrate parts of myself split off from each other.[29]

CONCLUSION

From the very beginning and throughout this work I have been criticizing and overcoming false Cartesian claims to an individualis-tic, isolated autonomy. The historical reduction in Chapter 1, the affirmation of the lived body, the discovery of the prescientific life-world, the grounding of reflection in perception, the linguistic turn, the phenomena of intersubjectivity, and finally the hermeneutical turn have all been steps in this process. Within the hermeneutical turn, there have been two main steps, a hermeneutics of restoration or receptive encounter with tradition, and a hermeneutics of suspi-cion. The move to the personal unconscious is the first step in this hermeneutics of suspicion. The personal unconscious functions as a middle term between personal consciousness and the socially un-conscious structures of capitalism, to be discussed in the next two chapters.

Looking forward to the next chapter, I can see that psychoanalysis, as one kind of critical social science, becomes an instance of and a model for critical social theory. The psychoanalytic encounter is an attempt through a reflective remembering to free oneself from re-pression and distortion.[30] Such a model, when generalized to the whole of society, becomes a model of unrestricted discussion carried on according to the four validity claims, bringing into question all forms of social repression, alienation, and distortion. In this way a hermeneutics of suspicion becomes a hermeneutics of liberation. Freedom, established eidetically in reflection upon the question, choice, and concrete relations with others, becomes concrete and fully itself here.

Freud tells us that the motive for sexual repression is economic; human eros is subordinated to the performance principle, a principle justifying the disciplining and repression of erotic activity and pleas-ure to the extent necessary for economic productivity. When the per-formance principle is linked to class exploitation in capitalism, a link to be discussed in the next chapter, then surplus repression is the result: a repression of eros occurring not for the sake of the individual person or persons, but for the sake of the dominating class. Alienation has not only an objective, economic aspect, but a subjective, sexual, erotic aspect as well. When the superego, after being formed in the initial, familial, Oedipal conflict, is informed subsequently by educational, religious, economic, and political authority interested in preserving the status quo, individuals can be socially conservative even when it is in their best interests to be radical and critical in thought and action. Thus a subjective resistance emerges to self-consciousness in word and in deed for which a traditional Marxist approach cannot account. A fully adequate dialectical phenomenology will take into account both the objective and the subjective aspects of repression.[31]

Freud thought that such repression was inevitable and necessary. If, as I shall show in the next two chapters, this repression is rooted in specific social structures that are historical, that have a specific beginning in time, and that, therefore, could end, then such alienation is neither necessary nor inevitable; nor is the conflict between eros and civilization. Surplus repression rooted in class domination could end, and there would remain only basic "repression," that form of discipline, authority, and organization necessary for society to get its necessary tasks done and fulfill its own real needs.[32]

In this chapter, I have begun to effect a union between eros and reason in dialectical phenomenology. A reason initially repressive of and hostile to the sexual and unconscious relates to and recovers the sexual and unconscious. An erotic reason emerges that is receptive, open to the other, dialogal, feminine as well as masculine, playful as well as serious, contemplative as well as active.[33] The theme of an "active receptivity," unifying opposites within itself and present already in perception, reflection, freedom, and intersubjectivity, reappears on the hermeneutical level as well. With such recovery of the erotic, I have taken one more step toward overcoming a limited, objectivistic, positivist, instrumental reason, oriented to means and not ends, to quantity and not quality, to things and not persons. I replace domination and repression of nature, sexual and otherwise, by a respectful openness to nature that is critically responsive and respectful of limits.[34] Such an overcoming is one of the main tasks of this book. I overcome both a subjective, transcendental

Husserlian reason and an objectivistic, positivistic, instrumental reason in dialectical phenomenology.

NOTES

1. Sigmund Freud, *A General Introduction to Psychoanalysis*, trans. Joan Riviere (New York: Pocket Books, 1953), pp. 38, 58–62.

2. Ibid., pp. 25–27, 32–43, 331–34. In exploring the unconscious and sexuality, I give a privileged place to Freud for three reasons. First, he is the one who discovered not only the method of psychoanalysis but the role of the unconscious and sexuality. Second, an integration of Freud with phenomenology has already occurred in Ricoeur's classic work *Freud and Philosophy*, and I can use his results. In this work an explicit step is taken away from an Husserlian model and toward an Hegelian, dialectical model of phenomenology. Third, I agree with thinkers such as Marcuse and Jacoby that post-Freudians such as Adler and Jung tend to back away from the radical, critical implications of Freud's discoveries. See Herbert Marcuse, *Eros and Civilization* (New York: Vintage, 1955), pp. 217–52, and Russell Jacoby, *Social Amnesia* (Boston: Beacon, 1975).

3. Freud, *Introduction to Psychoanalysis*, pp. 156–77, 196, 260–64.

4. Ricoeur, *Freud and Philosophy*, pp. 375–90.

5. Ibid., p. 385.

6. Ibid., pp. 386–90.

7. Ibid., pp. 390–92.

8. Ibid., pp. 392–95. Freud, *Introduction to Psychoanalysis*, pp. 58–59, 61, 128–31.

9. Ricoeur, *Freud and Philosophy*, pp. 395–406.

10. Ibid., pp. 406–408.

11. Ibid., pp. 422–30.

12. Freud, *Introduction to Psychoanalysis*, p. 112.

13. Ibid., p. 105. Habermas, *Knowledge and Human Interests*, pp. 246–73. Sigmund Freud, "Some Elementary Lessons in Psychoanalysis," in *The Complete Psychological Works of Sigmund Freud*, ed. James Strachey, trans. James Strachey, Anna Freud, Alix Strachey, and Alan Tyson, Standard Edition, 24 vols. (London: Hogarth, 1967), XXIII 282; and "New Introductory Lectures," in ibid., XXII 159; "Outline of Psychoanalysis," in ibid., XXIII 182, 196.

14. Sigmund Freud, *The Ego and the Id*, ed. James Strachey, trans. Joan Riviere (New York: Norton, 1962), p. 46; and "New Introductory Lectures," 80.

15. Freud, *The Ego and the Id*, pp. 20, 34–35. See Marcuse's *Eros and Civilization*, pp. 180–202, for a discussion of the distinction between a merely genital sexuality and an erotic sexuality. Freud, "New Introductory Lectures," 73–74.

16. Ricoeur, *Freud and Philosophy*, pp. 477–83.

17. Freud, *Introduction to Psychoanalysis*, pp. 202, 309–11, 334, 352–55, 359–60, 394.

18. Ricoeur, *Freud and Philosophy*, pp. 459–93.

19. Habermas, *Knowledge and Human Interests*, pp. 214, 228, 237–45, 246–300. Ricoeur, "The Question of Proof in Freud's Psychoanalytic Writings," in *The Philosophy of Paul Ricoeur*, ed. Reagan & Stewart, pp. 184–86, 89, 202–203.

20. Jacques Lacan, *Ecrits: A Selection*, trans. Alan Sheridan (New York: Norton, 1977), pp. 292–324.

21. Ricoeur, "Question of Proof in Freud's Psychoanalytic Writings," pp. 185–87. The first four criteria I derive from Ricoeur's essay; the fifth is my own.

22. Ibid., pp. 187–90. Freud, *The Ego and the Id*, pp. 19–29; and *Introduction to Psychoanalysis*, pp. 367–85.

23. Ricoeur, "Question of Proof in Freud's Psychoanalytic Writings," pp. 190–91.

24. See Chapter 6, p. 169.

25. Husserl, *Ideas*, p. 86.

26. Ricoeur, "Question of Proof in Freud's Psychoanalytic Writings," pp. 191–95. Freud, *The Ego and the Id*, pp. 19–29.

27. Freud, *Introduction to Psychoanalysis*, pp. 226–30.

28. Ricoeur, "Question of Proof in Freud's Psychoanalytic Writings," pp. 191–210.

29. On this question of contraries and opposites in psychoanalysis, see Freud, *Introduction to Psychoanalysis*, pp. 186–92.

30. Habermas, *Knowledge and Human Interests*, pp. 214, 228, 237–45, 246–300. Ricoeur, "Question of Proof in Freud's Psychoanalytic Writings," pp. 202–203.

31. Freud, *Introduction to Psychoanalysis*, pp. 38, 58–59, 61–62; and "New Introductory Lectures," 64. Marcuse, *Eros and Civilization*, pp. 20–95.

32. For a definition of basic and surplus repression, see Marcuse, *Eros and Civilization*, pp. 32–34. For a definition of repression as inevitable, see pp. 71–95, 117–26. The choice of "repression" as a term to describe the social order and discipline necessary for society was probably not one of Marcuse's happier choices.

33. Ibid., pp. 96–114, 144–202.

34. For a definition and critique of instrumental reason, see Max Hork-heimer, *Eclipse of Reason* (New York: Seabury, 1974), pp. 3–57. For instrumental reason as purposive rational action, see Habermas, *Towards a Rational Society*, pp. 91–94. Unlike Marcuse, I accept here Habermas' proposition that instrumental reason has its own legitimate domain. Where the problem lies is in its absolutization as the only form of knowledge.

8

Hermeneutics of Suspicion II: Dialectical Phenomenology as Social Theory

THERE IS not only a personal unconscious but also a social unconscious operating to some extent behind the backs of the participants involved. As I shall argue in this chapter, we must posit such a social unconscious in order finally to understand, explain, and evaluate the phenomena of reification, individualism, and scientism described in Chapter 1. In this chapter we return full circle to where we began in Chapter 1, the practical historical reduction. In so doing we expand into a new and higher viewpoint where we understand and criticize the self in its full historical and social dependence on capitalism as a form of life; we overcome, therefore, in an eidetic and critical manner the final vestiges of Cartesianism.

In contrast to an Hegelian return to the beginning, however, in which the philosophizing individual ends up reconciled with the status quo, ours is a return that is critical, that leaves the individual creatively unhappy and dissatisfied, and that points toward a future theoretical and practical praxis that would overcome the capitalist status quo.

As the first chapter began with an historically specific situation and texts and the previous two chapters have returned to such particulars, so also this chapter returns to the historically particular epoch of capitalism, grounding the phenomena of individualism, reification, and scientism. Capitalism is distinguished from other historical epochs, first of all, because it dissolves all immediate relationship to the earth. Communal property is dissolved in favor of private property, and even agriculture has been industrialized. Second, the laborer no longer owns the means of production as in medieval times. Third, the laborer no longer possesses the means of consumption but has to buy these with wages received. Finally, workers themselves are not among conditions of production, like slaves or serfs, but are themselves free to sell their labor power on the market to the highest bidder.

What led up to capitalism was, on the one hand, accumulation of money on the part of the capitalist and, on the other, the separation of labor from the means of production, instruments and raw materials with which he works. Because the capitalist buys up these means of production, they confront labor as alien. The subject–object relationship in capitalism at its most concrete level is labor confronting the means of production owned by capital as alien, as belonging to someone else. Rather than a subject–object unity, we have a subject–object split. By "capitalism," therefore, I mean a set of social relations in which workers are separated from means of production, in which the profit measured in money and going to the owners and managers of the means of production is the basic, overriding goal of the society, in which labor is free labor offering itself to capital in the market place, and in which market relations generally are characterized by freedom and equality. You do not have to buy from me nor I from you, but if we do engage in a transaction, we exchange equivalents.[1]

For many this chapter will be the most controversial in the book. What is least controversial is the formal necessity for a moment of critique or suspicion in phenomenology, already demonstrated at the end of Chapter 6. What is more controversial is that, in the area of social theory, the most appropriate move is radical rather than reformist. What is most controversial is the use of phenomenologically transformed and chastened Marxism or critical theory as the best model for suspicion in the social sphere. One can accept the first proposition without accepting the last two, and the first two without the last. As used in this volume, "Marxism" and "critical theory" will be synonyms.

Why am I employing a radically reflective, phenomenological Marxism rather than one that is reformist according to a Weberian model, for example, or a Schutzian model that grounds and makes use of Weber? One reason is that my model not only makes many of the same descriptive points about capitalism and its relation to scientism and positivism as Weber's, but embodies in itself a more phenomenologically sound model of reflective, dialectical reason. Reason for Weber tends to be formally or instrumentally rational according to the model of purposive rational action. Second, my model takes into account the unconscious dimension of psychological or social structures more adequately than a Weberian or Schutzian model, both of which give the moment of suspicion short shrift. Third, not only does my model incorporate discoveries about the life-world and temporality also present in Schutz's model, but there is the possibility of reflection on particular social structures not present in his model. Fourth, in my model there is a critical questioning and non-acceptance of alienating social structures more akin to the radical self-questioning orientation of phenomenology that tries, as much as possible, not to take anything for granted.[2]

Within phenomenology, two other possible models of suspicion I might employ are the Derridean and the Heideggerian. Derrida is inadequate for reasons discussed in the chapter on the self: an un-dialectical rejection of presence and identity, and affirmation of absence and *différance*. Derrida absolutizes the moment of suspicion or deconstruction and does not adequately relate it to a moment of hermeneutical retrieval. But taking a cue from Derrida, I shall move into a deconstruction that is also a reconstruction of Cartesianism—phenomenology in the next chapter. The reasons for rejecting a Heideggerian alternative I have argued for in the chapter on objectivity and shall develop further in the second part of this chapter.

What do I mean by a "phenomenologically transformed and chastened" Marxism? In general, even though I believe the intent and achievement of Marx himself escapes, for the most part, the charges of a materialistic, economistic reductionism,[3] I believe that much of later Marxism succumbs to such reductionism in theory and practice. For these reasons, dialectical phenomenology can and should absorb the genuine achievements of Marx while overcoming the problem of reductionism.

First, if a vulgar Marxism wishes to charge that all truth claims are false because they are ideology, disguised expressions of repressive class structures, then that claim refutes itself as a truth claim. What should become apparent in such vicissitudes are, as I argued in Chapter 6, the necessity and possibility of some intellectual claims having a certain distance from ideology.[4]

Second, instead of an economistic reduction of praxis to labor, I have already argued that praxis includes symbolic interaction, artistic expression, and theory with a practical, critical intent.[5] Third, a phenomenological basis, necessary but not sufficient, for rejecting the claim that political or cultural dimensions passively mirror an economic base is the argument already made that insight is enriching, that it gives us more than what is contained in the original perceptual experience.[6]

Fourth, building on the previous point, we can see how Marx could validly say that different parts of the social whole, economic, political, and cultural, both reciprocally determine one another and yet in a certain way give a primacy to the economic. To say that the economy determines the other areas can mean two different things. The economy in all epochs is determinant in the last instance, in the sense that it sets the limits within which human beings interact with one another at all levels of social life, and a non-economic level can emerge as dominant—for example, religion in the Middle Ages and politics in ancient Greece. "Determining" can mean "dominant." Only in a capitalist society is the economy dominant, but even this dominance co-exists with relative autonomy of other spheres such as the political and the cultural. As I shall argue later in this chapter, such relative autonomy allows the state and culture to influence the economy in many ways, setting up a legal framework within which production and exchange can go on, preventing depressions and recessions through government spending and welfare programs, and legitimizing capitalist social relations.

If one wishes to talk about causation, therefore, then we can posit a reciprocity between and among the economic, political, and ideological components of a social whole, with one of them being dominant. This causation has several different aspects to it. (*a*) There is the formal dimension, which has three different aspects. (1) The social environment influences actors or groups of actors by *motivating* them to act in certain ways rather than in certain other ways. A society given to emphasizing profit over human enjoyment in work will motivate actors, without forcing them, to have similar priorities. (2) There are structural relationships between and among aspects of the social whole under which an interpretative and explanatory hermeneutics attempts to understand and verify. As I shall show later in this chapter, there is a structural relationship between labor and capital, exchange value and scientism, production for profit and advertising. (3) Finally, as Goldmann has argued, there is at least a partial, formal homology between and among spheres of social life. As I shall show in Chapter 9, there is a similarity in structure between the Cartesian, Husserlian pure ego and the isolated self-interested economic individual; this homology justifies us in describing them both as bourgeois.[7]

(b) There is a dimension of efficient causality between and among spheres. If, as I have shown in Chapter 5, human beings act and intervene actively in the world, then dominant groups will be able to force their priorities on subordinate groups. If, as I shall show in this chapter, labor has to work on capital's terms because capital owns the means of production, then labor's goal of enjoying work will give way to capital's goal of higher profit. Labor works on capital's terms, because labor has to work in order to eat. Coercion rather than appeal predominates.

(c) Material and instrumental causality operates. One is the way in which capital develops science and technology, which are useful for cheapening labor and expanding profit. Materials produced by machinery at decreasing expense and machinery become more important as capitalism develops. (d) Final causality operates to the extent that the goals of the economic sector rule over and take precedence over other sectors. To an increasing extent, as I shall show in this chapter, it becomes necessary for capital to extend its sway over private consumption, culture, and the state. Control over consumption is crucial to keep people buying the goods capitalism produces, and control over the cultural and political is necessary to legitimate capitalist priorities. Causation as I shall describe it in this chapter is a complex unity of formal, efficient, material, instrumental, and final causation. Each is an aspect of the whole.

Fifth, if contemporary Marxism and critical theory is undergoing by its own admission a crisis of foundations, then phenomenology can help supply those foundations by giving descriptive, eidetic accounts of consciousness, embodiment, freedom, intersubjectivity, language, and the ideal speech-situation. Sixth, such an account of human beings in the world supplies the basis for a non-reductive "materialism." Seventh, such a non-reductive account implies the possibility of crises other than the economic: such as rationality crisis, economic crisis mediated through the state; motivation crisis, the erosion by capitalism of the social, cultural motivation necessary for its own survival and well-being; and legitimation crisis, capitalism's undermining the moral basis for its own legitimacy. Later in this chapter I shall develop these notions of motivation and legitimation crises.[8]

Eighth, my critique of capitalism and my alternative are phenomenology rooted in the ideal speech-situation, the community of rational inquirers and actors. Consequently there is a necessary fallibilism, indeterminacy, and ambiguity helping to overcome the dogmatism prevalent in much Marxist theory and practice. Ninth, my critique of scientism and technocracy and my account of the dialectical interaction between person and world, subject and object, help me to overcome the scientistic, technocratic tendencies of some Marxism, especially the Soviet version. In this sense my treatment coincides with a tendency of much Western Marxism such as Lukács, Gramsci, Korsch, and the Frankfurt School.[9]

Because the historical and experiential context of this book as an overcoming of Cartesianism is European, English, and North American, however, I will not engage in a sustained analysis and critique of Soviet state socialism, as necessary and important as such a critique and analysis would be.[10]

Tenth, in Chapter 3 I engaged in a phenomenological recovery of the concept of objectification. Such a recovery enables me to ground the Marxist concept of objectification, which is equivalent to that of expression in my sense, and which Marx uses to criticize Hegel.[11]

Eleventh, there is a growing tradition of phenomenological Marxism, including thinkers such as Paci, the later Sartre, Kosík, and Bologh. This chapter, and indeed to some extent this entire book, can be seen as arising out of that tradition.[12] In my opinion, Paci's attempt to integrate Husserl with Marx is unsuccessful because Husserl's transcendental orientation is incompatible with Marx's stress on human beings in the world. In contrast to Paci, I break with Husserl's transcendental ego completely and move clearly and decisively to an existential–hermeneutical phenomenology that is compatible with and includes Marxism.

My disagreements with the early Sartre on the questions of freedom and intersubjectivity should already be clear. The concept of freedom for which I argue in this book is one that is receptive, embodied, social, positive as well as negative, determinate as well as indeterminate. There is evidence that the later Sartre in *The Critique of Dialectical Reason* comes closer to this position.

However, rather than remaining in a sterile dichotomy between the descriptively eidetic and the structurally explanatory, my conception of dialectical phenomenology unites them as aspects of one whole and one method. Contrary to Sartre, I explicitly argue for the reality of structures in language, the personal unconscious, and the social unconscious not immediately present to conscious experience. The hermeneutical, and the explanatory as a moment of the hermeneutical, are not sufficiently present to mediate between description and critique in Sartre.

Also, there is insufficient distinction in the later Sartre between appeal and coercion, communicative political action and violence. This problem appears especially in his discussion of the fused group, a spontaneously formed, active, revolutionary gathering, and the pledge, a vow of fidelity to the group, undertaken with the sanction of death if the vow is violated. This inability or difficulty in affirming a non-violent, non-coercive political intersubjectivity may have its roots in the early Sartre's inability to recognize a non-coercive, non-dominating social intersubjectivity.[13]

While learning much from Kosík's classic work, I generate dialectical phenomenology as a method historically and phenomenologically from the ground up, do justice to linguistic, hermeneutical discoveries, and confront on an eidetic, descriptive level certain issues such as the nature of perception, objectivity, freedom, expression, and intersubjectivity in a way that he does not.

As the remainder of this chapter shows, I learn much and retain much from Bologh's notion of dialectical phenomenology as interpretation and critique of particular social structures. Nonetheless, I deem it necessary to integrate that kind of reflection with phenomenology carried on in an eidetic, descriptive manner to achieve a fully adequate, comprehensive dialectical phenomenology. Otherwise a lack of methodological clarity and clarity about foundations for critique can vitiate a phenomenology desiring to be as self-conscious and critical as possible. Also, I think it is necessary to include structural explanation in form and content more explicitly than she does.

This chapter will explore the relationship of phenomenology to ideology critique. In the next section there will be a movement from universal to particular as eidetic phenomenology functions as an element in and foundation for ideology critique. The following section will show how ideology critique in the Marxist, critical theoretical sense is already phenomenology and needs eidetic phenomenology. Here there will be a movement from particular to universal and their integration in the concrete universal.

PHENOMENOLOGY AS IDEOLOGY CRITIQUE

In the first chapter I began with a reflection on the concrete situation of human beings in twentieth-century Europe and America. I highlighted in my initial descriptions of such life reification, individualism, and scientism, three forms that alienation takes in the twentieth century. At this point I must effect a first confrontation between my eidetic account and these particular phenomena, which function in capitalist society both as lived phenomena and as ideologies, social rationalizations covering up, expressing, and legitimizing an irrational status quo.[14] There are ideologies, such as racism or sexism, other than those deriving from class domination, but capitalism subordinates all ideologies to its own ends.

A contradiction appears between my account of human subjectivity in the world and these particular phenomena. Reification, individualism, and scientism reveal themselves as irrational in the light of my account of personhood. Phenomenology, therefore, even on the descriptive, eidetic level, has an implicit critical thrust that I am now going to make explicit.

First, I can criticize reification on the basis of phenomenological method. The *epoche* or phenomenological reduction supplies a basis for criticism because the *epoche* has both a negative and a positive meaning. Negatively it is the deliberate setting aside of all commonsense or scientific notions about the world, including the notion that human beings are things or commodities. The *epoche* is the deliberately cultivated suspicion that the person is not a thing.

Positively the reduction reveals that the person is a subject, the discoverer and creator of meanings in the world. In relating to things and persons in the world, I am thematically aware of them, but prethematically, implicitly aware of myself as the agent performing the activity. For example, in perceiving the table across the room I am thematically aware of it as a thing and implicitly conscious of myself as the person perceiving the thing. Thematic or thetic consciousness of a thing presupposes a non-thetic consciousness of myself.

Second, subjectivity is temporal, and I have to understand subjectivity in a non-reified fashion. Temporality is not a series of thing-like instants, but a dynamic unity of past, present, and future in which these three dimensions of time are internally related to one another. When I listen to a person utter a sentence, I spontaneously retain each word as it slips into the past, give my attention to what is being said in the present, and anticipate the end of the sentence. Present, past, and future flow into one another, and any attempt to find a pure present, divorced completely from past and future, leads to an infinite regress of presents.

Third, the body-subject contrasts with the body-object. Capitalism, as I shall develop more fully in the next section, reduces human labor to abstract, mathematically measurable labor time, the human body to the goods that will keep it going or distract it, and human labor power to a commodity. Phenomenology shows that awareness of my body as subject is more basic. As I have already shown, the body cannot in its most original sense be an object or instrument, like a fork, knife, or pen, because I would require a second body in order to use the first as an instrument. In order to avoid an infinite regress of instruments, I must affirm the body as subject. The body is not an instrument but that which makes it possible for me to use instruments.

Fourth, the *epoche* implies the capacity to question the reified conditions of one's life. Such questioning is impossible without freedom, the capacity to conceive and realize possibilities. Because of the awareness of possibility, there is always a gap between what I am and what I am not. Though I have been married for many years, I can conceive the possibility of divorce or bachelorhood. Though I am a doctor now, I can imagine myself as a professor or politician.

Freedom is not simply negative, the capacity to question, resist, and say "no" to my surroundings, but positive, the ability to form projects and to realize them in the world. Freedom, as we have seen in the chapter on freedom, is a motivated freedom—"I choose because. . . ." I decide to go to Canada because I need a vacation. I choose Canada rather than New York because Canada is cheaper, cooler, and more of a change from my life in the Midwest. Even the attempt at a totally arbitrary act has its reason, the desire to prove myself totally independent of reasons and motives.

Individualism, which as an ideology affirms the isolated reality of people and things, I can criticize through reflection on intentionality. First of all, the experience of intentionality indicates that human consciousness is not closed in upon itself, but essentially open to what is other. All consciousness is awareness of an object not reducible to consciousness itself. As I have shown in the chapter on perception, to perceive an object sensibly is to be aware of a thing which is "there" in contrast to my own embodied "here," which is one, in contrast to my own multiple acts of perceiving; and which is given only through profiles, in contrast to the massive, certain, mute presence of my own lived body. Even the awareness of an ideal object, such as the mathematical proposition that $2 + 2 = 4$, is awareness of a meaning that transcends my own conscious states, because the meaning appears as a unity through a multiplicity of conscious acts. Human consciousness, rather than being isolated and atomistic, is flooded with otherness.

In perception and on all levels founded on it, the object is not an isolated atom or a series of isolated atoms. Rather, I perceive the table against the background of the room, do the mathematical problem against a background of prior knowledge and training, and remember the past love affair in its context of place and time and circumstance. I have to think of any figure or theme in relationship to something else, white in relationship to black, high to low, soft to loud. The perceived world, the reflective worlds of science, art, and philosophy, and the concrete world of capitalism are all organic totalities with internally related parts.

Therefore, not only is intentionality itself social, intrinsically welcoming otherness, but the world present to intentionality is social. Intentionality is aware of other persons, manifesting themselves as persons through their own embodied behavior. I experience the other as an embodied other because of the experienced differences between the way I experience myself and the way I experience her. For instance, I rule in my own body immediately "here," but relate to the other's body immediately "there." I can be totally certain that I am experiencing a pain, but only partially certain that the other is. Perhaps she is lying to me or playing a joke on me.

The other is one who contributes to the meaning of my world, who is essential to make it a fully objective world, whose viewpoint is continually complementing mine. The tree I am looking at, the scientific hypothesis I am considering, the poem I am trying to understand can all be misinterpreted by me. The other's viewpoint is necessary to correct, qualify, and deepen mine.

Such intersubjectivity manifests itself in the dependence of thought on language and the dependence of language on the body. Because human consciousness is an embodied consciousness in the world, it is essentially expressive. An idea is not complete in the mind apart from expression; rather, expression in language completes and clarifies the idea. The experience of artistic creation is the experience of discovering what one wants to say in the process of saying it. Human beings are born into a world of language and culture that they learn and appropriate. Once language is learned, it becomes habitual or sedimented, part of a linguistic whole out of which one utters any particular sentence or group of sentences and which can never be totally thematized. To talk intelligently about the game of baseball presupposes a knowledge of the game of baseball, its rules, its standard of excellence, its major teams. To discuss the artistic value of a Picasso painting implies a grasp of the history of modern art, its techniques, its goals, its important movements.

Because of this dependence on the other, language, and history, the human being is essentially finite, receptive, and social. As I have already shown, all understanding arises on the basis of questioning, and human beings understand the world and one another most fruitfully through conversation and dialogue, in which they advance through a dialectic of question and answer to the truth. Platonic dialogue is one example of such a dialectic; interpreting a text is another. In both instances, understanding arises not by imposition or domination, but by listening and questioning, allowing the other to have his say against me and running the risk of changing my own initial insights. Human understanding, even in its most intimate, private moments, is social. As Marx himself admits, I think for and with others. The language I use, the questions I ask, and the conclusions I arrive at are all heavily dependent on society.[15]

Technocracy is a paradoxical phenomenon, an ideology proclaiming the end of ideology, an affirmation of the values of tough-mindedness, precision, and control, and a claim to be value-free. The eidetic phenomenologist contributes to the effort of criticizing technocracy by showing that the main bulwarks of scientism, the physical sciences, social sciences, and formal logic, are founded on the life-world and consequently are derivative, not ultimate. The life-world is the pre-theoretical lived context in which perceptions occur. In addition to the theme of my perception, for instance, this person or table in front of me to which I am attending, there is the prethematic, lived, progressively widening context from which these objects emerge, the room, the building, the out-of-doors, the city, and so on. This total perceptual context or ground is the life-world. As I have indicated before, the life-world reached through phenomenology is never totally immediate, but saturated with language, tradition, and history. The reduction is never total, only partial. But as partial it has a value in allowing us to examine and criticize some presuppositions—in this instance, those of scientism.

Scientific inquiry begins and ends in the life-world. After being hit on the head by an apple, I raise questions about the law of falling bodies. After perceiving signs of development among species, I begin to think about the possibility of evolution. When hypotheses are formulated, they must be verified in experiments terminating in life-world perceptions. These experiments are socially conducted. Though the law of falling bodies is a scientific law, my awareness of others working with me on the same problem is prescientific. Though the theory of relativity is a scientific law, Einstein did not know Michelson through a scientific hypothesis but as a perceived member of the life-world.[16]

The dilemma for scientism is the following: if prescientific knowledge is merely subjective, then so is scientific knowledge because it requires "subjective perceptions" both in discovery and verification. If prescientific knowledge is objective, yielding its own kind of truth, then scientism topples to the ground because forms of knowledge other than science yield truth. Scientific knowledge has value and truth, but they are limited and derivative.

A similar kind of argument holds true, as we have seen in Chapter 2, for formal logic; the necessary presuppositions for formal logic are derived from the life-world. The notion of a universal truth valid for all times, places, and persons presupposes the life-world as the source of time, place, and intersubjectivity. The notion of a universal proposition applicable to many individuals presupposes the life-world, the context in which I encounter individuals. The possibility of a formal logic of consistent sense presupposes initial perceptions in which some senses are seen to be incompatible with others. "This color plus one makes three" is a judgment that makes no sense because the logic of addition is relevant to number but not to color in the life-world.

The life-world in one sense is distinct from science, but in another sense includes it, as one project among many. From this point of view, scientific knowing is one form of valid access to the world, along with other forms of knowing such as common sense, art, and philosophy. As a part within this whole, science enriches one's world. The world is a more meaningful world because of the discoveries of Einstein, Darwin, and Edison. However, these discoveries are products of a scientific activity that is always part of the whole, never the whole itself. As one project among many, science is neither inevitable nor necessary. It is equally possible that a person take up painting or music or stamp collecting.

Science reveals itself as founded in two senses: as dependent on a life-world distinct from it and as part of a life-world that includes it. A third kind of foundation emerges when we reflect on what we have been doing. For we have been reflecting in a phenomenological way on the limits and value of science. The critical justification or grounding of science is not itself scientific in a positive sense, but reflective and transcendental in articulating certain *a priori* structures of the life-world's relation to science. The dilemma for scientism is the following: if it wishes to be truly scientific and to justify itself, then it has to become philosophical, and such philosophical reflection emerges as one more counter-example to the all-embracing claims of scientism. On the other hand, if scientism cannot justify itself, then its claims are arbitrary, and what is arbitrarily asserted can be rationally questioned or denied.

IDEOLOGY CRITIQUE AS PHENOMENOLOGY

To say that phenomenology can serve as a part of and as a foundation for ideology critique, however, still does not go far enough. For a question remains concerning the ideology critique itself. Is it phenomenological or does it remain ultimately outside phenomenology?

The argument of this section is that ideology critique is itself phenomenological, but only if we transform, broaden, and deepen the

meaning of phenomenology. Phenomenology becomes not only reflection on universal structures common to any epoch, but reflection
on those particular structures that define particular historical epochs.
Phenomenology in the modern era, then, is not merely the reflection
of the isolated Cartesian individual on herself as an individual, but
the reflection on capitalism as a social structure that permeates and
defines individuals. Phenomenology becomes not only reflection on
the conscious relation between subject and object as that occurs in
any epoch, but reflection on conscious subject–object relationships
as they are defined by capital. Finally, phenomenology is not only
descriptive in an Husserlian sense, but dialectical in an Hegelian–
Marxist sense in that we reflect upon the alienating separation between subject and object in capitalism. Such reflection differs from
eidetic, descriptive phenomenology in having an explanatory, theoretical component.

The concrete social whole that emerges, then, is not merely one
defined by the eidetic relationships developed in preceding chapters.
"Capitalism" is the name we give to the social whole in its most concrete sense, a sense that defines our entire historical epoch in the
West. In contrast to other ages, ours is characterized by a separation
between worker and means of production. In contrast to other ages,
in ours most human beings have only their labor power to sell in the
market place. In contrast to other epochs, in ours production for
exchange-value and profit rules as a goal over production for use-
value. In contrast to other ages, in ours class division takes the form
of a division between capital, owning, controlling, and deriving the
primary benefit from means of production, and labor.[17]

The method, then, that emerges is dialectical phenomenology, in
which eidetics and critique, universal and particular, non-historical
and historical are united and related. Dialectical phenomenology
emerges as a negation and critique of positivism on a theoretical level
and a lived level. If positivism is irrational on the theoretical level,
capitalism as one form of lived positivism is irrational on a practical
level. To put the matter in Platonic terms, if capitalism is the dominant form that modern cave life takes, then philosophical liberation
from the cave requires a critique of and liberation from capitalism.

Such a movement from abstract to concrete, eidetics to ideology
critique, becomes necessary because phenomenology is interested in
moving from an un–self-conscious to a self-conscious form of life.

Such concerns motivate the *epoche* in Chapters 2 through 5, and the movement from limited wholes to broader, more concrete wholes. But to stop short of explicit reflection on and criticism of capitalism is to halt the movement toward a sufficiently self-conscious form of life. Phenomenology remains caught between an abstract affirmation of subjectivity and personhood in the first seven chapters and the concrete negation of that subjectivity in practice, between a theoretical rejection of positivism and the lived affirmation of it in practice.

To stay within the movement of phenomenology in the strict descriptive, eidetic sense is, therefore, to compromise the very orientation of phenomenology itself toward self-conscious thinking and living. I have already been forced into a hermeneutical, historical reduction in order to explain the historical origins of phenomenology, a movement into a hermeneutics of respect and a hermeneutics of suspicion, and a hermeneutical move into the personal unconscious in order to expand the meaning of subjectivity. Now I must move into history again through ideology critique in order to satisfy the telos of phenomenology. Without the interpretive grounding in the past and the critical orientation toward the future, eidetic phenomenology itself, as rooted in and including a phenomenology of time consciousness, remains incomplete, and, therefore, its orientation toward scientific completion is not satisfied. I have to transcend Husserl himself if I am to remain ultimately faithful to Husserl. In the previous section, I began this task by indicating how eidetic, Husserlian phenomenology itself can function as an element in ideology critique. Here I continue the process by considering ideology critique as phenomenology.

In this section I am very much indebted to Professor Bologh's enlightening work on Marx's method, *Dialectical Phenomenology*. As she puts it, the overriding rule for dialectical phenomenology is to be a form of reflexive theorizing. Reflexive or "analytic" theorizing moves from phenomena to finding their ground in a form of life[18]— in this case, capitalism. Reflexive theorizing contrasts with concrete theorizing, which treats phenomena as self-evident, natural, and complete in themselves. For example, alienation from work, which concrete theorizing treats as natural and inevitable, dialectical phenomenology traces back to its roots in capitalism as a form of life. A form of life is a set of unwritten rules or presuppositions that defines a given social formation, feudalism or capitalism. To ground phenomena in a form of life is to see them as essentially related to and proceeding from these rules or presuppositions. Alienated labor is traced back by Marx to its roots in the separation of worker and means of production owned privately by capital.

Marx's method in ideology critique is phenomenological in that it treats an object as essentially related to a conscious subject, dialectical in that it treats capitalism's separation of object and subject as problematical.

> Capitalism, an unself-conscious form of life, represses unity by separating subject from object. Such separation leads to a divided object, the exchange value and use value of the commodity, which in turn presupposes a divided subject, proletariat and bourgeoisie. A divided object (re)presents itself as a fetish, an object whose value seems to be independent of a subject. A divided subject (re)presents itself as internal conflict, class struggle.[19]

Class struggle can be understood analytically as a movement toward a self-conscious form of life in which a new unity between subject and object is constituted.

"Reading Marx phenomenologically and as a dialectical phenomenologist means reading his analysis of capital in terms of a separation of subject and object as his main achievement."[20] Because positivism also posits subjects as independent of objects and vice versa, capitalism is one form of positivism. Both capitalism and positivism treat the separation between subject and object as natural. Capitalism, then, is lived positivism; socialism as a fully self-conscious form of life is to capitalism on a practical level what dialectical phenomenology is to positivism on a theoretical level.[21]

Positivism as a one-sided focus on objects can give rise to idealistic, subjectivistic phenomenology as a one-sided reaction, Cartesianism in the narrow sense. Such subjective phenomenology can take two forms: that reality is whatever people think of it and that behavior must be understood in terms of individuals' intentions. A one-sided focus on the mind replaces a one-sided focus on the object. Instead dialectical phenomenology discovers a dialectical unity between subject and object in which neither one is reduced to the other.[22]

Positivism and idealism, objectivism and subjectivism alike reveal themselves as un–self-conscious forms of theorizing, uncritically reflecting the subject–object split within capitalism. Dialectical phe-

nomenology critically negates both forms by showing their rootedness in the form of life that is capitalism and by remembering the
subject–object unity that capitalism forgets. The false consciousness
or unconsciousness of such forms of theorizing is not deliberate or
morally culpable; rather, dialectical phenomenology shows how such
unconsciousness is explained by its rootedness in capitalism as a form
of life.[23]

We should not understand "form of life" in any economistic, reductionistic sense. Rather, it refers to a totality of internal relations,
a gestalt, if you like, between and among the economic, the cultural,
the political, and the social. To return to the earlier examples:
positivism and idealism have their own relative autonomy and interact with the economic by legitimizing it. Such forms of theorizing, however, are also parts and products of capitalism as a form
of life and, therefore, reproduce and reflect in distorted form relationships of that form of life.

As concretely practiced, dialectical phenomenology operates according to four reading rules or rules of interpretation.[24] The first of
these is to treat concepts as embedded in and deriving from a form of
life. As I shall show, "individualism" is a concept rooted in capitalism
as a form of life. The second is to treat individuals as grounded in
an historically specific form of life. As I shall also show, the bourgeois
individual is grounded in capitalism as a form of life.

The third rule is to recognize and treat a form of life as a totality
of internal relations. "Capital," for example, is essentially related to
labor and vice versa. Without capital, labor would have no means of
production with which to work and no wages. Without labor, capital
would have no one to work and, therefore, no commodities to sell for
a profit. The fourth rule is to treat a form of life as contradictory. I
shall show, for example, that there is a contradiction between the
ideals of freedom, equality, right to private property, and happiness
as these are lived and affirmed in the market place and the negation of
these ideals in the work place. As stated, therefore, these rules represent appropriate critical theoretical translations and applications of
the hermeneutical criteria developed in Chapter 6. The first three
rules, although not in a one-to-one manner, express and further
specify the criteria of consistency, comprehensiveness, and parsimony; the fourth, the canon of residues.[25]

Moving then to the phenomena of reification, individualism, and scientism, I have to ask what grounds them and accounts for them. Are they essential, in the sense of being part of or expressions of human nature in the life-world? The discussion in this book so far makes clear that they are not essential but rather contradict what is essential. For the phenomenological reduction has disclosed what the person is necessarily and essentially: incarnate, reflective, free, intersubjective, linguistic. Because the person is subject and not object, I have overthrown the thesis of reification eidetically and descriptively. Because the person is essentially social, historical, and linguistic, I must reject individualism. Because the human being is essentially spirit in the world rooted in the prescientific life-world and capable of many kinds of knowledge other than science, scientism is incorrect.

Are these phenomena natural, then, in the sense of being present in all historical epochs? Here again the answer has to be "no." The Middle Ages generally regarded a person as a child of God rather than as a scientific, economic object, a member of a community rather than as a rugged individual, and knowable philosophically and theologically in a predominantly religious context rather than as a scientific object. Reification, individualism, and scientism have developed and become dominant in the last four centuries. These phenomena are not necessary and eternal but have a date and historical origin, and therefore possibly an historical end.[26]

It is also not adequate to say, as Heidegger does, that technology is the problem.[27] First of all, this claim rests upon an illegitimate confusion between objectivity and alienation, already discussed in Chapter 3. Second, Heidegger does not adequately distinguish between science and scientism, legitimate technology and technocracy. There is all the difference in the world between the first member of both these pairs and the second. The first we experience as enriching and contributing to our life-world; the second, as impoverishing and alienating. As we experience when we photocopy an article, make a 'phone call, or read a published book, technology kept within proper limits can serve us rather than dominate us, and scientific knowledge conveyed in theories of evolution, relativity, and child development can and does illumine our life-world by adding to its intelligibility. What is impoverishing and alienating is an approach making science the only form of rationality and technology the only legitimate approach to the world; such moves exclude all other forms of life and turn the subject into an object.

Third, it is, therefore, illegitimate to talk as Heidegger does about technocracy as an event of being, as somehow proceeding from being. Being, as I have articulated it in this book, is the life-world conceived as unity of subject and object, person and world. Because scientism and technocracy cover up, violate, and contradict this unity, it makes no sense to talk about them as proceeding from being. Such talk ascribes a malevolence to being that is personally repugnant to me and phenomenologically unjustified.

Fourth, consequently one has to look elsewhere to answer the question why science systematically turns into scientism and technology into technocracy in this culture. If the life-world or being does not account for such dominance, then one has to look toward social relations, toward a specific form of life that would explain and account for the dominance of science and technology in this historical epoch. Since capitalism is the form of life that distinguishes this historical epoch from all others, one must try to see how reification, individualism, and scientism are grounded in capitalism as a form of life.

To show how such alienation is grounded in capitalism, I shall develop an argument in five steps: first, the dominance of exchange value over use value; second, the emergence of money in a context of free exchange; third; absolute surplus value; fourth, relative surplus value; fifth, late capitalism or welfare-state capitalism. These steps are logical, phenomenological, and historical steps in the development of and overcoming of such alienation and irrationality.

What are the conditions of existence for reification, individualism, and scientism? First of all, reification or objectivism implies the repression of a subject. Without subjectivity the world becomes lifeless, a collection of objects or things understood in terms of mere mechanical movements and physical forces. Reification implies a world in which objects are separated from subjects. Such separation presumes that a social form of life emerges at a certain historical moment. This separation is mediated through exchange value; exchange value comes between human subjectivity and its objects. The relationship between subject and object is dialectical in that the object produces the subject and the subject produces the object. This dialectical relationship may be formulated as a relationship of production. In labor, the subject produces the object as such, and the object makes possible and produces the subject as such.[28]

With the mediation of exchange value, the direct relationship of subject to object is broken. Exchange value is a mere mental calculation, but as exchange develops, an object takes on the symbolic character of exchange value. Every exchangeable item can now be exchanged for some given quantity of this objectified value, functioning as money. Money operates at this stage as a measure of exchange value and as a medium of exchange. With the objectification of exchange value in the form of money, a third function arises—that of representation of wealth in general. Money, as abstract exchange value objectified in a thing, can be amassed as general wealth, making possible the appropriation through money of any object.

Whereas previously objects were produced either for consumption or to buy other objects to be consumed, now it becomes possible to produce and exchange not for consumption but simply for making money. A new, subtle difference arises in the goal of production. Production is oriented no longer to objects of consumption, use values, satisfying concrete, real needs, but to objects as exchange values. Money becomes an end in itself, and everything else becomes a means. Objects of consumption imply a desiring, consuming subject. Exchange value, in contrast, is an objective thing in itself divorced from all subjectivity. "That item is worth four dollars."

With the emergence of making money, individual buyers and sellers appear in the market place each owning his own property, interested in pursing his own self-interest. Each buyer relates to the other instrumentally. I am interested in you insofar as you wish to buy my product, and you are interested in me insofar as you have something to sell. What unites buyer and seller is no common shared ethical community as such but only this instrumental relation. We relate to others as individuals, individualistically and serially. Because there is no real communal control over production, there is no guarantee that there will be buyers of my product when I go to market, and the possibility of economic crisis is present. The general flux of supply and demand is a fate outside anyone's control, and money, the measure of value of commodities, means of exchange, and now end in itself, supplies the community that the buyer and seller are unable to supply. Money is the real mind and community of all things.

Because there is a loss of the subject on the part of the object, the subject appears to be a thing in itself divorced from its object. As a result abstract labor emerges—labor conceived as a cost of production, with no relation to a specific object or subject. Hence abstract labor is calculated in terms of its exchange value. Its role as the subject of production is repressed, and it becomes a mere object of exchange, a commodity. The subject of production becomes capital, money, the representative of wealth in general functioning as the means for reproducing wealth. Money in the form of capital appears to be a subject determining production while labor appears to be a mere object used by capital. Labor power as an abstraction measured by money operating in capitalism as a way of life grounds the anonymous, impersonal, alienating character of contemporary mass society. Capitalism is an abstract way of life, in the context of which human beings relate abstractly to each other through the abstraction of money.[29]

To understand this strange reversal, we have to understand the essence of capital as exchange value. Exchange value refers to the exchangeability of one item for another. What basis could there be for determining exchange value? Utility might be one. We exchange one thing for another that we need and can use. The usefulness might determine its exchangeability. But this subjective aspect could not give rise, of itself, to some objective, universal measure that would ground exchange and economic science. To be able to say that a specific object has the value of so many other objects or is worth a certain amount independently of the needs and desires of exchangers, one presupposes some means by which quantitative comparison can be made. This proposition means and implies that every object must be comparable to every other in some respect; every object with exchange value must have something in common with every other. That which makes exchange value possible is the amount of labor time on the average that it takes to produce one object. Labor time is common to all objects of production and can be calculated objectively.

Hence labor time presupposes labor. I can distinguish exchange value from market value or price, which fluctuates according to supply and demand. Exchange value, in contrast, is inherent in the object itself as the embodiment of labor time. Once labor time takes the form of money, money not only represents labor time but replaces it in thought. Money appears as a thing in itself independent of any social determination. Exchange value, which is merely an abstraction from among producers–exchangers, appears inherent in the objects of exchange. The latter cease appearing to be objects of production, presupposing subjectivity, and appear to be embodied exchange values. Commodity fetishism appears, in which relations between and among persons take the form of relations among things. Reification of human beings is expressed by and grounded in such fetishism.[30]

Production for exchange value breaks down all previous relationships involved in production unmediated by exchange value. Money demystifies the world. In reducing all objects to exchange value, capital makes cynicism possible. Nothing remains sacred. Everything becomes reducible to its objective determinations and is "subject to universal prostitution." All subjectivity disappears from objects and with it spiritual value. Production for exchange value, then, heralds the domination of objective mind. Objects become separated from subjectivity; matter is separated from spiritual meaning or value, making possible the development of scientific reason.[31]

Beginning from a question of the origins or conditions of possibility for the separation of subjectivity and objectivity, a relationship I formulated as production, I examined the implications and consequences of that relationship being mediated by exchange value. The embodiment of exchange value in concrete form replaced the subject of production and in so doing removed subjectivity from the objects of production. The elimination of subjectivity makes the development of scientism and reification possible, and the process of exchange occurring between atomistic individuals grounds individualism.

Thus I arrive at the conclusion that modern, non-dialectical reason, objectivism and subjectivism, emerges historically with production for exchange value: the beginning of capitalism. Not only does capitalism make scientific rationality possible, but capitalism fosters its growth and development as well.

To understand the pivotal role of capitalism in the development of scientific thinking, we have to understand the importance of science to the production and accumulation of capital. This relationship presumes the need for continual revolutionizing of the means of production: technology and machinery. This need comes out of the need of capital to make money. Making money in the third sense as representative wealth becomes possible only when the owner does not hoard it but invests it in means of production and labor. Mere hoarding tries to corral for itself a finite supply of money in a finite market, which supply would soon dry up. By investing in production, the capitalist creates a source of more goods and more money. The infinite, rapacious thirst for money comes into its own and is implemented in principle with capitalism. The capitalist is a rational hoarder, and the hoarder is an irrational capitalist.

Abstract labor time, we have seen, is the substance of value. The capitalist invests money to make money. If labor time is the substance of value, the capitalist can make money only by appropriating surplus labor time or surplus value. Surplus value is that labor time over and above necessary labor time, the time necessary for the worker to be paid wages for the value of his labor power.

Surplus value cannot come from the sphere of circulation because there equivalents are exchanged. Consequently, it must come from the sphere of production. Within the sphere of production only three possibilities are present, materials of production, instruments of production, and labor. Neither of the first two can be the source of surplus value because they simply contribute to the product the value they already possess. It can only be labor that is creative in that it not only produces the value of its own labor power but produces surplus value. Labor as the source of surplus value, therefore, is a discovery enabling Marx to resolve the contradictions between two claims in bourgeois society and bourgeois economic science: within circulation equivalents are exchanged, and yet the capitalist invests money to make money.[32]

One has to distinguish, therefore, between labor power as a commodity, for which the worker receives an equivalent in wages, and labor as an activity in production, which creates value. One also has to distinguish between the sphere of appearance, circulation, and the sphere of essence, production, between what is immediately perceived and what is mediately, reflectively understood and judged. For the most part the actors within capitalism are unconscious of this distinction. Capital thinks that profit comes from cutting or raising prices, sharp, competitive advertising, its own initiative in investing, and other such activities; and labor is aware only of not being happy in work and not being well off financially outside work. The law of value functions behind the backs of the participants in the capitalist drama; for the most part, they are unconscious of this law. For this reason, reflection has to be phenomenological and dialectical in order to penetrate the veil. Yet, as we shall see, capitalism as a structure tends to discourage this kind of reflection and to bring about a positivism that leaves its own inner secret untouched and unrevealed.

Surplus value takes two forms historically, absolute and relative surplus value. The earlier form is absolute surplus value in which the capitalist strives to increase surplus value by lengthening the working day, from ten to twelve to fourteen hours. Because of physical and political limits among workers, however, extraction of surplus value is not likely or possible beyond a certain point. As workers' political resistance reduces the working day, capital has to extract surplus value another way, through lowering the relative amount of the working day that goes to the worker and increasing that going to capital. Such a result is achieved by cheapening the value of labor power through decreasing the value of those commodities such as food and clothing necessary to keep labor power alive. Labor power is worth less because the goods necessary to keep it going are worth less.

Capital achieves such cheapening of labor power through increasing productivity, making it possible to produce the same amount of goods in less time. Increasing productivity becomes possible through the introduction of machinery and technology. As capitalism develops, proportionately greater amounts of money are invested in machinery compared to labor, and such increased use of machinery increases the productivity of labor and allows more goods to be produced with less labor. Labor becomes increasingly superfluous in relation to machinery. Rather than the instrument of labor being a vehicle of the laborer's self-expression as it is in pre-capitalist epochs and even to some extent in the early stages of capitalism dominated by absolute surplus value, labor now becomes an appendage to the machine.

As capitalism develops, the mind and skill of the worker are transferred to the machine. To increase productivity, division of labor occurs. Labor is not only devalued but deskilled, and ultimately devalued because deskilled. The greater development of means of production can occur because of the revolutionizing effect of science and technology. Science and technology, rather than being external to the dynamics of capitalism, become internal to it as productive forces.

In the movement from absolute to relative surplus value, capital moves from a merely formal subsumption to real subsumption of labor to its imperatives. In early capitalistic production labor still has some residue of skill, craftsmanship, and pride in work. Capital gathers laborers together in one work place, but the work place is more loosely organized than occurs later and thus leaves some room for individual skill, initiative, and enjoyment in work. As capitalism develops by introducing more discipline into the work place, more division of labor, and more machinery, the feudal remnants of skill and pride in one's work tend to disappear. Capital, through the use of science and technology, moves from a merely formal subsumption to a real subsumption of labor and, therefore, comes more into its own. In the later nineteenth and early twentieth century this process of subsumption continues as capitalism moves more and more into the social and political spheres. Analogously to Hegel's absolute spirit tending to incorporate more and more into itself, capitalism continually strives to transcend limits and extend its sway. An essential part of the contradictory logic of capitalism is this dialectic between finite and infinite, of which the movement from absolute to relative surplus value is one example. Capitalism's boundless thirst for surplus value runs into limits, which it then attempts to transcend. The new solution, then, runs into other limits, which capital again tries to transcend.[33]

In early capitalism, the intervention of the state in the economy was minimal. The state simply secured the preconditions of capitalism by protecting bourgeois commerce in accordance with civil law, shielding the market from destructive side effects, satisfying prerequisites of production in the economy as a whole, and adapting the system of civil law to needs such as banking arising from the process of accumulation. The economy of early capitalism was free, unplanned, and competitive; and technological or scientific discoveries originated outside the sphere of production itself.

In late capitalism the state performs all the functions listed above, but also enters into the economy itself as an active participant and as a legitimator of the status quo. The state creates and improves conditions for the realization of capital by investing in unproductive projects (for example, armaments, space exploration), heightening productivity of human labor (education), guiding the flow of capital into sectors neglected by the autonomous market, relieving social and material costs resulting from private production (unemployment compensation, welfare), and strengthening the economy's competitive position abroad by supranational blocs, military presence, and imperialism. Such intervention becomes necessary to save the economy from self-destruction through overproduction and lack of demand, and to legitimate capitalist priorities.

Acting in concert with this changed role of the state are two other aspects of late capitalism, a planned economy, described by some as "monopoly capitalism," and the institutionalization of scientific and technological change. Big corporations, labor unions, and the government form a system that makes long-range planning by corporations possible, regulates demand, and controls wages and prices. Whereas early capitalism used scientific discoveries that happened to be at hand, late capitalism is systematically organized to develop science and technology—science and technology have become productive forces. Consequently a new sector of scientific workers, the "technostructure," has arisen in corporations and in the state.[34]

With the emergence and dominance of relative surplus value, the resulting subjugation of labor to machinery, integration of science and technology with itself, and finally the development of the interventionist state in the twentieth century, capitalism becomes fully itself and comes into its own. With its need to produce profit and to realize exchange value, capitalism strives to expand its markets and to extend its sway over more and more areas of human life. There are two forces inherent in the working of capital that lead to this result. On the one hand, there is the danger of satisfying a market such that demand for the product decreases and capital cannot realize the surplus value produced. Capital cannot sell all that it has produced and cannot continue to produce surplus value. Hence it must continually find or create new markets.

On the other hand, even if there is continual innovation in the market, consumers continue to need the product, especially if it is a perishable good. The profit realized from the first round of production results in an expanded amount of capital to reinvest. The capitalist realizes not only his original investment but a surplus as well. He must find an outlet for the amount originally invested, plus the amount over and above that realized in profit. A large investment with a correspondingly large amount of products requires a larger market. Each new round of production and selling leads to a larger total capital for reinvestment and the need for more markets. Thus over and above the greed or desire on the part of some individuals for increasing their wealth, there is a built-in mechanism for expanding the sway of capital over the world. This need to expand markets leads to the desire to change (improve or cheapen) the product in order to attract more of the market or create new markets. Science and technology provide capital with the means of doing that.

Further, increase in production requires expansion of consumption: quantitative expansion of existing consumption, creation of new needs by propagating existing ones in a wider circle, and production of new needs through the discovery and creation of new use values. The civilizing aspect of capital emerges in which it drives beyond any finite national or human limit, creates a system of general exploitation of natural and human qualities, and turns everything into an object of utility to be produced or consumed by capital. Everything becomes a means for capital. Advertising in the twentieth century is an example of such a process. Through the use of such human qualities as sexuality, repressive desublimation occurs, in which an erotic sexuality proper to the whole person and entering into all her activities in sublimated form becomes mere genital sexuality. Genuine and legitimate sexual liberation turns into the Playboy philosophy. In the first instance, the revolution occurs as genuine; in the second, as farce.[35]

Scientism, positivism, and objectivism become necessary to the working of capital. They are inherent in market rationality. A market orientation must eliminate non-calculable, non-monetary values from consideration. Positivistic science helps such elimination and legitimates it. Prediction, control, and domination suppress liveliness, desire, and playfulness. The latter now appear as irrational temptations drawing one away from the production for profit. As I have indicated, the latter requires the ability rationally (quantitatively) to calculate, predict, and control the behavior of markets and labor. Such control requires the domination over and suppression of everything not immediately subject to or useful for calculation, prediction, and control. As a result, a "surplus repression" of needs, desires, and activities not immediately useful to capital occurs in the utilitarian calculus. Such repression is "surplus" because it is not necessary, does not occur in the interests of people as subjects, but only for the sake of capital.[36]

At the same time as capital suppresses and dominates over all that cannot be appropriated to its own ends, it also produces and presupposes those other elements in a contradictory way. For example, it produces unemployment, a mass of people freed from capitalist discipline. It relies on and induces desire in order to market new products. It promises freedom to enjoy and indulge while providing the means and objects for that freedom and indulgence. The desire for freedom and enjoyment in work can lead to discontent with unenjoyable work and create a motivation crisis. Capital contains these contradictions by separating them. Market rationality is reserved for the sphere of production while the irrationality of desire and free play are reserved to the private domain of home, family, and friends. Sexism is subordinated to capitalism insofar as sexism justifies keeping women in the home as unpaid managers of consumption and insofar as male chauvinism becomes a supporting ideology for a technocratic, tough-minded market rationality.[37] But this separation creates its own tensions and dilemmas as private life requires economic support and hence must subordinate itself whenever necessary to the demands of economic life. Similarly from the side of capital, economic life must subordinate and manipulate private needs to meet its own needs for markets and labor. The failure of subordination threatens capitalism with crises, and the dialectic of finite and infinite continues.

All realms of human life, culture, politics, family life, become increasingly subject to the demands of capital as technique controls workers on the assembly line and in the office, voters in the political arena, and consumers in the social sphere. Scientism, positivism, and objectivism emerge as the forms of reason most appropriate to the full realization of capital. Science and technology become not only productive forces but ideology, expressing and legitimizing the one-dimensional reign of capital. As capital develops, grows, and comes more into its own, mass society grows in anonymity, impersonality, ambiguity, and loss of self. As the role of the father in family life declines because other agencies take over more and more of the functions of the family, capital through these agencies takes over the superego of the individual and bends him to its purposes.[38]

In late capitalism one contradictory form of such technocratic domination is that of a legitimation crisis mediated through the state. Because the state actively intervenes in the economy in order to control demand and fend off revolt, the state faces a legitimation crisis or the structural possibility of such a crisis. There is a contradiction between its role in securing accumulation favoring particular capitalistic interests and its role securing legitimation by appealing to norms stressing the good of all. Such norms implicitly presuppose the communicative ethic from which they emerge and by which they can be redeemed. The infinitude–finitude dialectic speaks out in new form.[39]

First, because the state intervenes in the economic process in a way that is obvious to people, capitalism can no longer pass off economic and political suffering as our inevitable, economic fate. We can and should publicly discuss and criticize criteria for these decisions. The state, therefore, is in a dilemma: the less it intervenes, the greater the danger of the economy's self-destructing through crisis. The more the state intervenes the greater the danger of a legitimation crisis.

If the government wishes to help out Lockheed, for example, then consistency demands that it also aid New York City financially if New York City needs the aid to survive and cannot receive it from elsewhere. One cannot consistently apply welfare-state principles in the one instance and laissez-faire principles in the other. One can attempt to solve the consistency problem by not aiding Lockheed, but then it and other similar capitalistic enterprises run the risk of self-destructing. Late capitalism, then, is posed on the horns of a dilemma. It can avoid self-destruction only through state intervention in the economy. But the more such state intervention occurs, the greater the possibility of a legitimation crisis because people can and should assess criteria for intervention publicly according to the norms of a communicative ethic.

Second, for real legitimation to occur according to the criteria of the ideal speech-situation, human beings should be active participants in the process of decision-making, not passive recipients of it. If there is to be appeal and not coercion, the participants in the discussion should be in equal positions of power, all should have an equal chance to have their interests voiced, and all reasonable alternatives should have a hearing. In late capitalism, none of these conditions is fulfilled. The rich and corporations own the means of production and consequently are in an unequal power position in relation to those whom they employ. The interests of these corporations receive a major share of the attention, publicity, and money, and minimize or exclude other needs, such as a clean, beautiful environment, rapid transit, or low-cost housing. Late capitalism also ignores or represses alternatives that threaten its priorities. Because of its structural inability to fulfill the conditions for legitimation, we have to judge late capitalism irrational.[40]

Third, democracy as it has developed in Europe, England, and America means free and equal participation by all. Western democracies have developed positively valuable institutions and traditions, such as freedom of speech and rights of public assembly, to facilitate such participation. If legitimation is to occur in a way that is favorable to capital, however, it must keep widespread democratic participation as low as possible. So that people remain sufficiently passive, rule of elites and ideologies of technological and scientific elitism repress or reduce democratic participation. A third contradiction arises between real and apparent legitimation.[41]

Fourth, to the extent that active participation is absent, political rule is always going to appear arbitrary and hence alienating. If someone claims to be governing in my name, either that person is ruling in my best interests or not. If not, and such is true in late capitalism, then that person cannot be legitimate. If the person or persons wish to be legitimate, then they must rationally convince me that they are ruling in my best interests. To convince me rationally they must enlist my participation and cease treating me as a passive being by manipulating me. Short of such rational persuasion, the person may claim to be ruling in my best interests, but what such persons arbitrarily assert I can rationally deny or question.

Someone could respond to this argument by saying that a sufficient amount of such participation is achieved when the people meet every two or four years to choose in primaries and elections between or among political candidates chosen by elites. Such a response presumes the arbitrary leap of faith that elites are acting not merely in their own or corporate interest, but in the general interest, and that they considered and evaluated in a fair manner candidates representing all possible alternatives, including those hostile to corporate priorities.

Finally, since the rulers in late capitalism claiming to rule in the interests of all are either a technological and scientific elite or politicians and managers advised by such an elite, they are in principle incapable of evaluating and defending their basic goals and priorities of society because positive science deliberately prescinds from value questions. The most that science can do is to ascertain the best means of achieving goals already in place. Legitimation, however, if it is to be fully rational, applies to the goals of a society and not simply to the means of achieving them. We have the choice, therefore, of either accepting the word of elites that the goals are in fact consonant with our best interests, a claim that the elite as a scientific elite cannot justify, or disagreeing with the elite. If we take its word on this matter, then we simply have made an irrational leap that whatever is is right. Democracy becomes whatever the current practice is. If we disagree with this question-begging approach and begin to think of rational alternatives to the system, then we have ceased being uncritically ruled by elites.

Capitalism, therefore, in contrast to precapitalistic times, has separated subject from object, individual from universal, mind from body, quality from quantity. As opposed to a one-sided immediacy in precapitalist times, a one-sided mediation has developed in which individuality, quality, and difference tend to be submerged. The monotonous uniformity of the commodity form, money, tends to produce a uniform, abstract form of life.

CONCLUSION

Late capitalism tends to shove to the side as anachronistic the rule of a prescientific, communal, ethical reason, symbolic interaction, and allows technological, scientific thought and practice, purposive rational action, to reign supreme. In the latter part of this chapter, by appealing to the universal criteria of a communicative ethic, I have shown how irrational such dominance and such exclusion are. In the previous section I moved from universal to particular; in this, from particular to universal criteria established descriptively and eidetically. In such complementary movement the concrete universal as union of universal and particular emerges, but with none of the implications for an absolute, apodictic, totally clear knowledge that such a notion has for Hegel.[42]

NOTES

1. Marx, *Grundrisse*, pp. 463–514. On the importance, for the emergence of capitalism, of the separation of the worker from the means of production and their concentration in the hands of capitalists, see Weber, *Economy and Society*, I 135–40, II 1393–99.

2. Schutz, *Phenomenology of the Social World*. Weber, *Economy and Society*, I 3–107. For a critique of Weber's concept of reason, see Jürgen Habermas, *Legitimation Crisis*, trans. Thomas McCarthy (Boston: Beacon, 1975), pp. 95–102.

3. See Melvin Rader, *Marx's Interpretation of History* (New York: Oxford University Press, 1979), for a convincing argument that Marx's model of society is an organic totality with mutually interacting, relatively autonomous aspects.

4. See above, pp. 172–73, 176–77.

5. See Chapter 2, pp. 56–58; Chapter 6, pp. 177–80.

6. See Chapter 2, p. 69.

7. Nicos Poulantzas, *Political Power and Social Class*, trans. Timothy Hagen (London: New Left Books, 1973), pp. 13–16, 27–33. Louis Althusser, *For Marx*, trans. Ben Brewster (New York: Vintage, 1970), pp. 111–13, 117–18, 200–13. Karl Marx, *Capital*, trans. Ben Fowkes, 3 vols. (New York: Vintage, 1977), I 175–76. For a definition of homology, see Lucien Goldmann, "Structure: Reality and Concept," in *The Structuralist Controversy*, edd. P. Marksey and E. Donato (Baltimore: The Johns Hopkins University Press, 1977), pp. 98–124; and *Marxisme et sciences humaines* (Paris: Gallimard, 1970), pp. 54–93. For the discussion of motivation, see above, Chapter 4, pp. 99–103; for the discussion of coercion and appeal, see Chapter 5, pp. 143–57.

8. Habermas, *Legitimation Crisis*, pp. 45–50. See Thomas McCarthy's Introduction, pp. vii–xxiv, for a good discussion of the contemporary crisis of critical theory.

9. Georg Lukács, *History and Class Consciousness: Studies in Marxist Dialectics*, trans. Rodney Livingstone (Cambridge: MIT Press, 1971), pp. 83–209. Karl Korsch, *Marxism and Philosophy*, trans. Fred Halliday (New York: Monthly Review Press, 1970), pp. 29–97. Antonio Gramsci, *Prison Notebooks*, ed. and trans. Quentin Hoare and Geoffrey Nowell Smith (New York: International, 1971). For a good discussion of the Frankfurt School, see Martin Jay, *The Dialectical Imagination* (Boston: Little, Brown, 1973).

10. See Herbert Marcuse, *Soviet Marxism* (New York: Vintage, 1961), for a criticism of the repressive, technocratic, undemocratic character of the Soviet experiment.

11. Marx, *Manuscripts*, pp. 108–15, 173–93.

12. Enzo Paci, *The Function of the Sciences and the Meaning of Man*, trans. Paul Piccone and James Hanson (Evanston, Ill.: Northwestern University Press, 1972). Sartre, *Critique of Dialectical Reason*. Karel Kosík, *Dialectics of the Concrete*, edd. Robert S. Cohen and Marx W. Wartofsky (Boston: Reidel, 1976). Bologh, *Dialectical Phenomenology*.

13. See Chapter 5, notes 17 and 28.

14. For technology and science as ideology, see Habermas, *Towards a Rational Society*, pp. 81–122. For individualism, see Marx, *Grundrisse*, pp. 83–85. For reification, see Lukács, *History and Class Consciousness*, pp. 83–122.

15. Marx, *Manuscripts*, pp. 137–38.

16. Husserl, *Crisis*, pp. 125–26.

17. Marx, *Grundrisse*, pp. 463–64.

18. The term "form of life" is initially used by Wittgenstein, *Investigations*, p. 8. For a creative use of this notion in a critical theoretical context, see Bologh, *Dialectical Phenomenology*, pp. 2–4.

19. Bologh, *Dialectical Phenomenology*, p. 8.

20. Ibid., p. 10.

21. Soviet Marxism, of course, is another form of lived positivism, into which a fully developed critical theory would have to conduct an inquiry and which has its own peculiar rules and presuppositions. I am focusing on capitalism because of its historical, logical, and phenomenological connection with Cartesianism, the central theme of this book.

Late capitalism, therefore, would have in common with state socialism the dominance of technocracy, positivism, and purposive rational action, and the minimizing or excluding of democratic participation. One way in which late capitalism differs from state socialism, however, is in the latter's dominance of the political sphere over the economic, whereas in late capitalism the economic sphere rules over the political. On this point, see Andrew Arato, "Critical Sociology and Authoritarian State Socialism," in *Habermas: Critical Debates*, edd. John B. Thompson and David Held (Cambridge: MIT Press, 1982), pp. 196–218. A fully adequate dialectical phenomenology would have to inquire into what distinguishes as well as unites late capitalism and state socialism. Capitalism as a form of life, then, is a ground, but not the only possible ground, for reification and scientism, also present in state socialism.

22. Bologh, *Dialectical Phenomenology*, pp. 6–10.

23. Ibid., pp. 4–6.

24. Ibid., pp. 27–30.

25. See Chapter 6, pp. 165–69.

26. Many thinkers from different traditions agree that individualism,

reification, and scientism have become dominant only in the last four centuries. See Marx, *Grundrisse*, pp. 471–514, 690–716, and *Capital*, I 492–639; Habermas, *Towards a Rational Society*, pp. 81–122; Heidegger, *Question of Technology*, pp. 3–35, 115–54; Husserl, *Crisis*, pp. 21–100; Weber, *Economy and Society*, I 80–81, 92–93, 119, 135–38, 147–48, 151, 155, 161–62, 223–26, and II 963–80, 1002, 1238–39, 1429–30; Ellul, *Technological Society*, pp. 3–227. Michel Foucault, *Discipline and Punish: The Birth of the Prison*, trans. Alan Sheridan (New York: Vintage, 1979).

27. Heidegger, *Question of Technology*, pp. 3–35. I would have to add, however, that Heidegger himself is not fully consistent on the issue. On the one hand, he seems to say that the end of metaphysics is technology and that objectification is necessarily alienating, as I showed in Chapter 3. On the other, he does seem to make at times some kind of distinction between technology and technocracy and to concede a legitimacy to technology within its own proper sphere. See *What Is Called Thinking?* pp. 32–36.

28. Bologh, *Dialectical Phenomenology*, pp. 8–9, 31–32. See Roslyn Wallach Bologh and James L. Marsh, "Dialectical Phenomenology as Social Theory" (unpublished), where some of the key ideas in the rest of this chapter, especially pp. 218–23, were initially developed.

29. Marx, *Grundrisse*, pp. 140–240. Weber, *Economy and Society*, I 81, 85–86, 92–99, 110.

30. Marx, *Capital*, I 125–77. In this argumentation we have Marx's implied answer to Böhm-Bawerk's critique of the value theory and his own theory of marginal utility, based on a qualitative criterion of the relative strength of subjective preference. This critique is the strongest, most influential that has been made of the labor theory of value. See Eugen von Böhm-Bawerk, *Karl Marx and the Close of His System*, ed. Paul Sweezy (New York: Kelley, 1966). There are three main problems with this critique. First of all, in making subjective preferences the source of value, he falls into the same problem as any qualitative explanation of value, based on use value, would have: subjective preferences as such are incommensurable and, therefore, there is no common measure established and no solid basis for economic science. Second, in arguing that Marx was inconsistent in assuming an identity between price and value in Volume I of *Capital* and then a difference in Volume III, Böhm-Bawerk misses a crucial feature of Marx's method in that it moves from very abstract, minimal determinations in Volume I, where methodologically Marx assumes an identity between price and value, to more concrete determinations in Volume III, where Marx removes such assumptions. See the *Grundrisse*, pp. 100–108, on this methodological point. Third, Böhm-

Bawerk's method is positivistic and undialectical, remaining on the level of appearance and not making the necessary movement from appearance to essence, price to value, circulation to production. On the necessity of such a movement, see Marx, *Capital*, I 279–80. As argued for in this book, this movement becomes necessary because there are social structures that are not immediately given.

As I indicate in this note and in note 33, there are many objections to value theory inside and outside the Marxist tradition. As I also indicate, I am not convinced by these objections. In my opinion, therefore, value theory still stands upright and can be employed as a resource in critical social theory.

But even if value theory were shown to be incorrect, the basic claims made in this chapter concerning the relationship between capitalism and individualism, reification, and scientism would still stand. Habermas' discussion of legitimation crisis and his critique of science and technology as ideology, even though I link them to value theory in this work, are not so linked in his. Other thinkers such as G. A. Cohen have argued that Marx's critiques of fetishization and reification are valid whether or not his labor theory of value is true. See Cohen's *Karl Marx's Theory of History: A Defence* (Oxford: Clarendon, 1978), pp. 115–33, 297–325.

Finally, thinkers inspired by Marx such as Michael Walzer (*Spheres of Justice* [New York: Basic Books, 1983], pp. 295–303) make ethical critiques of capitalism that are independent of value theory. Using Pullman's establishment of both a town and a company in the nineteenth century as an example, Walzer argues for the inseparability of economic and political democracy. Just as we would not accept as valid Pullman's claim to rule absolutely over the town because he had put his money and initiative into it, so we should not accept his claim to rule the company absolutely for the same reasons. Arguing *modus ponens*, we can say that if freedom and equality are legitimate and necessary in the town for certain reasons, then they are legitimate and necessary in the company for the same reasons. If A, then B; A, therefore B. Arguing *modus tollens*, we can say that if undemocratic economic control is valid in the company, then undemocratic political control is valid in the town. But because the latter is not valid, neither is the former. If A, then B; not B, therefore not A. Economic and political democracy are a seamless web; they go together or not at all.

31. Marx, *Grundrisse*, pp. 161–63, 221–35.

32. Marx, *Capital*, I 258–306. As Marx puts it, surplus value is the source of profit, which is surplus value considered in relation to the total investment of the capitalist. See *Grundrisse*, pp. 376–99, 434–43.

33. Marx, *Capital*, I 283–639; *Grundrisse*, pp. 690–727; *Manuscripts*,

pp. 170–93. For an historical discussion of the movement from formal to real subsumption as that occurred in England, see E. P. Thompson, *The Making of the English Working Class* (New York: Vintage, 1966). For an excellent discussion in Marx of the infinitude–finitude dialectic, see *Grundrisse*, pp. 401–23. For an excellent discussion of the way technology, science, and capitalism link up to one another in the United States, even in the nineteenth-century discoveries of the light bulb and the telephone, see David Noble, *America by Design: Science, Technology, and the Rise of Corporate Capitalism* (New York: Knopf ,1977).

In this discussion of real subsumption is Marx's implied answer to those critics such as Habermas who see the increasing importance of technology and trained technical talent as somehow invalidating the labor theory of value. Rather, relative surplus value is simply a more advanced way of exploiting labor, technology and science incorporated in machines are congealed labor, and even mental labor can be productive of surplus value when such labor is employed to produce profitable commodities. See Habermas, *Legitimation Crisis*, pp. 55–57; Karl Marx, *Theories of Surplus Value* I, ed. S. Ryazanskaya, trans. Emile Burns (London: Lawrence & Wishart, 1969), pp. 157–60.

34. Habermas, *Legitimation Crisis*, pp. 21, 35. John Kenneth Galbraith, *The New Industrial State* (New York: Signet, 1967), pp. 82, 16–17, 27–32, 190–91, 287–89. Paul Baran and Paul Sweezy, *Monopoly Capital* (New York: Modern Reader, 1966), pp. 5–51.

35. Marx, *Grundrisse*, pp. 401–23; and *The Eighteenth Brumaire of Louis Bonaparte*, ed. C. P. Dutt (New York: International, 1963), p. 15. Marcuse, *Eros and Civilization*, pp. ix–x, 71–95. For an excellent Marxist discussion of the development of advertising in twentieth-century America, see Ewen, *Captains of Consciousness*. For an excellent non-Marxist discussion making many of the same critical points, see Galbraith, *Affluent Society*, pp. 114–30.

36. See Marcuse, *Eros and Civilization*, pp. 32–34, for a definition of "surplus repression." For my initial use of the term, see the end of the preceding chapter, pp. 195–96. For an economic argument that American capitalism is wasteful and that if the United States eliminated wasteful production, the average length of the work week could be reduced from thirty-five to twenty-three hours a week while retaining the same amount of real consumption and production, see Samuel Bowles, David Gordon, and Thomas Weisskopf, *Beyond the Waste Land: A Democratic Alternative to Economic Decline* (Garden City, N.Y.: Doubleday Anchor, 1983), pp. 150–78. These authors argue that almost half the gross national product in 1981, $1.2 trillion of $2.6 trillion, was waste production and consumption.

37. See John Kenneth Galbraith, *Economics and the Public Purpose* (Boston: Houghton Mifflin, 1973), pp. 29–37, for a discussion of women as paid managers of consumption. For a discussion of sexism as supportive of an ideology of technocratic, militaristic tough-mindedness, see Marc Feigen Fasteau, *The Male Machine* (New York: McGraw-Hill, 1974), pp. 158–208. For a discussion of worker discontent in the strike at Lordstown rooted in desire for more enjoyable work, see Stanley Aronowitz, *False Promises: The Shaping of American Working-Class Consciousness* (New York: McGraw-Hill, 1973), pp. 21–50. For a discussion from a non-Marxist point of view of this contradiction between desire for enjoyment and the requirements of discipline in a capitalist society, see Daniel Bell, *The Cultural Contradictions of Capitalism* (New York: Basic Books, 1976).

I do not wish to give the impression here of simply reducing sexism to economic, class domination. My position is that racism and sexism are distinct forms of oppression, relatively autonomous but ultimately subordinate to the domination exercised by capitalism. My reasons are, first, that capitalism is distinctive of the modern in a way that racism and sexism are not; they existed in pre-modern eras. Second, in the West and areas colonized or controlled by it, capitalism is more universal than racism and sexism. Capitalism is present not only in countries like the United States, where women and racial minorities have, to a significant extent, achieved recognition of their basic rights, but in countries in Latin America, where women and racial minorities have not even begun to be liberated. Third, "classism" is more deeply entrenched in our society than racism and sexism. We have committed ourselves institutionally in the United States to an overcoming of racism and sexism in a way that we have not to the overcoming of "classism." Fourth, capitalism as the dominant, most comprehensive form of life in the West and in countries controlled by it can use or twist racism for its own ends assymetrically. Capitalism can use racism and sexism for its own ends in a way that is difficult or impossible for sexism and racism to use capitalism. Capitalism's historic use of racism to fragment the working class and to justify lower pay to certain groups is an example of the first tendency; the difficulty that blacks have had in this country in moving from formal, political equality to full economic equality with whites is an example of the latter.

I wish to distinguish, therefore, among a vulgar Marxist reduction of racial and sexual exploitation to class exploitation, a thesis of co-equality among racism, sexism, and "classism," and a theory that affirms class exploitation in the West as most dominant, thoroughgoing, universal, and definitive of our social situation. According to this third alternative, racism and sexism in our society remain relatively autonomous, significant forms of exploitation with their own logics and origins. These forms, however, are ultimately subordinate to capitalism.

Even though we in the United States have gone a long way toward achieving racial and sexual justice, we still have a long way to go. Also, critical theory has a great deal to learn from black and feminist accounts and critiques of society and the Marxist tradition itself. Unfortunately, the scope and framework of this book do not allow me to pursue and develop these lines of argument further. For an example of an important feminist work, from which critical theory has much to learn, see *Feminism as Critique*, ed. Seyla Benhabib and Drucilla Cornell (Minneapolis: University of Minnesota Press, 1987).

38. Marcuse, *Eros and Civilization*, pp. 71–95. See Weber, *Economy and Society*, I 147–48, 161–64, 223–26, II 963–1001, 393–99, for a discussion of the way in which formal, technical rationality extends into all spheres of modern society and is linked to capitalism. I do not wish to overstate the thesis of one-dimensionality, however. On this point I agree with Habermas against Marcuse that even though one-dimensionality is a tendency in modern capitalism, nonetheless the orientation toward total administration brings into play counter-tendencies and the possibility of other kinds of crises, such as legitimation or motivation crises. Also, legitimate traditions in our institutions such as free speech and freedom of the press resist such one-dimensionality. See Habermas, *Legitimation Crisis*, pp. 50–60, 68–94.

39. Habermas, *Legitimation Crisis*, pp. 68–75.

40. Michael Harrington, *The Twilight of Capitalism* (New York: Simon & Schuster, 1976), pp. 236–92. Ewen, *Captains of Consciousness*. Stuart and Elizabeth Ewen, *Channels of Desire* (New York: McGraw-Hill, 1982). Bowles, Gordon, & Weisskopf, *Beyond the Waste Land*, pp. 150–78. James O'Connor, *The Fiscal Crisis of the State* (New York: St. Martin's, 1973), pp. 150–78. Galbraith, *New Industrial State*, pp. 352–60. Ernest Mandel, *Late Capitalism*, trans. Joris De Bres (London: New Left Books, 1975), pp. 248–407. Bowles, Gordon, & Weisskopf show that even if we adopt a conservative estimate of real defense need, the United States wasted $49.8 billion dollars on military production in 1980.

41. Liberals, Marxists, and others agree on the fact, although not the desirability, of technocracy and scientific elitism. See Habermas, *Towards a Rational Society*, pp. 81–122. Ellul, *Technological Society*, pp. 229–318. Galbraith, *New Industrial State*, pp. 71–82, 176–88, 304–24. Robert Dahl, *Who Governs?* (New Haven: Yale University Press, 1961), pp. 223–325. Peter Bachrach, *The Theory of Democratic Elitism* (Boston:

Little, Brown, 1967), pp. 59–92. C. Wright Mills, *The Power Elite* (New York: Oxford University Press, 1956), pp. 3–9, 269–97. Jack L. Walker, "A Critique of the Elitist Theory of Democracy," *American Political Science Review*, 60 (1966), 285–95.

42. On the concrete universal, see Hegel, *Logic of Hegel*, pp. 287–97; and Chapter 6 above, pp. 170, 179.

9

The Emergence of
Dialectical Phenomenology

IN THE LAST CHAPTER we are left with the task of consolidating results through reflecting on dialectical phenomenology as a method. I choose to achieve this goal by reflecting in a hermeneutically suspicious manner on Cartesianism and a descriptive, eidetic phenomenology growing out of such Cartesianism. In the previous chapter I used dialectical phenomenology to reflect on capitalism as a form of life. In this chapter I use dialectical phenomenology to reflect on itself in relation to its other, Cartesianism and an excessively Cartesian phenomenology, and to capitalism as a form of life. In the previous chapter I stressed the content and object of dialectical phenomenology; in this chapter, the form and method of dialectical phenomenology.

I have been reflecting throughout the book on Cartesianism, in both a broad and a narrow sense. In a broad sense, Cartesianism posits a dualism between a non-extended ago and a world of extended substances. To these two realms, there correspond two different sciences, a philosophical reflection on the ego and a science of extension, leading to and grounding subjectivism and objectivism, idealism and positivism. In a narrow sense, especially as it develops within phenomenology, Cartesianism in this reflection on the ego often dialectically negates scientific objectivism. Progress as that takes place historically and in the development of this book lies in the gradual recovery of and integration with the objective social world. Intentionality, language, the lived body, freedom, the other person, the unconscious, and the life-world of capitalism all represent stages in this progressive recovery of the world.

Cartesianism can be either self-conscious or un–self-conscious of itself as grounded in a form of life. If it is self-conscious, then it will inquire into the grounds of itself in a form of life. Insofar as it is not self-conscious, it contradicts its own movement toward self-grounding and is inconsistent.

In precapitalist times men and women were tied immediately to the land, to other people, and to themselves. Working people owned their means of production, lived close to the soil, and knew their feudal lord personally. We must take care, however, not to romanticize this era. Feudal lords exploited serfs, but for the sake of use value rather than exchange value: fighting wars against opposing lords, giving parties, and enhancing the lord's enjoyment of life in general. Making money as a main preoccupation existed on the margins of society. Religious rather than economic values dominated.[1]

With the emergence of capital, with money-making as the dominant way of life, with the primary role of the state becoming the preservation and increase of private property, there is a movement from immediacy to mediation. The subject is split off from the object, mind from body, production for the sake of profit from work for the sake of enjoyment. With the worker separated from the means of production, capital brings the two together on its terms and exerts control over labor and means of production for the sake of profit. As even Adam Smith tells us, there would be no investment without the hope of profit.[2] With the one-sided mediation of capital and the subjugation of all human activity to the abstractions of money and exchange value, a yearning develops to return to the past. The basic root of conservatism lies in this divorce between immediacy and mediation.

With the advent of money and capital as dominant, the old ethical and religious community, based upon the subordination of exchange to use value, dissolves. The only kind of society that can survive and prosper is one that has incorporated money-making as a way of life into itself. What emerges, as Locke and Hobbes describe in their versions of the state of nature, is a multiplicity of separate, isolated individuals, each pursuing her own self-interest, each looking out for himself, each watching out for number one.[3]

In such a society, there emerges "freedom, equality, property, and Bentham": there is the right of each to pursue her own individual interest up to the point where she violates the rights of other individuals; equality insofar as each confronts the other as an independent person in the market place and they exchange goods equal in value; property insofar as each has the right to appropriate what he has worked up through personal labor; and "Bentham" insofar as all this activity governed by an invisible hand is supposed to lead to the greatest happiness of the greatest number.[4]

Such a movement to capitalism initially appears as, and to some extent is, liberation of the individual from feudal shackles. In feudal times there was personal dependence of the individual on those above him and objective dependence on society; in capitalist times there is personal independence and objective dependence. Workers are no longer tied to the land or to particular lords; they can work for whomever they choose. However, freedom, equality, property, and Bentham turn into their opposites in the sphere of production. Freedom turns into absolute subjugation within production, rigid division of labor, progressive de-skilling, and ruthless subordination of workers to the demands of the machine. Equality turns into inequality as the capitalist appropriates unpaid labor time as the source of his profit, and the gap between rich and poor increases. Property, the right to appropriate the fruits of one's own labor, turns into the capitalist's right to appropriate the fruits of other people's labor, and the greatest happiness of the greatest number into general unhappiness.[5]

As their limits and contradictions appear, therefore, capitalist freedom, equality, property, and happiness reveal themselves to be historically limited, not to be identical with freedom, equality, property, and happiness as such. In spite of their contradictoriness, however, there is great development of productive forces—means of production, science, technology, machinery—made possible by the subordination of quality to quantity, use value to exchange value. Capital does not contemplate, revere, and respect the natural world, but rather exploits, rapes, and plunders it for raw materials, development, and profit. Respect and awe before nature as a manifestation of God give way to domination of nature.[6] Such development of productive forces creates the conditions for a rich, many-sided individuality. Because the subject is cut off from the object, labor from means of production, physical labor from mental labor, in capitalism this individuality remains, to a significant extent, truncated and unfulfilled.

Capitalism as a form of life is a totality of essential, internal relations, one set of which is the relation among the economic, the political, and the cultural spheres of social life. Because economic domination implies a power relationship between classes in society, there inevitably is a political relationship between and among classes. Because capitalism is a social system with free, intelligent human beings in it, there is a question not only of systems identity but of social identity.[7] Because power relationships have to be understood, expressed, and legitimated, the awareness that people in a culture have of the cultural domain is essentially, internally related to the political and economic. What we have is a social gestalt that is analogous to the perceptual gestalt.

Because Cartesianism is a part and product of capitalist culture, we must interpret and criticize Cartesianism in relationship to capitalism as a form of life. If Husserl argued for the necessity of a phenomenology of phenomenology,[8] then in a sense different from Husserl's, we must engage in a hermeneutical, suspicious reflection of phenomenology on itself, as it is rooted in capitalism. To do less is to fail to be fully critical and self-conscious and, therefore, to fail to live up to the telos of phenomenology itself. The final steps in transcending Cartesianism mean seeing through it and beyond it as part of a bourgeois form of life. Fully transcending Cartesianism, the basic form and mode of Western philosophy for the last four centuries, means transcending capitalism theoretically and practically. In this book the overcoming of Cartesianism is part of such a praxis, at once theoretical and practical, of overcoming capitalism.

Husserlian, eidetic phenomenology, as well as Heidegger, Merleau-Ponty, Marcel, Sartre, and others, begin and contribute significantly to this project but in the end do not go far enough. As we have seen, Husserl in the *Crisis* traces on the level of ideas the rise of dualism, of scientism, of positivism, and shows how that history is integral to the self-becoming of phenomenology itself. Phenomenology, in order to comprehend itself adequately, has to become not only eidetic–descriptive, but also hermeneutical, critical, and dialectical.

Heidegger as well, in *Being and Time*, develops an analysis of the crowd in its anonymous, objectivizing features. But in refusing to go further and to ground these structures in capitalism as a form of life, he makes them essential *existentialia*, necessary and yet somehow able to be transcended in authentic being toward death. Heidegger's remains a truncated, inconsistent phenomenology. Marcel bemoans the dominance of having over being, but does not inquire into the socioeconomic grounds of such dominance. As reinterpreted in the context of dialectical phenomenology, "having" is a phenomenon peculiar to a form of life in which human beings define themselves as commodities, define their worth in terms of how much they possess, and subordinate all else to the pursuit of profit. Being is on the level of quality or use value; having is on the level of quantity, of exchange value. Having rules over being to the extent that exchange value dominates over use value. Later Heidegger talks about technocracy as a way of life and definition of reason in the twentieth century, but again does not ground that phenomenon in late capitalism as a form of life. Technocracy as a phenomenon, therefore, he does not account for, adequately explain, or interpret.

Marx in his reflection on thinkers such as Smith and Ricardo, thinkers whom he greatly respected, tried to develop what was incomplete in them or inconsistent or unexplained or undeveloped. In so doing he not only brought to light their limits as bourgeois thinkers, rooted in capitalism as a form of life, but transcended them while incorporating their valid insights.[9]

Similarly, we too, in reflecting on the phenomenological tradition that begins with Husserl, are reflecting on what is incomplete, as in Husserl's critique of scientism; or inconsistent, as in Heidegger's simultaneous affirming of a reified, inauthentic life embodying necessary, essential features and yet calling on us in *Being and Time* to transcend such inauthenticity; or unexplained, as in Marcel's account of the dominance of having in the twentieth century; or undeveloped, as in Ricoeur's movement to suspicion essential to hermeneutics. In so doing we are interpreting and criticizing phenomenology's unconsciousness of itself as rooted in capitalism as a form of life, and arguing that phenomenology has to become critically conscious of itself in this manner if it is to fulfill its own telos toward fully self-conscious thinking and living. A merely bourgeois phenomenology, uncritical and unconscious of itself as bourgeois, is a truncated phenomenology.

I do not mean to sound reductionistic here. There is an autonomous logic to the history of philosophy that I do not wish to deny. This kind of concern I have already taken into account by arguing that capitalism is a form of life with economic, political, and cultural aspects; these aspects mutually determine one another, and are not reducible to one another. There is a relative autonomy of philosophy with respect to the socioeconomic domain. Such autonomy is relative and not absolute, because all reflection is founded on perception but not reducible to it. Since all perception is socially determined and mediated through institutions such as language, and educational, economic, political, and religious organizations socially determine and mediate perception, this social, historical context founds reflection.

Descartes in particular has his own relatively autonomous motives for making certain moves. Some of these motives were desires for certainty, for philosophy as rigorous science, for intellectual and personal autonomy. In these motives and in the results of his inquiry there are elements that point beyond capitalism as a form of life, elements that I have exploited in the course of this study.

In some respects Descartes anticipates later developments in capitalism. For instance, the physical science that he argues for is only fully integrated with capitalism some centuries later. But just as Marx argued that we have to understand Smith and Ricardo in their historical context if we are to understand them completely, so also must we understand Descartes. Insofar as capitalism is a form of life, a totality of internal relations including more than the economic, Descartes and Cartesianism are part of that form of life as it originates and develops.

To discuss the "bourgeois" character of Cartesianism is to use a term that is qualified, descriptive, and critical, in a negative and a positive sense. We qualify the term insofar as Descartes is bourgeois in a limited, not a total, manner, in an inconsistent, not a totally consistent, way, because there are traditional, medieval elements in his thought as well as modern, novel elements. "Bourgeois" is descriptive insofar as it indicates that Cartesianism is a philosophical approach both influenced by the emerging capitalist socioeconomic context and exerting its own unique influence on that context in such a way that there is a somewhat homologous fit between the philosophy and the context. "Bourgeois" is critical in a positive sense insofar as many modern and contemporary methods of philosophy having their origins in Descartes, such as phenomenology, linguistic analysis, Hegel, and critical theory, are positive achievements with a great deal of insight and truth. The best of these achievements attain greater clarity about their contradictory relationship to capitalism and bring those contradictions into the light of day. The term "bourgeois" is negatively critical insofar as it indicates a form of life and a form of thought to be overcome and transcended. Such overcoming, however, does not imply total rejection; such a stance would be totally un-dialectical. We should not entirely reject bourgeois philosophy or capitalism in its economic and political aspects, but retain their valid aspects in a new synthesis and a new, more adequate form of life.[10]

In the above senses, this book in philosophy is bourgeois, building on and incorporating the achievements of modern philosophy but also pointing beyond itself toward a new form of life and a new praxis. As a final step toward achieving this goal, we need to reflect on Carte-sianism's relation to capitalism as a form of life by considering in a Marxist "conceptual deconstruction" four different aspects of Carte-sianism, four different kinds of false bourgeois presence.[11] First of all, Cartesianism is a philosophy of freedom, of personal autonomy, of subjectivity. In thinking that it can so detach itself through universal doubt from all ties to the past and to tradition, Cartesianism shares in the illusory independence and individuality characteristic of indi-viduals existing under capitalism. It is paradoxical that this very illusion of freedom from social ties becomes possible only in a system that fosters and makes possible this illusion. In the new subjective in-dependence of the bourgeois era, the objective dependence of the individual on society is less obvious, concealed, mediated. In a society that dissolves immediate social ties in favor of the community of money, the illusion of total autonomy and independence arises. Des-cartes and Husserl in his *Cartesian Meditations*, therefore, in an un-critical, un–self-conscious way reflect and legitimize the false inde-pendence and autonomy of the bourgeois individual. Throughout this book we have been trying to see through and overcome this illusion.

Second, in a society where the subject is separated from the object, subjective labor power from the objective means of production, men-tal labor from physical labor, we expect to find such dualism in the most profound philosophical expressions of the bourgeois era. Con-sequently, Descartes moves to subjectivity, doubts the relationship of subject to object, and separates mind from body; and Husserl uses the *epoche*, tries to achieve a presuppositionless starting point, affirms the transcendental ego as the souce of all meaning, and undertakes a search for strict apodicticity. Conversely, we need to ground such dualism and subjectivism in a form of life that is itself dualistic and subjectivistic. Descartes' philosophy emerges as distinctively bour-geois, in contrast to Aquinas', for example, for whom everything is in place, confidence about community reigns supreme, the subject is immediately related to the object, mind to body, the natural world to the cultural world, human beings to God. Aquinas in such claims is as distinctively medieval and feudal as Descartes is modern and bourgeois in his. Indeed, we could interpret the preoccupation with certainty and with finding a solid basis in the subject as a result of the loosening of social ties and the rise of a disconcerting pluralism of methods. The search for a total, rock-like security in the subject is both an effect of the rise of capitalism and a response to such an event. The legitimate triumph of ambiguity is, therefore, an implicit response to and critique of one-sided attempts at certainty and autonomy.

The move into the ego as a mode of philosophizing seems to be distinctively bourgeois. Such a mode of philosophizing, where the self has to reclaim itself in opposition to a harsh, alienating world inviting one to forsake oneself, corresponds to a form of life that renounces subjectivity in favor of objectivism, interiority in favor of exteriority, authentic life in favor of inauthentic life. Such a form of philosophizing stands in stark contrast to the dialogal model in Plato's *Dialogues* and the disputation model in Aquinas. Both these modes of thinking took place confidently in a taken-for-granted context of community. With the dissolution of community by money and capital, such confidence dissolved.

As the subject split apart from the object, therefore, the self had two choices. It could give itself over to the object by playing into Heidegger's "crowd" or Marcel's "having" or various philosophies of the object, scientism, positivism, empiricism, logicism; or it could move into itself in reflection and freedom and try to recover itself. The latter move, even though it is one-sided, was basically the more progressive path and the one taken by various philosophers of interiority from Descartes on, such as Kant, Nietzsche, Kierkegaard, Husserl, Heidegger, and other phenomenologists. To a greater or lesser extent and with greater or lesser consciousness, philosophies of interiority became attempts to liberate oneself from one-sided objectivism. Philosophies of interiority became philosophies of liberation; one freed oneself from the tyranny of the bourgeois object by moving into the freedom of the subject.

With such a radical move into interiority, we begin to see through the self-enclosed bourgeois individual, merely externally, instrumentally, problematically related to objects or to other people. The whole of this book has been a progressive seeing through of such self-enclosedness. We have discovered that persons are not merely inside themselves, but outside themselves intentionally related to the world; that that world is intersubjective; that others can be related to in a way that enhances freedom; that through language one is bound up in history and tradition. Phenomenology as bourgeois reflection on bourgois interiority closed off from the world tends to explode that interiority and, therefore, to transcend itself as bourgeois. Phenomenology as radical reflection on the division between subject and object tends to overcome such division and to relate subject to object. The movement to critical social theory is the final stage in the self-becoming of phenomenology.

Because we overcome a false interiority, we also overcome a false exteriority. We see through the myth of an object in itself, totally cut off from human intentionality. We see that the object is constituted, produced, created through a work of discovery, creation, labor, praxis. We see through the object as fetish, value free, totally cut off from human purposes, desires, goals, presuppositions.

In overcoming false interiority and false exteriority, phenomenology not only reconstitutes and rediscovers the world but also reconstitutes itself as intersubjective, dialogal, Socratic, non-totalitarian. Dialectical phenomenology does not reject interiority but inserts it into an intersubjective context of play and work, openness and critique, contemplation and action. Phenomenology becomes a continuing, ongoing attempt to practice and attain the ideal speech-situation. Such phenomenology is not a mere return to the naïveté of Socrates but an incorporation of Socratic method into a broader, richer context in which people are aware of their interiority, their individuality, their freedom, their subjectivity in a way undreamed of by Socrates. Phenomenology becomes a way of thinking and living the "rich, many-sided individuality" that would have been impossible prior to the bourgeois experiment in thought and social practice.[12]

Because phenomenology as dialectical is inherently non-bourgeois, it is in stark contrast with the way philosophy is often done in American universities where each professor is an entrepreneur with a group of consuming students, externally related to other faculty, pursuing his own teaching and research, handing down the truth to passive students like a banker handing out money.[13] Phenomenology as dialectical is fully radical or revolutionary in its demand to return to the things themselves, in its insistence on personal responsibility in seeing things for oneself, in its intersubjective, dialogal, non-totalitarian approach to experience, in its radical methodology practiced from the *epoche* on through the hermeneutical turn into openness to tradition and suspicion toward that tradition. In form and content, theory and practice, such phenomenology is opposed to all arbitrary impositions of power. In its practice of the *epoche*, phenomenology is an attempt to see through the one-sided fetishism of the object and the one-sided autonomy of the subject; critical theory is simply the last step in an increasingly deepening *epoche*.

Third, we might expect capitalism's dominance of quantity over quality, of exchange value over use value, and of the machine over labor to be reflected somehow in Descartes. We find him, therefore, in his discussion of the piece of wax in the *Meditations*, affirming the objectivity of primary, scientifically known qualities over subjective, secondary qualities, and we see him adopting a deductive, mathematical model of certainty and method for philosophy itself. Conversely Husserl has already shown the roots of scientific objectivism, scientism, and positivism in Descartes' philosophy. Capitalism as lived positivism is the proper context for such emerging tendencies. Capitalism is an abstract form of life in which money is more important than enjoyment in work, abstract labor more important than concrete labor, and profit more important than human beings.[14]

Indeed Heidegger himself has shown not only that the move into technological domination is distinctively modern, but that this domination itself is rooted in an abstract, one-sided subjectivity. The move into subjectivity as the ruling principle of the modern era makes possible technological domination as the most important form of subjective self-assertion. Technological domination is subjectivistic in its very attempt to be totally objective; objectivism and subjectivism coincide here. Correspondingly, the abstract subject, the Cartesian ego or the transcendental ego of Husserl or Kant, mirrors the abstract object, where exchange value dominates over use value, and the barter principle legitimating equivalent exchange mediates such domination. Capitalism is a society ruled by abstraction, one-sided mediation, both on the side of the object and on the side of the subject. As Kant himself says, the transcendental unity of apperception founds the unity of the scientific object.[15]

The dominance of technocratic capitalism imposing a one-dimensional, positivistic form of thought and life on the world has led to the desacralizing of the world, an emptying of its depth, a reduction of the person to simply a set of functions. Radical, descriptive, dialectical phenomenology is an effort to overcome such reductionism, to overcome one-dimensionality in thought and practice, to become aware of "the dearest freshness deep down things,"[16] to recover "currents whereby life can be reborn in regions of the mind which have yielded to apathy and are exposed to decomposition."[17] Even in its eidetic, descriptive aspects, therefore, phenomenology is implicitly radical insofar as it rediscovers and affirms the dimensions that a technocratic capitalism represses. In its recovery of the life-world, intentionality, subjectivity, freedom, consciousness, language, and tradition, phenomenology rediscovers not only domains of human life worth knowing for their own sakes, but also truths about the human condition essential for any critical theory that wishes to be sure of its foundations and rationally to resist the onslaught of technique—technology linked to the structure and goals of capitalism.[18] Eidetics and description are already implicitly radical and critical; critique requires eidetics and description if it is to be fully grounded and self-conscious.

Dialectical phenomenology is contemplation as well as critique, knowledge for its own sake as well as knowledge directed toward the transformation of society. Because the contemplation tends to go counter to one-dimensionality, such contemplation is already critical. Because critique is critique of instrumental reason, it must guard, lead to, and be grounded in contemplation of various kinds: scientific, interpersonal, aesthetic, philosophical, religious. If not, then such critique merely turns into a form of the instrumental reason it is criticizing. Dialectical phenomenology, in theory and practice, is an example of knowledge for its own sake. In theory and practice it is a critique of instrumental reason. In the play of question and answer, contemplation and critique, in the delight of recovering experience in all its freshness, in giving way to the desire to know as eros of the mind, in a reverence for experience born out of the piety of thinking,[19] dialectical phenomenology transcends instrumental reason. In reviving the atrophied faculty of wonder, such phenomenology is an implicit protest against the reduction of thought in work, politics, culture, and education to mere utility, professionalism, careerism. In the phenomenological encounter in which the thinker returns to the things themselves, the thinker discovers a most profound paradox: the most valuable things in human life are the "useless" activities that are ends in themselves—love, knowledge, art, friendship, commitment to the other. It is these activities that a one-dimensional, technocratic capitalism washes away.

Finally, the dominance of dualism, separation, and dichotomy in capitalism gives rise to philosophies characterized to a greater or lesser extent by *Verstehen*, either–or antagonisms between opposites conceived as ultimate. To the extent that Cartesianism is dualistic— and it is not simply dualistic because Descartes also attempts to mediate between opposites—phenomenological and dialectical thinking arises to overcome such dualism. However, a merely theoretical overcoming, such as occurs in Hegel and in eidetic phenomenology, is not sufficient because capitalism as a dualistic form of life remains. The contradiction between a theoretical overcoming of dualism, true enough in itself, and practical, lived dualism remains. Theoretical overcoming of Cartesianism, necessary as a first step, points toward the practical overcoming of capitalism as a form of life. What the positive content of such a practice is takes us beyond the limits of this book; that question I shall consider in another work.

Phenomenological theorizing points toward a practice necessary for itself as theory, because only with the overcoming of capitalism will the rational become real. Indeed, because capitalism as a form of life includes not only socio-economic and political but also cultural and ideological aspects, theory is a form of practice, a necessary first step and part of the overcoming of capitalism as an irrational form of life.

From the very beginning of this book there has been a progressive overcoming of "either–or" in favor of "both–and." Through the notion and experience of intentionality, we see that the subject is essentially related to the object, inner to outer, consciousness to expression. Through reflection on the lived body, we have seen that the mind–body dichotomy is a false one, and through the reflection on the activity of knowing, that sense and intellect, perception and reflection require one another. Through reflection on language, freedom, and intersubjectivity, we have seen that the dichotomies between determination and indetermination, structure and event, self and other, activity and passivity, openness to tradition and critique of the tradi-

tion are false. Through reflection on the personal and social unconscious, we overcome a merely immediate consciousness necessarily
opposed to the unconscious and excluding it in a false autonomy.
Finally, through reflection on capitalism as a form of life, we see that
such a social system fosters, encourages, and develops dualism, dichotomy, division, and repression. In thinking for ourselves "eroti-
cally" this play of opposites, we have rediscovered for ourselves
Hegel's bacchanalian revel. In this play of opposites, we begin to
think irreverently as well as reverently, negatively as well as positively, playfully as well as cogently.[20]

Phenomenology, therefore, insofar as it is merely subjective, individual, and private, uncritically reflects capitalism as a form of life.
The historical result of Descartes' science of extension, positivism,
insofar as it is merely objective, anonymous, and publicly verifiable, reflects capitalism in a different, objectivistic way. Phenomenology and positivism as one-sided negations of each other reflect
the subject–object split in capitalism. Dialectical phenomenology
emerges as the critical negation of these one-sided forms because it
relates subject to object, mind to body, individual to society. *Aufhebung* in the Hegelian sense is operative here with its double sense of
negation and preservation. Negation occurs insofar as we reject one-
sidedness, and preservation occurs insofar as we retain phenomenology's valid insights into subjectivity and positivism's insight into
objectivity.

Dialectical phenomenology is critical as long as it thinks a subject–
object unity that is violated in practice: the practice reveals itself as
irrational in the light of what is thought. As long as it affirms the
value of self-conscious living violated by un–self-conscious living in
practice, dialectical phenomenology must remain at odds with this
practice. As long as capitalism affirms subjectivity in principle and
violates it in practice, rejects positivism in principle and embraces
it in practice, dialectical phenomenology will be radical and critical.
Philosophy, if it is to fulfill its historical telos, must become revolutionary.

Western philosophy since Descartes, then, has been bourgeois men
and women trying to think themselves out of their intellectual and
social predicament. If Husserl is correct up to a point that transcendental phenomenology is the telos of modern philosophy and we are

correct in our *Aufhebung* of Husserl, then it follows that dialectical phenomenology is at least one reasonable candidate to fulfill this telos. Both Cartesianism in its narrow sense and positivism are bourgeois; the secret telos of modern philosophy is to think beyond and to overcome this bourgeois form of life.

If philosophy remains bourgeois, merely subjectivistic or merely objectivistic, it cannot fulfill its basic telos toward radicality and self-conscious living. If Socrates is correct about the unexamined life not being worth living and capitalism is the dominant modern version of the unexamined life, then living the examined life in its full sense means ceasing to be bourgeois. If philosophy remains unconsciously bourgeois, then it has not asked all the relevant questions. If it remains consciously bourgeois, then it is in conscious bad faith, at odds with itself, inconsistent, ambiguous in a bad sense.

What I have done in the book is to show how phenomenology, and by implication the whole of modern Western philosophy, can and should lead to dialectical phenomenology if it is faithful to itself. Only with the final step into critical social theory does one achieve full rationality, do full justice to the phenomena, and reconcile theory and practice fully. Short of the move into critical social theory, we have not asked crucial questions and not explained crucial contradictions.

The dilemma for phenomenology, then, is this: either it moves into critical theory or it does not. If it does, then it is fully self-conscious and faithful to itself. If it does not, then it remains obscurantist, dishonest, and less than fully comprehensive—obscurantist because it does not ask all the relevant questions, dishonest because it ignores the lived negation of personhood that is capitalism, and less than fully comprehensive because it does not consider all the phenomena, only those that can be explained in abstractly universal, eidetic terms. As phenomenology, then, it remains incomplete even as an account of the phenomena.

To affirm freedom eidetically and to ignore the lived negation of freedom in the work place and the market place is to be incomplete and abstract. To affirm subjectivity and individuality abstractly and to ignore their lived negation in the conformist society is to remain incomplete. To affirm the value of self-conscious living and to ignore its absence in such practices as advertising is to be incomplete. Phe-

nomenology that does not move to critical theory remains ideological in the worst sense, an abstract affirmation of personhood that
ignores its violation in practice and therefore implicitly legitimizes
the system.

However, the movement to critical theory is a movement within
the larger movement that is phenomenology. Phenomenology must
go beyond critical theory in reflecting on universal foundations. Just
as phenomenology is critical and needs to be self-consciously critical,
critical theory is phenomenological and needs phenomenology. It is
phenomenological in the sense of reflecting dialectically on the relationship between subject and object in capitalism. It needs phenomenology in the eidetic, descriptive sense if it is to be sure of its foundations, of the criteria for critique, of the meaning of reason. Critical
theory cannot talk about false consciousness without being clear
about what consciousness is. It cannot be a philosophy of freedom
without knowing what freedom is. It cannot talk about capitalism's
misusing persons without knowing what a person is. A fully nondogmatic critical theory, then, which not merely asserts but justifies
its claims in a fully self-critical manner, requires phenomenology. A
critical theory that is free not only of bourgeois content, capitalism,
but also of bourgeois form, positivism, requires the most severe, radical grounding in subjectivity possible. Otherwise the self generating
the critique remains shrouded in darkness. A critical theory aiming at
self-consciousness remains supremely unconscious of itself.

Present in the history of philosophy since Descartes and in this
book are not only a dialectic between dialectical phenomenology, on
the one hand, and positivism and idealism, on the other, but also a
dialectic within phenomenology itself between the Husserlian, Cartesian mode and the Hegelian, Marxist mode—the first stressing the
abstract universal common to all epochs, and the second stressing the
concrete, particular, historical epochs. The result of this dialectic is
the concrete universal as unity of universal and particular. Universal
and particular imply each other and are not thinkable apart from
each other. "Capitalism" as a particular life-world is not thinkable
apart from "life-world" in general; nor is alienated labor thinkable
apart from "labor" in general. Universal grounds for critique such as
the four validity claims remain incomplete as long as they are not
applied to particular social structures; critique of particular structures

is arbitrary if there is no clarity about the universal grounds for critique.

In insisting on the necessity of eidetic, descriptive phenomenology as a basis for interpretation and critique, I may seem to be falling into the foundationalism so strongly criticized by Rorty, Derrida, and others.[21] However, what is objectionable in foundationalism, the recourse to a pure, private, immediate, strictly apodictic Cartesian ego, is the main target of my book. The claim that there are putatively universal, eidetic structures known fallibilistically in a non-presuppositionless manner evades the fire of the post-modern critique. The aim of this book is to chart a third way between the Scylla of a strict Cartesian foundationalism and the Charybdis of a post-modern rejection and transcendence of modernistic rationality.

Not only does such a post-modernism have self-referential problems, using evidential rationality to overcome rationality, argument to criticize argument, concepts to transcend concepts, but questions can arise concerning the descriptive adequacy of its own account of experience. Is rationality essentially logocentric, technocratic, dominating, and alienating, or are there essential distinctions between and among alienating and non-alienating objectification, perception and reflection, common sense and science, science, morality, and art? Is rationality basically conceptual, systematic, probative, objective, leaving no room for pre-conceptual, questioning, playful elements, or is the full story the account of rationality as a unity of pre-conceptual and conceptual, question and answer, subjectivity and objectivity, playfulness and seriousness? If the latter is the case, then post-modernism's cult of *différance* leads to an ironic suppression of difference.

Again we may contrast post-modernism's rejectionistic approach to the tradition of modern philosophy with my dialectical approach, which gives a "yes" and a "no" to this tradition. As I have argued in the book, we should not simply reject the tradition but see it as a contradictory, dialectical unity of light and darkness, truth and falsity, liberation and domination. Once again there is the irony of a post-modern cult of *différance* leading to denial of crucial differences within the tradition.[22]

The philosophy and reality of the Cartesian subject has to be overcome in a determinate, not a simple, negation. The alternative to the

Cartesian subject, therefore, is not a post-modern death of the sub-ject, but a de-centered, post-bourgeois self, embodied, intersubjec-tive, linguistic, bound to tradition, related to and mediated by un-conscious psychological and social structures.

The debate, then, between a critical modernist such as I and a post-modernist such as Heidegger, Derrida, Rorty, or Foucault is this: Who has the most rational account of rationality? The post-modernists are arguing, not for irrationality, but for a more ade-quate account of rationality that implies a jettisoning of evidential, Western rationality. Both critical modernism and post-modernism aim at thinking and creating a more humane future. The question that arises in this debate, then, is what counts as a forward move in philosophy and social theory.

Emerging as an answer in this book is that the criteria for such a forward move are performative consistency, descriptive adequacy to experience, and hermeneutical comprehensiveness concerning the tradition. Is not a performatively consistent account of and critique of rationality preferable to one that is not? Is not a descriptive account of the different kinds of rationality and different aspects of rationality preferable to an account reducing rationality to one of its kinds or aspects, scientific, calculative, coercive, dominating? Is not an ac-count of the modern philosophical tradition doing justice both to its light and to its darkness more comprehensive and nuanced than an account that simply sees this tradition as dominating, calculative, logocentric, covering up and obliterating being, *différance*, nature? Is not an interpretation of modernity integrating both its liberating and its pathological aspects, present when such rationality is sub-ordinated to the aims of class and group domination, preferable to an interpretation that merely equates such rationality with such pathology?[23]

At this point we see again the necessity of the Marxist, critical theoretical turn if phenomenology and modern, Western rationality are to be redeemed. Dialectical phenomenology not only legitimates and grounds such rationality as legitimate, but shows that its abuse in the service of class domination is *irrational* by the standards of critical modernist rationality. The problem with capitalist rationality is not too much but too little rationality. The development of modern science, for example, is a good thing in itself; the use of science in the transition from the formal to the real subsumption of labor to capital is pathological. The move to reflectivity, interiority, and critique, indebted to Descartes is a positive way, is in itself good; the perverting and twisting of this movement into the cult of the rugged, bourgeois individual is pathological.

Now, a post-modernist could object to such criteria for making a forward move. Maybe there are other criteria; maybe the problem is in asking for criteria. But either the post-modernist simply asserts this claim in an arbitrary manner, or he has to argue it in a speech situation that presumes the transcendental precepts and validity claims. He is caught in a dilemma of self-contradiction *vs.* arbitrariness. If he enters into conversation and argument, then he is presuming the very modernistic, evidential rationality he wishes to deny.

The critical modernist is fallibilistic to the extent that she admits her claims and criteria are always open to further argument and correction. What she insists on pointing out to the post-modernist is that in making his critique of reason he inevitably and unavoidably makes claims, uses arguments, employs concepts in a way that seems self-contradictory. It is provocative and fashionable in a post-modernist vein to say, for example, that "All judgments are police actions." Since this claim is a judgment, however, it becomes as untrue and repressive as the claims it is criticizing. Does it not presuppose the structure of experience, understanding, and judgment to the extent that one reads or hears the words, understands the meaning of the sentence, and affirms or denies the truth of the proposition? Does such a claim do justice to the putatively non-violent, non-coercive judgments we experience in a Socratic situation, a conversation between friends, or a dialogue between lovers?

Is such a judgment—"All judgments are police actions"—one that makes ultimate philosophical sense, or is it a form of anti-philosophical philosophizing from on high carried on without a careful, prior, descriptive inquiry into experience? Is it a form of loose, anti-philosophical talk that finally does not stand up to careful scrutiny? If so, then post-modernism's claim to "give a more rational account of rationality" is in trouble.

To the extent that eidetic description grounds and guides hermeneutics and critique, such description is legitimately foundational in a very broad sense. Such descriptions, however, never reach an un-

mediated, pure experience, as I have shown, and the influence between eidetics and interpretation–critique runs both ways. It may
be that hermeneutics and critique call into question what we deem
true and essential. It may be, for example, that apodicticity in the
strict sense is just rooted in the emerging bourgeois individual's need
to deal with the crisis of social relations. It may be that the demand
for a presuppositionless account is an illegitimate "prejudice against
prejudice." Eidetics grounds interpretation and critique; interpretation and critique complete and test eidetics.

Dialectical phenomenology insists, then, on the concrete universal
as a unity of universal and particular. The concrete universal as
object is capitalism as a form of life; as subject it is dialectical phenomenology; and as a unity of subject and object it is this interpretation and critique of capitalism by dialectical phenomenology. Accordingly, what has emerged is dialectical phenomenology as social
theory with a hermeneutically respectful, a descriptive, and a hermeneutically critical aspect. The hermeneutically respectful inquires
into the past as lived and thought, the past from which dialectical
phenomenology springs; the descriptive inquires into present experience, eidetic structures, and egological–ontological grounds; and the
hermeneutically critical is basically oriented toward future praxis.
Included in the eidetic analysis are both a universal ontology of life-
world structures and a communicative ethic developed in the chapter
on intersubjectivity.

CONCLUSION

The question we have been concerned with from the beginning of
the book is the question about the self: What does it mean to be a
self? If the argument of this book is correct, authentic selfhood is incompatible with capitalism; the bourgeois subject is an incomplete,
self-contradictory, mutilated subject. Such a conclusion may cause
the reader to draw back, to question previous conclusions, to doubt
previous premises. Yet if Cartesianism is in error, if scientism, positivism, and logicism are one-sided, false forms of theorizing, and if
capitalism grounds these ways of thinking, then the conclusion seems
to hold. To take seriously the self and the notion of reason as dialectical phenomenology that flows from such self-definition is to

be at odds with the basic premisses and fundamental orientation of capitalism.

Authentic appropriation of one's own interiority is revolutionary in a threefold sense: as self-reflexive, as ethically and socially critical, and as metaphysical–religious. Insofar as we have been focusing primarily on the first and to some extent on the second form of this radicality, subsequent volumes will develop the second and third more fully. What underlies all three versions of radicality is intentionality as self-transcendence: transcendence of the extroverted self lost in the "they" toward an authentic self, transcendence of unconscious bourgeois theory and practice toward a fully self-conscious theory and practice, transcendence of a merely finite concern with immanence toward being and God.

What has emerged is the movement from theoretical reason to practical reason, subjective to objective spirit, eidetic phenomenology to critical theory as achieved in principle. The move from theoretical reason to practical reason is one that takes place for the sake of theoretical reason itself. Reason is not fully theoretical unless and until it comprehends itself as practical. True reason is unity of theoretical and practical reason or, as the Hegelian, Marxist tradition describes it, praxis.[24]

The argument has been, then, that until we overcome capitalism we do not achieve fully authentic selfhood. If Heidegger's authentic self has to escape from the clutches of idle talk, curiosity, ambiguity, and falling, and if these social phenomena are grounded in capitalism, then authentic selfhood is impossible without the overcoming of capitalism. If Marcel's dominance of having over being is rooted in capitalism, then being will not fully emerge until we overcome capitalism. If scientism as Husserl describes it in his *Crisis* is grounded in capitalism, then we must overcome capitalism to overcome scientism. Capitalism is the secret, hidden worm at the heart of modern philosophy and modern life in Western Europe and America, eating away at their essential core. The loss of self and of being, commented on so much by Heidegger, is to a significant extent a political problem. Neither philosophy nor human life is reducible totally to political thinking or politics, but the political remains an essential, important dimension both of philosophy and of human life. To suppress the ethical and political is not only to mutilate philosophy but to privatize human life in a way that is inescapably bourgeois.[25]

NOTES

1. Marx, *Grundrisse*, pp. 463–514.

2. Adam Smith, *An Inquiry into the Nature and Causes of the Wealth of Nations*, ed. Edwin Canaan (Chicago: The University of Chicago Press, 1976), p. 54.

3. John Locke, *Two Treatises of Government*, ed. Peter Laslitt (Cambridge: Cambridge University Press, 1963), pp. 307–18, 327–44, 361–69. Thomas Hobbes, *Leviathan*, ed. C. B. Macpherson (Harmondsworth: Penguin, 1978), pp. 183–201.

4. Marx, *Capital*, I 279–80.

5. Ibid. I am indebted to Carol Gould, *Marx's Social Ontology* (Cambridge: MIT Press, 1978), pp. 1–39, for her discussion of the various kinds of dependence and independence, as they are treated in relevant portions of Marx's *Grundrisse* (see, for example, pp. 163–65).

6. Marx, *Grundrisse*, pp. 157–65, 409–10, 705–706.

7. Habermas, *Legitimation Crisis*, pp. 1–17.

8. Husserl, *Cartesian Meditations*, pp. 29–30.

9. Louis Althusser and Etienne Balibar, *Reading* CAPITAL, trans. Ben Brewster (London: New Left Books, 1970), pp. 20–34. See above, Chapter 1, pp. 1–5, 16–23, for my initial discussion of and use of Marcel and Heidegger and of Husserl's *Crisis*, and notes 2, 4, 14, and 36–59, for my initial references to these thinkers. For my discussion of the inadequacy of the later Heidegger's critique of technology, see Chapter 8, pp. 217–18. For Heidegger's argument in *Being and Time* for moving to authenticity, see pp. 312–82 of that work.

10. Such is the authentic intent of Marx, rather than any vulgar, simplistic rejection of the bourgeois as such. See Shlomo Avineri, *The Social and Political Thought of Karl Marx* (Cambridge: Cambridge University Press, 1970), pp. 62–63, 87–89, 143–49, 182–84, 200–203, 208, 238.

In referring to the bourgeois character of Cartesianism, I am, in keeping with good, hermeneutical principles, referring to the content of the text rather than any private, autobiographical facts about Descartes. See Ricoeur, *Interpretation Theory*, pp. 89–95, and Chapter 6 above, pp. 161–64. Descartes' aristocratic background, as Albert William Levi describes it in *Philosophy as Social Expression* (Chicago: The University of Chicago Press, 1974), pp. 165–231, is no valid argument against the point I am making, which is based on the content of Descartes' thought as presented in his texts. However, taking a cue from Levi, I do not wish to overstate the bourgeois character of his thought. Rather, we see Descartes as a thinker at the intersection of the traditional and the modern, the aristocratic and the capitalistic, reflecting these impulses in a contradictory way; see Levi's text, esp. pp. 218–19, 226.

11. In using the term "conceptual deconstruction," I am inspired not only by Derrida but by Adorno in *Negative Dialectics*, trans. E. B. Ashton (New York: Continuum, 1973). See Michael Ryan, *Marxism and Deconstruction* (Baltimore: The Johns Hopkins University Press, 1982), pp. 73–81, and Martin Jay, *Adorno* (Cambridge: Harvard University Press, 1984), pp. 21–23, for the similarities between Derrida's and Adorno's methods. I agree with Ryan and Adorno that deconstruction has to be linked more explicitly with social critique than Derrida usually does. Against both Derrida and Adorno, I argue not only for a negative moment in reflection, but also for positive moments of eidetic descriptive and hermeneutical retrieval. "Suspicion," as I have argued for it in this volume, thus sublates both "deconstruction" and "negative dialectics," retaining aspects of both but integrating them with positive moments. It goes without saying that I reject completely the anti-philosophical motifs present in both these methodologies.

12. See Marx, *Grundrisse*, pp. 197, 325, 705, 712, 832, for a discussion of this notion of the individual in a communist society, for which capitalism creates the condition.

13. See Paulo Freire, *Pedagogy of the Oppressed* (New York: Seabury, 1973), for a criticism of the banking concept of education and a more radical, active questioning concept of education as praxis.

14. Descartes, *Meditations*, pp. 67–69, 108–12.

15. Heidegger, *Question of Technology*, pp. 131–35. Immanuel Kant, *Critique of Pure Reason*, trans. Norman Kemp Smith (New York: St. Martin's, 1965), pp. 141–75.

16. Gerard Manley Hopkins, "God's Grandeur," in *A Hopkins Reader*, edd. W. H. Gardner and N. H. McKenzie (Oxford: Oxford University Press, 1970), p. 66.

17. Marcel, *Creative Fidelity*, p. 12.

18. Ellul, *Technological Society*, pp. 13–19. I am borrowing the term "technique" from Ellul, but using it in a different, phenomenological Marxist sense. See Chapter 1, p. 5.

19. Heidegger, *Question of Technology*, p. 35.

20. See Hegel, *Phenomenology of Spirit*, pp. 27–28, for this discussion of the bacchanalian revel proper to philosophy.

21. See Richard Rorty, *Philosophy and the Mirror of Nature* (Princeton: Princeton University Press, 1979), pp. 3–9, for a definition of foundationalism. See Derrida, *Grammatology*, pp. 3–72, for a general statement of his project of deconstruction as a critique of logocentrism and immediate presence.

22. For different post-modern accounts of modern history and philosophy, see Theodore Adorno and Max Horkheimer, *The Dialectic of Enlightenment*, trans. John Cumming (New York: Seabury, 1972), pp. 3–42; Derrida, *Grammatology*, pp. 6–26; Heidegger, *Question of Technology*, pp. 3–35, Foucault, *Discipline and Punish*.

23. Unfortunately, John Caputo's *Radical Hermeneutics* (Bloomington: Indiana University Press, 1987) appeared after I had completed this volume. This provocative, insightful, well-written, courageous critique of Western *Ratio* deserves more critical consideration than I have been able to give it in this book. Nonetheless certain points of comparison and contrast between his effort and mine are clear. (*a*) Caputo interprets the tradition of modern philosophy and phenomenology along a post-modern line of development, extending from Kierkegaard and Nietzsche through Husserl and Heidegger to Derrida; this interpretation contrasts with my critical modernist reading, moving from Descartes and Husserl through Merleau-Ponty and Ricoeur to Habermas and Marx. (*b*) Caputo performs a deconstructive critique of the modern philosophical tradition that is similar to and yet different from my "suspicion" exercised toward that same tradition, a suspicion mediated by eidetic description and hermeneutical retrieval. (*c*) In criticizing the pathology of Western rationality, Caputo "politicizes" reason in a way that I find extremely insightful and important. See especially his remarkable pages on the university's involvement in dominating economic and political structures (pp. 228–35). (*d*) A legitimate target for both of us is the individualistic, unmediated, totally certain Cartesian ego. Both of us engage in critiques of immediate presence. (*e*) Nonetheless certain differences between us emerge, similar to those discussed in the above paragraphs, on the questions of performative consistency, descriptive adequacy to experience, and hermeneutical comprehensiveness. (*f*) The most fundamental difference between us is the following: Is the tradition of modern, Western rationality simply to be overcome or is it to be redeemed dialectically?

24. For a classic formulation of this concept of praxis, see Karl Marx, "Theses on Feuerbach," in Marx and Engels, *German Ideology*, pp. 121–23.

25. It would be erroneous to oppose one extreme, a privatized human consciousness, to that of another, a totally politicized consciousness with no room for private, personal life. On the dangers of this latter alternative, see William Earle, *Public Sorrows and Private Pleasures* (Bloomington: Indiana University Press, 1976). Ideally, public and private should mediate each other and complement each other without being reducible to each other. In this volume I have tried in the chapters on reflection, the free self, and the personal unconscious to give full, legitimate play to this private, personal moment.

Adorno, Theodor. *Negative Dialectics.* Trans. E. B. Ashton. New York: Continuum, 1973.

——, and Horkheimer, Max. *The Dialectic of Enlightenment.* Trans. John Cumming. New York: Seabury, 1972.

Althusser, Louis. *For Marx.* Trans. Ben Brewster. New York: Vintage, 1970.

——, and Balibar, Etienne. *Reading* CAPITAL. Trans. Ben Brewster. London: New Left Books, 1970.

Apel, Karl Otto. *Towards a Transformation of Philosophy.* Trans. Glynn Adey and David Frisby. London: Routledge & Kegan Paul, 1980.

Arato, Andrew. "Critical Sociology and Authoritarian State Socialism." In *Habermas: Critical Debates.* Edd. John B. Thompson and David Held. Cambridge: MIT Press, 1982. Pp. 196–218.

Arendt, Hannah. *The Human Condition.* Garden City, N.Y.: Doubleday Anchor, 1959.

Aronowitz, Stanley. *False Promises: The Shaping of American Working-Class Consciousness.* New York: McGraw-Hill, 1973.

Austin, J. L. *How To Do Things with Words.* Edd. J. O. Urmson and Marina Sbisa. 2nd ed. Cambridge: Harvard University Press, 1975.

Avineri, Shlomo. *The Social and Political Thought of Karl Marx.* Cambridge: Cambridge University Press, 1970.

Ayer, A. J. *The Concept of a Person, and Other Essays.* New York: St. Martin's, 1963.

——. *Language, Truth, and Logic.* New York: Dover, 1950.

Bachrach, Peter. *The Theory of Democratic Elitism.* Boston: Little, Brown, 1967.

Baran, Paul, and Sweezy, Paul. *Monopoly Capital.* New York: Modern Reader, 1966.

Bell, Daniel. *The Cultural Contradictions of Capitalism.* New York: Basic Books, 1976.

Blanshard, Brand. "The Case for Determinism." In *Determinism and Freedom.* Ed. Sidney Hook. New York: New York University Press, 1965. Pp. 3–15.

Böhm-Bawerk, Eugen von. *Karl Marx and the Close of His System.* Ed. Paul Sweezy. New York: Kelley, 1966.

Bologh, Roslyn Wallach. *Dialectical Phenomenology: Marx's Method.* London: Routledge & Kegan Paul, 1979.

——, and Marsh, James L. "Dialectical Phenomenology as Social Theory." Unpublished.

Booth, Wayne C. *The Rhetoric of Fiction*. 2nd ed. Chicago: The University of Chicago Press, 1983.

Bowles, Samuel, Gordon, David, and Weisskopf, Thomas. *Beyond the Waste Land: A Democratic Alternative to Economic Decline*. Garden City, N.Y.: Doubleday Anchor, 1983.

Braverman, Harry. *Labor and Monopoly Capital*. New York: Monthly Review, 1974.

Busch, Thomas. "Coming to Terms with Jean-Paul Sartre." *Philosophy Today*, 24 (1980), 187–235.

Caputo, John D. *Radical Hermeneutics*. Bloomington: Indiana University Press, 1987.

Carr, David. *Phenomenology and the Problem of History*. Evanston, Ill.: Northwestern University Press, 1974.

Casey, Edward. *Imagining: A Phenomenological Study*. Bloomington: Indiana University Press, 1976.

Cohen, G. A. *Karl Marx's Theory of History: A Defence*. Oxford: Clarendon, 1978.

Comte, Auguste. *Introduction to Positive Philosophy*. Ed. and trans. Frederick Ferré. The Library of Liberal Arts. Indianapolis: Bobbs-Merrill, 1970.

Dahl, Robert. *Who Governs?* New Haven: Yale University Press, 1961.

Derrida, Jacques. *Dissemination*. Trans. Barbara Johnson. Chicago: The University of Chicago Press, 1981.

——. *Margins of Philosophy*. Trans. Alan Bass. Chicago: The University of Chicago Press, 1982.

——. *Of Grammatology*. Trans. Gayatri Chakrovorty Spivaks. Baltimore: The Johns Hopkins University Press, 1974.

——. *Positions*. Trans. Alan Bass. Chicago: The University of Chicago Press, 1981.

——. *Speech and Phenomena*. Trans. David Allison. Evanston, Ill.: Northwestern University Press, 1972.

——. *Writing and Difference*. Trans. Alan Bass. Chicago: The University of Chicago Press, 1978.

Descartes, René. *Meditations on First Philosophy*. In *Philosophers Speak for Themselves: From Descartes to Locke*. Edd. T. V. Smith and Marjorie Grene. Chicago: The University of Chicago Press, 1940. Pp. 49–113.

Dufrenne, Mikel. *The Phenomenology of Aesthetic Experience*. Trans. Edward Casey, Albert Anderson, Willis Domingo, and Leon Jacobson. Evanston, Ill.: Northwestern University Press, 1973.

Earle, William. *Public Sorrows and Private Pleasures.* Bloomington: Indiana University Press, 1976.

Eliot, T. S. *The Four Quartets.* New York: Harcourt, Brace & World, 1943.

Ellul, Jacques. *The Technological Society.* Trans. John Wilkinson. New York: Vintage, 1964.

Ewen, Stuart. *Captains of Consciousness: Advertising and the Roots of the Consumer Culture.* New York: McGraw-Hill, 1976.

——, and Ewen, Elizabeth. *Channels of Desire.* New York: McGraw-Hill, 1982.

Fasteau, Marc Feigen. *The Male Machine.* New York: McGraw-Hill, 1974.

Feminism as Critique. Edd. Seyla Benhabib and Drucilla Cornell. Minneapolis: University of Minnesota Press, 1987.

Foucault, Michel. *Discipline and Punish: The Birth of the Prison.* Trans. Alan Sheridan. New York: Vintage, 1979.

——. *Language, Memory, Counter-Practice.* Ed. Donald Bouchard. Trans. Donald Bouchard and Sherry Simon. Ithaca, N.Y.: Cornell University Press, 1977.

——. *Power/Knowledge.* Ed. Colin Gordon. Trans. Colin Gordon, Leo Marshall, John Mepham, Kate Soper. New York: Pantheon, 1980.

Freire, Paulo. *Pedagogy of the Oppressed.* New York: Seabury, 1973.

Freud, Sigmund. *The Ego and the Id.* Ed. James Strachey. Trans. Joan Riviere. New York: Norton, 1962.

——. *A General Introduction to Psychoanalysis.* Trans. Joan Riviere. New York: Pocket Books, 1953.

——. "New Introductory Lectures." In *The Complete Psychological Works of Sigmund Freud.* Ed. James Strachey. Trans. James Strachey, Anna Freud, Alix Strachey, and Alan Tyson. Standard Edition. 24 vols. London: Hogarth, 1967. XXII 3–182.

——. "Outline of Psychoanalysis." *The Complete Psychological Works of Sigmund Freud.* Ed. James Strachey. Trans. James Strachey, Anna Freud, Alix Strachey, and Alan Tyson. Standard Edition. 24 vols. London: Hogarth, 1967. XXIII 138–207.

——. "Some Elementary Lessons in Psychoanalysis." In *The Complete Psychological Works of Sigmund Freud.* Ed. James Strachey. Trans. James Strachey, Anna Freud, Alix Strachey, and Alan Tyson. Standard Edition. 24 vols. London: Hogarth, 1967. XXIII 279–86.

Gadamer, Hans-Georg. *Truth and Method.* Trans. Garrett Barden and John Cumming. New York: Seabury, 1975.

Galbraith, John Kenneth. *The Affluent Society.* New York: Mentor, 1958.

——. *Economics and the Public Purpose*. Boston: Houghton Mifflin, 1973.

——. *The New Industrial State*. New York: Signet, 1967.

Goldmann, Lucien, *Marxisme et sciences humaines*. Paris: Gallimard, 1970.

——. "Structure: Reality and Concept." In *The Structuralist Controversy*. Edd. P. Marksey and E. Donato. Baltimore: The Johns Hopkins University Press, 1977. Pp. 98–124.

Gould, Carol. *Marx's Social Ontology*. Cambridge: MIT Press, 1978.

Gramsci, Antonio. *Prison Notebooks*. Ed. and trans. Quentin Hoare and Geoffrey Nowell Smith. New York: International, 1971.

Habermas, Jürgen. *Knowledge and Human Interests*. Trans. Jeremy Shapiro. Boston: Beacon, 1971.

——. *Legitimation Crisis*. Trans. Thomas McCarthy. Boston: Beacon, 1975.

——. *The Philosophical Discourse of Modernity*. Trans. Frederick Lawrence. Cambridge: MIT Press, 1987.

——. "A Review of Gadamer's *Truth and Method*." In *Understanding and Social Inquiry*. Edd. Fred Dallmayr and Thomas McCarthy. Notre Dame: University of Notre Dame Press, 1977. Pp. 335–63.

——. *Theory and Practice*. Trans. John Viertel. Boston: Beacon, 1973.

——. *Towards a Rational Society*. Trans. Jeremy Shapiro. Boston: Beacon, 1970.

——. *Zur Logik der Socialwissenschaften*. Frankfurt: Suhrkamp, 1970.

Hampshire, Stuart. *Thought and Action*. New York: Viking, 1960.

Harrington, Michael. *The Twilight of Capitalism*. New York: Simon & Schuster, 1976.

Hartshorne, Charles. *Creative Synthesis and Philosophical Method*. La Salle, Ill.: Open Court, 1970.

Hegel, Georg Wilhelm Friedrich. *The Logic of Hegel*. Trans. William Wallace. 2nd ed. London: Oxford University Press, 1892.

——. *The Phenomenology of Spirit*. Trans. A. V. Miller. Oxford: Clarendon, 1977.

Heidegger, Martin. *Being and Time*. Trans. John Macquarrie and Edward Robinson. New York: Harper & Row, 1962.

——. *Discourse on Thinking*. Trans. John Anderson and E. Hans Freund. New York: Harper & Row, 1966.

——. *On the Way to Language*. Trans. Peter Hertz. New York: Harper & Row, 1971.

——. *The Piety of Thinking*. Trans. James G. Hart and John C. Maraldo. Bloomington: Indiana University Press, 1976.

——. *Poetry, Language, Thought*. Trans. Albert Hofstadter. New York: Harper & Row, 1971.

——. *The Question Concerning Technology, and Other Essays*. Trans. William Lovitt. New York: Harper & Row, 1977.

——. *What Is Called Thinking?* Trans. Fred D. Wieck and J. Glenn Gray. New York: Harper & Row, 1968.

Hobbes, Thomas. *Leviathan*. Ed. C. B. Macpherson. Harmondsworth: Penguin, 1978.

Hopkins, Gerard Manley. "God's Grandeur." *A Hopkins Reader*. Edd. W. H. Gardner and N. H. McKenzie. Oxford: Oxford University Press, 1970. P. 66.

Horkheimer, Max. *Eclipse of Reason*. New York: Seabury, 1974.

Hosker, William. "The Transcendental Refutation of Determinism." *Southern Journal of Philosophy*, 11 (1973), 175–83.

Hume, David. *A Treatise on Human Nature*. Ed. L. A. Selby-Bigge. Oxford: Clarendon, 1888.

Husserl, Edmund. *Cartesian Meditations*. Trans. Dorion Cairns. The Hague: Nijhoff, 1960.

——. *The Crisis of European Sciences and Transcendental Phenomenology: An Introduction to Phenomenological Philosophy*. Trans. David Carr. Evanston, Ill.: Northwestern University Press, 1970.

——. *Experience and Judgement*. Ed. Ludwig Landgrebe. Trans. James S. Churchill and Karl Ameriks. Evanston, Ill.: Northwestern University Press, 1973.

——. *Formal and Transcendental Logic*. Trans. Dorion Cairns. The Hague: Nijhoff, 1969.

——. *Ideas*. Trans. W. Boyce Gibson. London: Allen & Unwin; New York: Macmillan, 1931.

——. *Logical Investigations*. Trans. J. N. Findlay. 2 vols. New York: Humanities Press, 1970.

Jacoby, Russell. *Social Amnesia*. Boston: Beacon, 1975.

Jaspers, Karl. *Nietzsche*. Trans. Charles F. Walraff and Frederick J. Schmit. Tucson: University of Arizona Press, 1965.

——. *Philosophy*. Trans. E. B. Ashton. 3 vols. Chicago: The University of Chicago Press, 1969.

Jay, Martin. *Adorno*. Cambridge: Harvard University Press, 1984.

——. *The Dialectical Imagination*. Boston: Little, Brown, 1973.

Jordan, James N. "Determinism's Dilemma." *Review of Metaphysics*, 23 (1969), 48–66.

Kant, Immanuel. *Critique of Pure Reason*. Trans. Norman Kemp Smith. New York: St. Martin's, 1965.

Kierkegaard, Søren. *Concluding Unscientific Postscript.* Trans. David Swenson. Princeton: Princeton University Press, 1941.

———. *Either–Or.* Trans. Walter Lowrie. 2 vols. Garden City, N.Y.: Doubleday Anchor, 1959.

———. *Fear and Trembling and The Sickness Unto Death.* Trans. Walter Lowrie. Garden City, N.Y.: Doubleday Anchor, 1954.

———. *The Journals of Søren Kierkegaard.* Ed. and trans. Alexander Dru. London: Oxford University Press, 1938.

Korsch, Karl. *Marxism and Philosophy.* Trans. Fred Halliday. New York: Monthly Review Press, 1970.

Kosík, Karel. *Dialectics of the Concrete.* Edd. Robert S. Cohen and Marx W. Wartofsky. Boston: Reidel, 1976.

Lacan, Jacques. *Ecrits: A Selection.* Trans. Alan Sheridan. New York: Norton, 1977.

Levi, Albert William. *Philosophy as Social Expression.* Chicago: The University of Chicago Press, 1974.

Lévi-Strauss, Claude. *Structural Anthropology.* Trans. Claire Jacobson and Brooke Grundfest. Garden City, N.Y.: Doubleday Anchor, 1967.

Levison, Andrew. *The Working-Class Majority.* New York: Coward, McCann, & Geoghegan, 1974.

Lindbloom, Charles. *Politics and Markets.* New York: Basic Books, 1977.

Locke, John. *Two Treatises of Government.* Ed. Peter Laslitt. Cambridge: Cambridge University Press, 1963.

Lonergan, Bernard. *Insight: A Study of Human Understanding.* New York: Longmans, Green, 1957.

———. *Method in Theology.* New York: Herder & Herder, 1972.

Luhmann, Niklas, and Habermas, Jürgen. *Theorie der Gesellschaft oder Sozialtechnologie—Was leistet die Systemforschung?* Frankfurt: Suhrkamp, 1971.

Lukács, Georg. *History and Class Consciousness: Studies in Marxist Dialectics.* Trans. Rodney Livingstone. Cambridge: MIT Press, 1971.

McCarthy, Thomas. *The Critical Theory of Jürgen Habermas.* Cambridge: MIT Press, 1978.

Mandel, Ernest. *Late Capitalism.* Trans. Joris De Bres. London: New Left Books, 1975.

Marcel, Gabriel. *Creative Fidelity.* Trans. Robert Rosthal. New York: Noonday, 1964.

Marcuse, Herbert. *Eros and Civilization.* New York: Vintage, 1955.

———. *One-Dimensional Man.* Boston: Beacon, 1964.

———. *Soviet Marxism.* New York: Vintage, 1961.

Marsh, James L. "An Inconsistency in Husserl's *Cartesian Meditations.*" *New Scholasticism,* 53 (1979), 460–74.

Marx, Karl. *Capital.* Trans. Ben Fowkes. 3 vols. New York: Vintage, 1977.

——. *Economic and Philosophic Manuscripts of 1844.* Ed. Dirk J. Struick. Trans. Martin Milligan. New York: International, 1964.

——. *The Eighteenth Brumaire of Louis Bonaparte.* Ed. C. P. Dutt. New York: International, 1963.

——. *Grundrisse.* Trans. Martin Nicolaus. New York: Vintage, 1973.

——. *Theories of Surplus Value* I. Ed. S. Ryazanskaya. Trans. Emile Burns. London: Lawrence & Wishart, 1969.

——, and Engels, Friedrich, *German Ideology, with Supplementary Texts.* Ed. C. J. Arthur. New York: International, 1981.

Merleau-Ponty, Maurice. *Consciousness and the Acquisition of Language.* Trans. Hugh Silverman. Evanston, Ill.: Northwestern University Press, 1973.

——. "In Praise of Philosophy." In *The Essential Writings of Merleau-Ponty.* Ed. Alden L. Fisher. New York: Harcourt, Brace & World, 1969. Pp. 17–26.

——. "On the Phenomenology of Language." In *The Essential Writings of Merleau-Ponty.* Ed. Alden L. Fisher. New York: Harcourt, Brace & World, 1969. Pp. 214–29.

——. "Phenomenology and the Sciences of Man." In *The Primacy of Perception.* Ed. James Edie. Evanston, Ill.: Northwestern University Press, 1964. Pp. 43–95.

——. *Phenomenology of Perception.* Trans. Colin Smith. New York: Humanities Press, 1962.

——. "The Primacy of Perception and Its Philosophical Consequences." In *The Essential Writings of Merleau-Ponty.* Ed. Alden L. Fisher. New York: Harcourt, Brace & World, 1969. Pp. 47–63.

——. *The Prose of the World.* Ed. Claude Lefort. Trans. John O'Neill. Evanston, Ill.: Northwestern University Press, 1973.

——. "The Relations of Soul and Body and the Problems of Perceptual Consciousness." In *The Essential Writings of Merleau-Ponty.* Ed. Alden L. Fisher. New York: Harcourt, Brace & World, 1969. Pp. 138–81.

——. *The Visible and the Invisible.* Trans. Alphonso Lingis. Evanston, Ill.: Northwestern University Press, 1968.

Meszaros, Istvan. *Marx's Theory of Alienation.* New York: Harper & Row, 1970.

Mills, C. Wright. *The Power Elite.* New York: Oxford University Press, 1956.

Nietzsche, Friedrich. *The Antichrist.* In *The Portable Nietzsche.* Ed. and trans. Walter Kaufmann. New York: Vintage, 1967. Pp. 565–656.

——. *Beyond Good and Evil.* Trans. Marianne Cowan. Chicago: Gateway, 1955.

——. *On the Genealogy of Morals.* Trans. Walter Kaufmann. New York: Vintage, 1967.

——. *Thus Spake Zarathustra.* In *The Portable Nietzsche.* Ed. and trans. Walter Kaufmann. New York: Vintage, 1967. Pp. 103–449.

——. *Twilight of the Idols.* In *The Portable Nietzsche.* Ed. and trans. Walter Kaufmann. New York: Vintage, 1967. Pp. 463–563.

Noble, David. *America by Design: Science, Technology, and the Rise of Corporate Capitalism.* New York: Knopf, 1977.

O'Connor, James. *The Fiscal Crisis of the State.* New York: St. Martin's, 1973.

Ollman, Bertell. *Alienation: Marx's Conception of Man in Capitalist Society.* Cambridge: Cambridge University Press, 1971.

Paci, Enzo. *The Function of the Sciences and the Meaning of Man.* Trans. Paul Piccone and James Hanson. Evanston, Ill.: Northwestern University Press, 1972.

Poulantzas, Nicos. *Political Power and Social Class.* Trans. Timothy Hagen. London: New Left Books, 1973.

Rader, Melvin. *Marx's Interpretation of History.* New York: Oxford University Press, 1979.

Ricoeur, Paul. "Explanation and Understanding." In *The Philosophy of Paul Ricoeur.* Edd. Charles E. Reagan and David Stewart. Boston: Beacon, 1978. Pp. 149–66.

——. *Freedom and Nature: The Voluntary and the Involuntary.* Trans. Erazim V. Kohak. Evanston, Ill.: Northwestern University Press, 1966.

——. *Freud and Philosophy.* Trans. Denis Savage. New Haven: Yale University Press, 1970.

——. "The Hermeneutical Function of Distanciation." *Philosophy Today,* 17 (1973), 129–41.

——. *Hermeneutics and the Human Sciences.* Ed. and trans. John B. Thompson. Cambridge: Cambridge University Press, 1981.

——. *History and Truth.* Trans. Charles Kelbley. Evanston, Ill.: Northwestern University Press, 1950.

——. "Husserl and Wittgenstein on Language." In *Phenomenology and Existentialism.* Edd. E. N. Lee and M. Mandelbaum. Baltimore: The Johns Hopkins University Press, 1967. Pp. 207–17.

——. *Interpretation Theory: Discourse and the Surplus of Meaning.* Fort Worth: Texas Christian University Press, 1976.

——. "The Question of Proof in Freud's Psychoanalytic Writings." In *The Philosophy of Paul Ricoeur.* Edd. Charles E. Reagan and David Stewart. Boston: Beacon, 1978. Pp. 184–210.

Rorty, Richard. *Philosophy and the Mirror of Nature*. Princeton: Princeton University Press, 1979.

Ryan, Michael. *Marxism and Deconstruction*. Baltimore: The Johns Hopkins University Press, 1982.

Ryle, Gilbert. *The Concept of Mind*. New York: Barnes & Noble, 1949.

Sartre, Jean-Paul. *Being and Nothingness*. Trans. Hazel E. Barnes. New York: Citadel, 1964.

——. "Consciousness of Self and Knowledge of Self." In *Readings in Existential Phenomenology*. Edd. Nathaniel Lawrence and Daniel O'Connor. Englewood Cliffs, N.J.: Prentice-Hall, 1967. Pp. 113–42.

——. *The Critique of Dialectical Reason*. Ed. Jonathan Ree. Trans. Alan Sheridan-Smith. London: New Left Books, 1976.

——. *Existentialism and Human Emotions*. Trans. Bernard Frechtmann and Hazel E. Barnes. New York: Philosophical Library, 1957.

——. *The Transcendence of the Ego*. Trans. Forrest Williams and Robert Kirkpatrick. New York: Noonday, 1957.

Saussure, Ferdinand de. *Course in General Linguistics*. Edd. Charles Bally and Albert Sechehaye. Trans. Wade Baskin. New York: McGraw-Hill, 1976.

Schutz, Alfred. *The Phenomenology of the Social World*. Trans. George Walsh and Frederick Lehnert. Evanston, Ill.: Northwestern University Press, 1967.

——. *The Structures of the Life-World*. Trans. Richard Zaner and H. Tristam Englehardt, Jr. Evanston, Ill.: Northwestern University Press, 1973.

Skinner, B. F. *Beyond Freedom and Dignity*. New York: Vintage, 1971.

Smith, Adam. *An Inquiry into the Nature and Causes of the Wealth of Nations*. Ed. Edwin Canaan. Chicago: The University of Chicago Press, 1976.

Sokolowski, Robert. *Presence and Absence*. Bloomington: Indiana University Press, 1978.

Taylor, Mark C. *Kierkegaard's Pseudonymous Authorship*. Princeton: Princeton University Press, 1975.

TeHennepe, Eugene. "The Life-World and the World of Ordinary Language." In *An Invitation to Phenomenology*. Ed. James Edie. Chicago: Quadrangle, 1965. Pp. 133–46.

Thompson, E. P. *The Making of the English Working Class*. New York: Vintage, 1966.

Tracy, David. *The Analogical Imagination*. New York: Crossroad, 1981.

Walker, Jack L. "A Critique of the Elitist Theory of Democracy." *American Political Science Review*, 60 (1966), 285–95.

Walzer, Michael. *Spheres of Justice*. New York: Basic Books, 1983.

Weber, Max. *Economy and Society*. Edd. Guenther Roth and Claus Wittich. 2 vols. Berkeley: University of California Press, 1978.

Whitehead, Alfred North. *Process and Reality*. New York: Macmillan, 1929.

Wittgenstein, Ludwig. *The Blue and Brown Books*. New York: Harper & Bros., 1958.

——. *On Certainty*. Trans. Denis Paul and G. E. M. Anscombe. New York: Harper Torchbooks, 1969.

——. *Philosophical Investigations*. 2nd. ed. Trans. G. E. M. Anscombe. New York: Macmillan, 1958.

——. *Zettel*. Edd. G. E. M. Anscombe and G. H. von Wright. Trans. G. E. Anscombe. Berkeley: University of California Press, 1967.

Wolfe, Alan. *The Limits of Legitimacy: Political Contradictions of Contemporary Capitalism*. New York: Free Press, 1977.

Wolin, Richard. *Walter Benjamin: An Aesthetic of Redemption*. New York: Columbia University Press, 1982.

INDEX

Adorno, Theodor, 171
Alienation, as mistakenly equated with objectification, 81; Definition of, 1; in coercion, 151–52; Kinds of, 3; Relation of, to inauthenticity, 112
Ambiguity, ix–x, 185, 205; as related to objectivity, 121–22; Definition of, 23, 31–32; Distinction between good and bad versions of, 33; in explanation, 30; in interpretation, 171–72, 176, 177, 185; in Merleau-Ponty, 29, 33; in perceptual experience, 27, 29, 107; in the concrete universal, 179; in the experience of freedom, 92–93, 106; in the self, 107; Limits of the triumph of, 32–38; Negative sense of, 2; Triumph of, 23–32, 246
Analogy, Argument from, 131
Apodicticity, as an ideal of truth, 12, 15, 23, 30; in a strong sense, 38–39, 132, 245; in a weak sense, 38–39, 70, 132
Appeal, Definition of, 155; described, in contrast to coercion, 148–55
Aquinas, St. Thomas, 166, 245
Aristotle, 161
Ayer, A. J., 4, 94

Being, Definition of, in relation to the life-world, 87, 218
Belonging, in relation to distanciation, 176–77
Bentham, Jeremy, 241
Blanchard, Brand, 95
Body-subject, lived body, in contrast to body-object, 250
Böhm-Bawerk, Eugen von, 233–34n30
Bologh, Roslyn Wallach, 205–207, 214–16

Canons, of interpretation, 165–67; of scientific method, 84
Capital, Essence of, as exchange value, 220; Relationship of, to science, 221ff., 240
Capitalism, as contradictory unity of subjugation and liberation, 239ff.; as lived positivism, 215, 248; as modern version of the cave, 213; Aspects of late version of, 224–25; Distinction between early and late versions of, 224–25; Distinctiveness of, from other epochs, 200–201, 213; Links of, with non-dialectical reason, 221; Power and contradictoriness of late version of, 225–30
Caputo, John D., xi, 261n23
Cartesianism, Cartesian, ix, xii–xiii, 16, 166, 177, 188, 204, 213, 215; as bourgeois, in narrow and broad sense, 244–45; as criticized by dialectical phenomenology, 239ff.; as dualistic, 250–51; as ideology, Four different aspects of, 245–51; Cartesian ego as expressive of capitalism, 248; Cartesian individual, 243; Narrow and broad meaning of, xii, 239; Relation of, to capitalism as a form of life, 242ff.; Transcendence of, in the project of overcoming capitalism, 242
Causation, Aspects of, in society, 203–204
Class consciousness, Levels and aspects of, 142–43
Commodity fetishism, Relation of, to reification, 221
Consciousness, as embodied, 210; as intentional, 45–47; as related to the unconscious, 188; as temporal, 35–38; as unified, 107–11;